HOMO SCHIZO II

The cover is from Pablo Picasso's "Girl before a mirror," 1932, the original of which rests with The Museum of Modern Art, New York City, and a photograph of which was lent by the Princeton University Art Library.
The text was processed by the Princeton University Computer Center, with photo-composition by the Princeton University Press, and printed at the Princeton University Print Shop by xerography in a limited edition.

HOMO SCHIZO II

Human Nature and Behavior

by
Alfred de Grazia

Metron Publications
Princeton, N.J.

Library of Congress Cataloging in Publication Data
de Grazia, Alfred, 1919-
  Homo Schizo II: Human Nature and Behavior
  Includes index
    1. Psychology. 2. Medicine. 3. Human Behavior
I. Title.
ISBN: 0-940268-02-7
Printed in the U.S.A. Limited first edition
Address: Metron Publications, P.O. Box 1213,
    Princeton, N.J. 08540, U.S.A.

12

To Harold Dwight Lasswell

(1902 - 1978)

Almus frater magnus idearum

FOREWORD

My thesis here comes close to a remark once made by Mark Twain: "The human race consists of those who are dangerously insane and those who aren't." Humans, that is, are naturally somewhat crazy, by all definitions of that term among practicing psychologists.

A book on human nature, especially if it contains a theory of instincts, needs an apology. *The International Encyclopedia of Social Sciences* of 1968 carried no article on human nature. Its direct predecessor, the *Encyclopedia of Social Science* of 1932, did publish such an article, written by John Dewey, where he opined that social experiments might ultimately reveal the limits of what humans could achieve and tolerate; we hope that they have not yet done so.

Some 16,000 articles and reports in psychology were noted in *Psychological Abstracts* in 1979. None was grouped under the heading of "human nature." There was no such heading. In the area of information storage and retrieval, what is not indexed tends not to exist. Researchers usually follow marked paths. Lionel Tiger and Robin Fox presented a book on *The Imperial Animal* recently with nary a peep or growl about human nature, although, if I read it aright, that is precisely the subject.

My teachers at the University of Chicago, a fashion leader in matters intellectual before World War II, generally regarded the search for "human nature," and "instincts," too, as futile. It was the heyday for stressing cultural influences and cultural differences. "Human nature" was suspected of being a tool of conservative theologians and politicians. The ordinary man had made it a vehicle of his biases, his hopelessness, his social darwinism and his need to generalize, no matter how foolishly.

In respect to the concept of instinct, McDougall and Freud were influential. But the one by overclassifying the phenomena of instinct, and the other by using the term broadly and vaguely, aroused suspicions of it. G.H. Mead, in the vanguard of imperialism for the concept of culture during the 1920's, substituted "impulse" for instinct. There came a period of "motivation," "values," and "drives" and now, too, one can see certain nuclear meanings that are handled by "reflexes," "genetic factors," and "genetic predisposition."

So the term "instinct," too, went by the board of *Psychological Abstracts*. A third term to which I refer often is "schizophrenia" and here, I am privileged to say, a computer printout of the *Abstracts* will convey hundreds of titles every year. As we shall see, however, "schizophrenia" is scarcely less diffuse and troublesome a term than "human nature" or "instinct."

To me the term "human nature" signifies the traits most distinguishing humans from other life forms. A model or system of behavior can be constructed of these traits such that their interrelations are perceived, along with the mechanisms energizing them. As will be observed from the chapters to follow, the half-million studies in psychology that accompanied the near demise of the two terms, "human nature" and "instinct," nevertheless changed what can and cannot be said about them. I may remark, as did Konrad Lorenz once, upon returning home from some American disputation over whether behavior was all learned, "I think I have taken some of the stink out of instinct."

Empirical research, both macroscopic and microscopic, now offers pertinent data in abundance. New perspectives are invoked. The study of the brain has made excellent progress as, for instance, in the comparative study of cerebral hemispheres. The French newspaper

Le Monde, quoted a Delegate to the World Congress of Biological Psychiatry in 1981 to say: "Psychiatry will slip away from the psychiatrists if they don't want to do biology." Ethology and socio-biology are aggressively pushing into the realms of anthropology and sociology. Chimpanzees have been house guests. Women have lived as neighbors to gorillas. More and more of animal instincts are observed to be subsumable under deliberate decisions and experiential learning. We have more systematic knowledge, as well, about the human social condition and what brings it about. Also, physical reconstruction of human nature has become theoretically possible, if some pronouncements upon gene-splicing, cloning, drugs, and brain surgery are to be believed.

Although many books are related to questions of human nature, few works attack the subject head-on. Almost all of these latter are old. They may come out of any field of knowledge, but usually emerge from philosophy, theology, anthropology, psychology, and political theory. The present work derives in part from twenty years of teaching political psychology and the sociology of invention, and from a decade of studying prehistoric and ancient cultures which were undergoing ecological disturbances and creating myths and legends meanwhile. It connects ultimately with a merged set of pragmatic, psychological and anthropological traditions that were especially well represented at the University of Chicago a generation ago. I am indebted beyond words to that community of scholars.

The sequence of chapters can be explained in a few sentences. First I seek a usable concept of the normal human being. I cannot find it, for it sinks into the quagmire of ideas concerning man as a rational animal. Thereupon I look for a description of the mentally ill today, and how they are treated. It appears that psychotherapy is seeking vainly to reduce bizarre behavior, but such behavior crops out in normal people too as their perverse inheritance.

So both the disturbed and the normal gyrate around a central complex of behavior (including mental activity) that is schizoid, and this schizoid complex cannot be reduced to "normal." The "normal rational person" is a fiction, undiscoverable in reality, unsupportable and misleading theoretically. The concept of "normalcy" becomes a portion of a statistical distribution of the population whose behavior is appropriate. Thus, a person who eats moderately is sane; one who is a glutton is sick. One who kills in self-defence behaves reasonably; one who kills in a religious sacrifice is mad.

Conventional behavior makes a poor key to human nature. A more workable key can be fashioned from the traits assigned to schizophrenia. Schizophrenia is not an aberration of human nature but a powerful and influential expression of the basic personal and social format. It becomes especially conspicuous when social structures are displaced or destroyed.

I find that it emerges from a general genetic failure of the human instinctive system, a blocking of responses. This instinct-delay brings self-consciousness, a plurality of selves, whose disorganization imparts a continuous, unstoppable and ineradicable fear. The fear transforms into a drive for total interior and exterior control. There occur a set of strategies for coping with the fear. Language and science coordinate the strategies. The ideas of the good, true, and beautiful that eventuate convince the human being that, if not a divine creation, he is at least the monarch of nature.

An analysis of human nature is likely to prove pessimistic. Although it may deny "original sin," it uncovers too many lapses and contradictions in human behavior to conclude with a happy prognosis. Nonetheless, I cannot but feel that the bio-psychiatry of *homo schizo* presents human nature in a perspective which scientists and philosophers will readily comprehend. From understanding to research, and then on to description, and finally to applications is a familiar path in our times.

Table of Contents

HOMO SCHIZO II

chapter one

THE NORMALLY INSANE

Niccolò Macchiavelli, the clear-headed founder of modern political science, was not above a little harmless hallucinating:

> When evening comes I return to the house and enter my writing-room, and on the threshold I take off my everyday clothes full of mud and mire and put on royal and court robes, and properly re-clothed I enter the ancient courts of the men of antiquity where, received by them affectionately, I pasture on that food that alone is mine and for which I was born, where I am not too timid to speak with them and ask them about the reasons for their actions; and they in their courtesy answer me; and for four hours of time I feel no weariness, I forget every trouble, I do not fear poverty, death does not dismay me: all of myself I transfer into them.[1]

This is acceptable behavior. The relatives of a young farm lad who behaved so would think him rather mad. An atheist regards similar behavior in a working priest as a typical and appropriate feature of the great delusion of religion. It verges on the delusory, the megalomanic, the impractical, the hallucinatory. Abandoning the living to identify with the dead; treating words as voices; speaking to several people a thousand years apart in defiance of time and space. The genius of Machiavelli lay in his ability — cultured or genetic — to abandon himself to his mad world and afterwards to return to everyday chores, but more than this, to draw upon his conversations for writing that has been for several centuries a by-word for realism and the scientific approach to politics.

Identification — a set of projections of himself to a wide net of characters — and control, the ability to grasp them and organize them within his personal ego system: we see these qualities fairly sharply. But we also see a typical syndrome of human nature — the conventional and the alienated rubbing shoulders, so to say: the security blanket of his authoritative clothing that admitted him to the great company; the compelling obsessiveness to tie his life experiences into the mainstream of his culture; as well as the other qualities which I have already labelled. Thus does schizotypicality crop up in Machiavelli.

A book could be easily filled with material to show that "People do the strangest things." It is not difficult to prove that all humans are a bit crazy. Quirks, exhibitionism, phobias, dizziness, hang-ups, depressions, avoidance, suspiciousness, acid stomach, fear of abandonment, nightmares and other symptoms of stress and troubles of the mind abound in ordinary experience. To have psychological problems is normal, even universal. "Do you know, Martha, I think everybody is crazy, except thee and me," said the Quaker to his wife, "and sometimes I'm not so sure about thee." Most people can joke about the prevalance of psychic disturbances. "It's a funny world." And it takes but a minute to get them to agree that politics, the world of public affairs, is a circus of abnormal behavior. An informant of the F.B.I. in the Abscam exposés, which recently disgraced a number of American officials, repeatedly declared on network television that "congressmen are crooks, perverts, and alcoholics."

I do not intend to fish in these shallow waters. Down deep the big fish swim. There we can expect to locate the

monstrous forms of an idea, that the human being is
essentially and normally "insane," that what we call
normal human thought and behavior are derivatives,
vitally important to be sure, of the same schizotypical
core that manifests itself in those whom we label insane.
If everybody, at some time, acts a bit crazy, it is not
because they are departing from their normal human
state but because they are reaching for their normally
insane nature.

Of course, then, the term "insane" should have to be
dropped. "Insane" is a deviation from a standard, that of
"sanity." If the standard is "insane," then the deviations
must be something else — sanity? It is uncomfortable to
say so, but, yes, in a way, although and until a better term
should be found. For the insane of society are no more
fixed and pure representatives of the core of human
nature than the sane. All of humanity, sane or insane,
normal or abnormal, typical or untypical, forms globally
around the core of human nature that we can best
describe with the word "schizoid."

Human nature is a set of qualities to be found only
among people. Of course we must keep a wary eye on the
animal kingdom and its curators, the ethologists, who
persist in finding identities between animals and men
where once only large differences were thought to exist.
We must avoid saying what is human nature, only to find
that it is animal nature as well.

At the same time, we cannot get around the fact that
our chromosomes and culture manage to fashion hundreds of differences between animals and humans. No
matter how close the similarity, no animal trait is precisely typical of humans. We differ in every way conceivable, just as, for that matter, humans differ as individuals
in every respect, no two people being alike. Withal this
book must confine intself to those qualities which ae both
distinctively human and important as such.

But, granted that a quality may be proven distinctive,
who is to say that it is important? We must say, partly
begging the question, that what is important in human
nature is whatever has the greatest effect in producing
those human traits and activities that we regard as most
important. This leads directly to the human mind; the

nub of human nature is in the mind. In the "minds" — because, whatever the propensities of the individual mind, the human species does not exist except in transacting minds.

We have then before us *homo sapiens*. We declare that we shall make of him more specifically *homo sapiens schizotypus*, *homo schizo* for short.[2] We would strip from our tunics the noble title of *homo sapiens sapiens*, which is often now accorded us, reserving it for a species of some future event and time. So drastic an action may not be taken, however, without due process of law, and our book is intended as a hearing on the allegation that *homo sapiens sapiens* is not the wise wise man and cannot by nature be so.

What is the nature of *homo sapiens* that he should be relegated to the status of schizotypicality? According to Pascal, "Men are so necessarily mad, that not to be mad would amount to another form of madness." Mainly the nature of the human is that he is either normally insane or insanely normal, or both. If either or both, he is not the man we thought he was. Whereupon we should analyze his nature more critically than has been the custom, and learn what makes him behave so, and what we can expect of him. Dunbar points out that "Through the study of the unusual or deviant, the obscurity of many normal processes is penetrated. Just as the mutant is the ultimate ancestor of the race, so the deviant is often the common denominator of processes too complex to be broken down in the norm."

In searching for the roots of human nature, I have to use a number of concepts that are modern, psychiatric, and originally invented for the diagnosis of disease, beginning with the very word schizophrenia. However I also use the terms of old science, like human nature and instinct, and the jargon of the computer age, and of electricity and politics. For the assault upon the problem of the human constitution and its origins levy verbal troops from everywhere. If the assault is successful, there will be time enough to provide these with the linguistic uniform that new science invariably prescribes.

A first step, then is to show how *homo sapiens* is insanely normal, implying paradoxically that the concept of normality is quite confused in practice, and ends in contradictions. It cannot then be a helpful idea, if its meaning collapses from one moment to the next. It is like a tall pole without a base, which can stand upright only so long as you steady it; nor does it matter where you stand to steady it.

"Normal" is an interesting word of the 18th century Enlightenment; it is a late arrival to our language. Its function was probably being served before by words such as "good" and "healthy." It comes from geometry, hence science, directly from the Latin *norma*, the right angle rule used in drawing. From "rule," came "mold," "unit," a point of comparison. Then a century later "normal" came to be a state of a living being or an organ which is not affected by any pathological modification, as in a "normal human oral temperature." Later it acquired the senses of "devoid of exceptional character," "conforming to the most frequent type" (typical), "occuring according to habit," a "normal person." So we see an object needed by the new applied physical sciences which is expanded abstractly to include a model or verbal rule; already it is forcing its way as an objective concept into the moral sphere; then we watch it attach itself to an undiseased state of a living being (which concerns us here) and ultimately to the statistical type or the ordinary (which we also consider).

The problem when the world deals with human nature becomes apparent: the non-pathological state, and the ordinary or typical, are mingled in the idea of a normal human being. The normal person should be of the normally healthy majority. The trouble is that there is neither a normal standard state, nor a normally healthy majority. On those matters closest to the important code of human nature, we cannot decide on what should be termed "non-pathological." And on even those traits which are conventionally deemed healthy, we cannot find a great concentration of individuals to cluster.

The normal engages the range of the abnormal, even some of its extremes, and the abnormal is a set of improvisations on the normal. We do not end up with a rational person of healthy mind and of someone who is broken down into insanity as with a bad fall off a bicycle. Rather there is the human being whose essential functions are the same, *homo schizo*, who is always behaving "madly," but as one of his defense mechanisms divides people into the sane and insane according to largely societal canons. The prudent approach in these circumstances is to locate a foundation for normality. By all tokens, it should be in the idea of sanity. The human species has to be composed of normal sane people; else it is a contradiction in terms. But suppose that we find mostly insane people; then something is wrong with the definition of insanity, or of normality. So we go in search of the normal great majority of sane human beings.

To define who is normal is not like sounding the concert pitch for the orchestra. Various writers emit their own authoritative sounds, and these and many others bring in their peculiar instruments, whose construction and qualities defy brief classification. There are those for example who offer an anatomical definition of man. They measure heights, head shapes, dentition, and so on. They have a rather precise job. For they know in advance that they are dealing with contemporary man. They can categorize sub-races, sex differences, blood groupings, and ranges of variation on many other traits.

They know that some people have small brain cases but are observably intelligent. They know that the Congo Pygmies are human, although a foot below average in height and their brains are smaller, but they have a reputation for unusual cleverness, complex polyphonic music, a large repertoire of legend, and great skill in hunting; they intermarry with tall neighbors of different race. There have been giants on the earth, too, bones and records tell us, and legends have them "normal," though on occasion more "wicked" than the story-tellers — just very big. Many others traits vary around the world and within peoples: hairiness, skin color, eye color, head shape, etc.

CULTURED MAMMALS

Today we are witness to rapid progress in brain and central nervous system chemistry and electricity. Soon we shall be able to define every mental aberration by a test result showing a surplus or deficiency of a chemical or gas or electrical charge in critical locations. This achievement will not define human nature but will certainly facilitate efforts at controlling behavior deemed sick or criminal. The normal may thus be precisely measured. Moreover, those elements of the abnormal that are regarded to have positive value, that is, those elements of the abnormal that we seek to make normal, such as "altruism," or "intelligence," or "dexterity," can probably be manipulated electro-chemically so as to produce specifically acceptable behaviors within a larger set of undesired behaviors.

Try as we may, with dozens of testing instruments, we cannot find a genetically non-miscegenable, intellectually inferior (or superior), uncivilizable, ungodly, mother-marrying, physically defective, short-lived, crawling (or arboreal) unselfconscious, mythless breed. We find genetic sports, who are six-digited specimens, brain-damaged, sickle-celled, or have prodigious IQ's, and so forth, again all among normal human groups. A host of human variations exist, none of them obviously in fundamental contradiction to normalcy, either as usually defined or as schizoid normal. When a person has suffered some neurological disorder or brain injury, noone can object to his being labelled sick — mentally ill, if his voluntary behavior is altered — and, even though the injury has effects much like that of ordinary psychic abnormality, and even if his treatment, too, is that tendered the mentally ill, we perceive the case as exceptional and as another class of illness.

Sometimes we get the impression that the animal kingdom supplies a baseline for normal behavior in humans. To be called "a healthy animal" is ground for pride in some quarters — images of exuberant spirits, strong musculature, and high sexual potency come to mind. Everyone has his favorite animal story to show how human a beast can be — whether a dog, a cat, a pig, or a bird, not to mention elephants, octopus, dolphins and monkeys. And it is generally true that well-cared-for animals are healthy and not crazy, while demented humans do not seem to take proper care of themselves,

being often enfeebled, unkempt, and of ungovernable or
poor appetite.

Ethologists, who lend animals their full attention, are
often taken in by their charges and come to see in them
all too much conduct that is human. Still it is to be admitted, as the latest returns from the field come in, fewer and
fewer human activities lack a close analogy or counter-
part in some other species. One after another, the
"unique" traits of *homo sapiens* are washed away. Chimpanzees talk, flatworms reason, seagulls adapt, the
devoted dog performs religious rites before his god, the
ordinary biological cell contains the human code of life.

The best that can be said of man is that he does more
of everything and does it more consistently and continuously. And the best of human performers are mad, for is it
not true, what Lombroso said, that genius and madness
are akin, that only by his product is the creative genius
released from the burdens of the unsuccessful madman?
It is certainly true in politics. In the benighted United
States, a man who drinks his urine and bathes in it is
locked up, while in India, not for that, of course, he may
be Prime Minister.

"Of the 113 geniuses that have most helped civilization, 37 percent to 40 per cent were psychotic, 83 per cent
to 90 percent were psychopathic or sociopathic, and 30
percent of the most important were commited." So says
Johnson.[3]

All the figures are questionable, including the 113 to
begin with, but nevertheless impressive in the round.
Painstaking investigations of cultures, from the deep forest primitives of the Philippines to the penthouse dwell-
ers of Manhattan, bring to light only cultural forms that
are readily analogical, even homological, with all other
cultures. They can all become the life style of whoever
happens to become engaged in them from infancy. This
transferability, universality, and relativity of culture, is
highly important to the definition of normalcy. It enables
one to say that whatever may seem to be abnormal behavior in one culture will be found to have a normal place in
some other culture. Properly directed hallucinating is a
gift, or a symptom of insanity, according to cultural norm;
in a doubting and liberal culture, as for instance the

United States today, one may discover even psychologists who cultivate hallucinating, whether for religious reasons, adventure, or self-experimentation. Practically every symptom of nervous disease disappears into the tolerant maw of culture.

Intercourse among uncles and nieces is taboo in some cultures while in other cultures uncles teach their nieces how to copulate. Judging by its lurid prominence in writings, an instinct to commit incest seems more likely than an instinct to avoid it. Most commentators have viewed the stern injunctions against incest that are so widespread as proof of the intensity of the instinct. Yet N. Bischoff argues a propensity to avoid incest, which is not strong enough "to determine but only to motivate our behavior."[4] Thus, we are free enough to act contrary to our nature; but we are not free enough to do so with impunity. Individuals are not transferable so easily in practice as in theory. By the time their abnormality becomes developed, they are too encrusted with the rest of their culture and too enmeshed in their failures or careers to make a computer date *via* the Human Relations Area Files with a culture normally harboring the abnormality. So they appear to be condemned to being treated as sick.

SAMPLING FOR THE NORMAL

Perhaps, however, one's society is changing, and one may discover a niche of acceptability. The poet Oscar Wilde was a public homosexual ahead of his time. He was jailed. Today he would meet only with mild, and extralegal, disapproval in his mating habits. English law has changed, following upon a change in elite opinion.

People are not at all sure of behavior occuring within their own cultures, whether in Singapore or Chicago. "You can't imagine the things that go on!" a tendentious paranoid third of the population will tell you. And they are correct, even if their attitude can lead to some undesirable social distrust that pulls at the weak fabric of social consensus. There are many kinds of abnormal "things that go on," conspiracy, for example, as when gangsters,

politicians, businessmen and any other group for that
matter plot actions better kept undisclosed, for tactical or
moral or legal reasons. There are undisclosed criminal
offenses, to which the American people confess in great
numbers to priests, psychiatrists, and interviewing
strangers. It appears that nearly everyone has committed
at least a couple of crimes that he knows about and can
recite.

Of the conspiracies and crimes, a great many are moral
in nature. Child-abuse, spouse-abuse: these are examples. Millions of such cases occur; are they normal behavior? Are they crime or illness? Or both? Benevolent associations and fiction writers try to catch up with them, and
the latter at least win only a reputation for caricature and
morbidity, harping upon the "abnormal." Not forseeing
how uninhibited literature would become, a French
writer, Jules Barbey d'Aurevilly, addressing himself to
famous writers, in his short stories about diabolic women
of a century ago, said "Ask them how much incest is to be
found in families, whether of the poorest or highest class,
and see if literature, which is accused of being so
immoral, has ever dared to tell of them, even to frighten
the reader," complaining that one had to go to the ancient
examples of Myrrha, Agrippina and Oedipus, although,
all around, there were cases to be found.

But then there is the category of abnormalities called
madness, or mental illness, which the legions of science
strive to segregate from acts of conspiracy, immorality,
and crime. Possibly they are moved by an instinct of terri-
toriality — for without a field of study there cannot be a
fat herd of scientists. More largely, they are searching for
their identity in their object, as a shepherd for his flock, a
priest for his parishioners.

We cannot speak individually to a whole people, asking them whether they belong to the psychiatrist's flock.
But we have learned to sample a population, assuring
that those sampled truly stand for the whole, and we can
interview these. Perhaps here the search for the normal
person can end. If there is anything that is uniquely
human and normal to mankind, it will have emerged from
the great factory of the mind to find its way into the communication of ideas, thoughts, and feelings. All other

normality can be consigned to our generic kinship with apes, fish, and bacteria.

The result of such surveys of mental health give scant comfort to expectations of normality. They disclose more people to be sick than well, many more. And if one adds, to the self-confessed illnesses, the sickness that is not disclosed, because of the suppression of recall or the inadequacy of the questioning, the scene darkens and many more of the normal become abnormal.

In one study of sample of householders of a rural Canadian county, as many as 69% were deemed to be psychiatric cases.[5] Most others had troublesome mental problems. Only 17% were classified as "well." To be "well" then is to be statistically abnormal.

In a middle-class white section of New York City, a different sample survey of mental health was conducted.[6] Here 1660 adult residents were interviewed at length by trained workers and the materials adjudged by psychiatrists. Some 18.5% were deemed mentally "well." A third had mild symptoms, and the rest, about half, suffered moderate or severe symptoms of mental illness. Again the "well" or "normal" are statistically abnormal.

Other studies can be cited. A recent World Health Organization report gives a figure of 40 millions for the gravely sick of mind in the world; another 200 millions are too ill to function well. One in every six Englishwomen are receiving care for mental disorder, one in every nine men. Deliberate self-therapy must treble these figures. Then, too, people go in and out of treatment, self-administered or not. A third of the American population, where hallucinations are neurotic or psychotic, nevertheless hallucinate from time to time. From one-third to one-half of normal perons aged 12 to 35 years report episodic symptoms of dissociation or depersonalization. A third, not necessarily the same two-thirds, suffer neurotic anxiety or worse. Practically everyone engages in psychosomatic illness from time to time. There appears to be little doubt: the normal is abnormal, and the abnormal is normal, statistically, intraculturally, and crossculturally.

When one adds up the diagnosed ill, the ambulant ill, the suffering normals, the individually destructive, the sexually differentiated, the genetically abnormal, the culturally and criminally diverse and perverse, the infantile and the senile, and proceeds to some type of summation, the remainder, if they have a strong sense of normality, can be classified as megalomaniacs. Feeling bad is the norm, in one or more of a thousand ways. Mental suffering must be on an immense scale throughout the world. The "normal" human being is not the healthy animal he is supposed to be.

Throughout history, anxiety has been recognized as an inherent part of man's being. Discussion of the origins of anxiety has become explicit in the 20th century and is a frequent theme in today's literature. The definition of anxiety is as varied as the experience itself, and its biological basis is obscure. While anxiety may be thought of as an unpleasant state, characterized by uneasiness and apprehension, it is also a strong motivating force in many forms of behavior and, like fear, has fundamental adaptive and perhaps evolutionary significance.[7]

Perhaps the very idea of "normality" is a sickness. Psychopaths and neurotics often hate abnormality or atypicality in others, as Hitler hated gypsies and a meticulous drill sergeant may dislike a tall recruit who stands out from the line. One must consider whether the idea of the normal human is not some unrecognized myth, functioning to hold an individuated lot of persons in a tighter society. If so, we should dredge up the myth, for it may be blocking our understanding of human nature.

THE IDEAL PERSON

An obvious relative of such a concealed myth would be the idea of the "noble savage." Something like the idea of the "noble savage" is to be found going back thousands of years. The "Golden Age" of mankind fascinated many ancient historians and peoples. It was an age of easy subsistence, warmth, equality, and peace. The Romans associated the Golden Age with Saturn; they stored their weapons in his temple when at peace.

Upon the Age of Discoveries, from the 16th to the 18th centuries, and despite much evidence to the contrary, Europeans conjured a vision of happy primitive peoples living in a benign state of nature, even foregoing governments, taxes, war, and civil strife, to which the Europeans were habituated. Jean-Jacques Rousseau, whose deservedly famous *Confessions* frankly recited his many "abnormal," "neurotic" behaviors, played a greater role than any other writer in building up the myth.

He felt a compulsion to reveal his shocking evil and errors. He was the son of a watchmaker, an obsessive occupation, and was himself a musician. He suffered from paranoia, strong ambivalences, incontinence, phobias, hallucinations. He enjoyed being spanked on the rump. He believed his portrait, though excellent, was part of a conspiracy to make him look like a monster.

Rousseau yet claimed that the human being was born with natural reason and good motives. In his educational writings, he argued that to confine or restrain the pupil was to pervert him. Anthropologists, while they could not deny the most astonishing "perversions" among the peoples whom they were newly studying, nevertheless added the idea of relativity: that is, if all is not good, then it is at least different and hence we must not insist upon our absolute standards of the good.

Rusticism, the belief in simple rural existence and its virtues, has been a chronic "neurosis" since times immemorial. One encounters the idea among people of all classes even, or especially, in America today, while only three per cent of the population are farmers; many politicians play upon the rustic theme.

Sigmund Freud, of all people, may be perceived, in his essay on *Civilization and Its Discontents,* to assign mental malignancies to the burden of discipline and complexity attributable to civilized life. He, at least, explains how impossible it is to take up the rustic life again. But he does not doubt that there was and can be a rustic life. And there is little doubt he regards the human

being as potentially happier if ever he would return to
the "normal" of his mentality. Given his many different
writings, this can only be regarded as a contradiction and
a minor nuisance, still it is capable of distracting him in
his search for the origins and condition of human nature.

Psychologists, disobeying the first principle of science — factuality — have been loath to lay their cards on
the table. "The mentally ill person, helped to discover
the origins of his illness, will use the knowledge to cure
himself, to become normal." So goes an ordinary principle by which many psychologists operate. Finding oneself, coming to terms with oneself, and similar slogans
amount to the premise that there is a normal human self
that is within us all, a core that, when struck, will resonate natural goodness.

Attempts to elaborate scientifically the syndrome of
normality scarcely produce an integrated core of rationality, goodness, or creativity. They elicit conventional syn-
dromes. They tend to bring out diffuse characteristics
that are tolerable. It seems almost as if, in striking paral-
lelism with the myths of the noble savage and the rustic,
they are turning back towards a docile and agreeable
hominid. Johnson remarks that "tests show that so-called
normal individuals have little imagination, limited interests and social activities, limited aspirations, and no
ambition."[8]

Gaillant presents material on life careers that reveal
students testing "normal" to be less subject to illnesses
that are of psychosomatic origins.[9] The finding is not
soothing, for it points back to the association of creativity
with mental illness, and lets one wonder whether normality is a "success story" blocking (psychophysical) illness but questionable as to the grounds of success, which
can itself be grounded upon mental operations basically
abnormal.

A schoolmaster or legislator might define the normal
person as one who imitates well the norm, who obeys the
authorities, who eats moderately, does not take drugs,
sleeps well, fulfills sexual desires within suggested limits, accepts responsibilities when charged with them, has
only appropriate fears and associates these with the real
source of danger, is hygienic, loves one's family, is

careful in dealing with strangers, feels gratitude, and believes in gods.

Not only are such persons unusual, but they do not constitute an integral psychological type wherein contradictions are absent. They, too, must be the results of high test-scoring on separate items of inquiry. More than this, however, is a fact which will be looming up as crucial to this book, that "normal" qualities, such as moderation, hygiene, responsibility, belief in gods and others as well, are qualities that are sculpted out of a basic natural "insanity."

In everyday behavior, there are clichés for every symptom of mental disease.

Consider only the following. Others readily suggest themselves.

> *dissociation:* "I'm not myself today."
> *fear and control:* "Afraid of her shadow.." "Get
>   hold of yourself.."
> *anhedonia* (masochism): "Suffering is good for
>   the soul."
> *aversiveness:* "Don't trust a stranger." "Keep
>   them at arm's length."
> *paranoia:* "The walls have ears." "May God
>   strike me dead if..."
> *catatonia:* "All things come to those who wait."
>   "Rest is the best cure." "I hate to get up in the
>   morning."
> *obsession:* "Genius is 99% hard work." "I can't
>   help but feel that.."
> *cognitive disorder:* "Pray for peace." "Keep the
>   family together."
> *megalomania:* "Aim for the stars." "Nothing is
>   impossible."
> *aggression:* "We need law and order."
>   "Equality." "National Security."

Each trite expression feeds upon a human dimension that also feeds general schizophrenia. Each can be linked to others, too. "National security" is a slogan with paranoic, obsessive, and fearful as well as aggressive nuances.

But is not "national security" also, at some times, in some places a reasonable demand, raised in defense against a measurable threat? Yes. I have said that it fits into a reciprocating scheme of madness and normality. It may be correct under the circumstances to arm one's nation. Should those who disagree, however, be categorized as insane, or merely as ignoramuses? And the pacifists? And, further, is it not the pride of the human animal that it can plan its "national security" far ahead of this day; and is it not true that it will be especially paranoid, aggressive, nationalistic-identifying, and obsessive characters who will be most insistent upon this human far-sightedness? We shall say more of such matters as we go along.

The average person lives a life of "madness." Analyze his or her activities minute by minute in the course of the day. It is loaded with sleep (a life-suppressor); dreams (by definition insane) while asleep; waking fantasies of glory, sex, escape; guilt feelings; nursing animosities; feelings of inferiority; futile gestures; self-doubts; moments of mania; laughter; doing what "is bad for me;" reminiscing; praying; ruminating; brooding; projecting false pictures; making required and excessive purchases; repeating routines uncomprehendingly or automatically; relapsing blank-minded; playing psychological games with co-workers and others — at the end there is a "product" which justifies the passage of the day, lends meaning, provides ego support if assured so sufficiently by others (whom one in turn assures also). Where the brutish activity of sleep and feeding and physically moving about ends, what must be human begins, but this human is almost entirely madness, redeemed by defining "work instrumentalism" and "realistic appraisals of self and others" as sane behavior, perhaps 10% of the total of life.

Rarely, a scientific writer, (Harold Lasswell is one of them) will so much as frankly acknowledge that he is interested in advancing a certain kind of person in society, an "ideal man and woman," an "ideal citizen," in effect, whose etiological dynamics psychiatrists (and statesmen) should explore, understand, and propagate.[10]

The "normal" is waived in favor of the "ideal."
Indeed, one suspects that it is precisely in order to control the true normal population that the ideal norm is set
up. He is what he is, not because he is a natural man, but
because he might be artificially created to go against
nature!

Lasswell speaks of the values for which humans
strive. These are a type of instincts; they are generalized
appetitive urges that crop out in many ways. The values
are power, respect, rectitude, safety, wealth, well-being,
enlightenment, and affection. The objective of public
policy should be to develop the sharing of these among
the people of the world. The means to the end is the creation of democratic characters who are willing and ready
to share. "Failure to develop democratic character is a
function of interpersonal relations in which low esti-
mates of the self are permitted to develop." Reminiscent
of Alfred Adler's "inferiority complex," a prevalent low
estimate of oneself leads people to wish to deprive others, thence misunderstanding and aggression, among a
host of other neuroses and psychoses.

The democratic man, then, has an intact ego, open to
thought and impression; is possessed of many values and
disposed to share them with all. He is free from disabling
anxieties and increasingly in command of the flow of
energies from his unconscious self. Lasswell grants the
difficulty of creating a dominating psychic type: "The
task is nothing less then the drastic and continuing
reconstruction of our own civilization, and most of the
cultures of which we have any knowledge."

Lasswell frees himself from the rustic fallacy: a new
kind of man is to be created, whose life is to be supported
by especially designed institutions, a utopia, to be sure,
but one unencumbered by dreams of normalcy and myths
of a golden age. We shall see below whether, in fact,
there is a potential within the human being to create or
develop, much more to sustain, such a type. To Thomas
Hobbes, writing several centuries earlier, the idea would
be ludicrous: man is naturally conflictful, party to a war of
all against all, and capable only of receiving a brutal reg-
imentation by a sovereign. Indubitably, history bears
down on this side of the scales.

Our arguments here against the prevalance of "normal people" are not intended merely to "broaden our minds" regarding normality; many writers have done this job well. Nor are we aiming to set up an ideal type, which has an elite that can create artificial normalities. We assert rather that the very logic, the very substructure, the very physiology of the concept of normality sought for as a base for judging abnormality is not present.

SELF-AWARENESS

What is there in the jumble of physiques, cultures, behaviors, in this preponderance of crimes, immorality and aberrations among the normal, that we can fix upon as unique to the human species, and that is found in the sick and the well, in criminals and judges, in leaders and followers, in Patagonia and Canada, in the first days of the human species down through history to the present.

The answer is well-known, and might perhaps have been written in the beginning. It is self-awareness. Whatever recognizes itself is human. Whatever can see itself without a mirror is human.[11] Whatever thinks that it thinks: *cogito ergo sum*, is human. Whatever doubts is human. But the ramifications of self-awareness are so many that they may be categorized in the dozens and detailed in the thousands. We need not go farther with them here. Essentially we can say that with a couple of possible minor exceptions, involving heavy training, animals and plants are not self-reflective: they may be conscious to any degree of sharpness, ranging from rock-like inanimacy to laser-like concentrations of attention.

Only by the most strenuous efforts can we deprive a human of self-awareness, and then only temporarily, without lethal consequences, and without genetic effect. Never can a human maintain an alert consciousness without lapsing from time to time into sensations of self-consciousness.

Pause, for a moment, to consider the fantastically complex mind that is operating in a self-aware schizo-phrenic. The classical tell-tale symptom is the auditory hallucination, which the patient(1), describes to the doctor (or a friend) (2), as a voice of another (3), which the patient hears (4), and is the patient (5), talking to himself (6), and which the patient asks the doctor to believe (7), but also asks the doctor to deny (8), because he the patient is sick (9), and denies the voice is real (10), although he admits (11), and argues against the correctness of the message of the voice (12), which in fact we know (13), is not uttering anything at all (14), and sometimes the patient hears several voices speaking in unison (15..n), or uttering different messages (16..n).

Traits ordinarily attributable to human nature are derivatives from the basic fact of self-awareness. For instance, Aristotle's famous sentence, "Man is a social animal,": seems to accord to sociability a unique human quality. Social, even political, behavior is characteristic of many animal species, and in a meaningful sense plants that must live in clumps can be termed social.

Going beyond this obviously inadequate characterization of man, we should also comment that this sociability, when it becomes particularly the human kind of sociability, has to be an appendage of individual self-awareness. It is not, cannot be, "herd behavior." Human individuation is rife within the human group. Regardless of how they are raised and trained, the style in which they live, and whether they are criminal or judges, moral or immoral, mentally sick or well, in or out of groups and crowds, humans are self-conscious. If not self-conscious in the immediate, flashing sense, they are coasting along with all the momentum of self-awareness imparted by the motive force of their total prior life-experiences.

Not only are all mental diseases diseases of self awareness, but also all mental operations, diseased or not, are inflicted or shaped by self-awareness. The ability to go mad is almost entirely human, no matter how madness is defined. And if, in the end, all that is uniquely human is exposed and one is prompted to exclaim: "But that *is* madness," we had better redefine madness, and medicine, and policy, and philosophy. Again, my position is not far from those psychotherapists who say that all mental illness is centered upon problems of the ego. It will take some paragraphs now to tell how true this is, and to begin to use the diseases of the ego to construe the elements of human nature.

The redoubtable Cardinal Richelieu, ruling minister of France under Louis XIII, had said "Give me a sentence a man has spoken, and I'll give you enough to hang him." The same expression might end "...and I'll show you that he is demented." Nor have modern police-states been unaware of the new alternative. The Soviet government often prefers to treat political opponents as mad, rather than treasonable; the Chinese communist government of Mao popularized the term "brainwashing," implying that its political dissidents had cluttered and dirty minds. The early Italian Fascists, more earthy and ironic, force-fed opponents with large doses of castor oil to purge them. Apropos, the French word for "asylum" has only the two meanings: "political asylum" for fugitives from a country's law, and a "mental asylum."

Our grounds for suspecting the ordinary person of some admixture of madness are already considerable. Indeed the very excesses of pursuing the distinction of being mad contain more than a hint of obsessive compulsion, prompted by self-doubts. Politics aside, what is the punitive and aggressive impulse to be called that drives men to segregate indistinct orders of people in order to call them by special names — anonomania? Nonetheless, our fidelity to scientific method bids us continue, this time reversing the order and asking, "What is mental illness, the class of abnormally ill and atypical?"

One may search for a classification, expecting to find an acceptable set of categories for ordering the millions of mentally ill for contemplation and analysis. No such classification exists, to our way of thinking. One can choose among many systems, each with its defects — too lengthy, too brief, lopsided, stressing any given specialist's area of expertness and giving him this a reason for preferring it. Eugen Bleuler's scheme of 1911 is still influential, although by now encrusted with novelties and frills.

From Bleuler's work we can derive roughly two

groups, one of organic lesions and strongly hereditary, the other less hereditary, with strong social components.[12] So we have a first list consisting of: congenital mental defectives; cretinism and idiocy; cerebral tumors; paresis; and senile dementia.

Then we have a second list containing: drug addiction; paranoia; hysteria; neurasthenia (obsessive-compulsive ideas); neuroses; schizophrenia; epilepsy; and psychosomatic disorders.

The first category can be excluded from consideration here because the elaboration required to integrate its components into our theory of human nature would take up too much space, and furthermore is unnecessary, since the second category leads us more directly to the points we wish to make. The second group has been of course heavily discussed so that, again, we may save time and conserve attention by omitting descriptions and comparative treatment. I exhibit the list only to say that the symptoms that constitute all of these diseases have in one way or another, and by some, though not necessarily most, psychologists, been dealt with also as symptoms of schizophrenia and will be so considered for our purposes here. Few if any of their indications exclude them from what can be termed general schizophrenia. Once we abstract and re-route the major symptoms of insanity, we find that a not-too-rare concept of schizophrenia can hold them all neatly.

Alcoholic intoxication simulates mental illness in many ways, beginning with the wide variability of its symptoms, a fact that has baffled attempts at its analysis despite the ready access to experimental and natural subjects. We note that fears, both existential and immediate, promote the use of this drug (and others) and that withdrawals from intoxication are often accompanied by panic; tranquillizers are sometimes supplied to reduce such agitation. A drunk may suffer distorted perceptions and cognition; slowed reaction speeds; hallucinations and "flights of fancy"; mania, recklessness, megalomania; depression; paranoiac aggression; change of roles and depersonalization; reduced bodily control; and heightened associational ability and creativity.

All mental illnesses may be encountered in some

single episodes, it would appear: can it be that there is only one mental illness, and that alcohol can induce it. If so, alcohol must be pressing upon the core of human nature from all-around, not only figuratively but literally. Perhaps all instinctual responses are slowed down, and at the same time all inhibitions are overwhelmed by the stimuli to respond. So the stimuli roam throughout the brain, seizing upon any neural outlets they can find, riding upon any neurotransmitters that are available. Irrelevant behavior of many kinds ensues. Ultimately, the sleep reaction is triggered in the "lower" animal sections of the central nervous system; there comes a significantly deep sleep, possibly death. Later on, much will be said to put psychosomatic illness in its proper place as a mimic of all mental illness, rather like alcoholism, so we shall not discuss it here.

THE HUMAN DISEASE

"Schizophrenia" is a widespread affliction. Its provenance is worldwide and has little regard for social class. Dunham reports its worldwide rates as "quite comparable," with a prevalence between two and nine per thousand.[13] His narrow definition, of course, leaves us the task of showing that some 90% may be "schizotypical." J. Murphy also found comparable rates of indigenously defined schizophrenia (non-hospitalized cases) in Sweden (5.7 per 1000), Canada (5.6), and among Eskimo (4.4) and Yoruba (6.8). "Explicit labels for insanity exist in these cultures...Almost everywhere a pattern composed of hallucinations, delusions, disorientations, and behavioral aberrations appear to identify the idea of 'losing one's mind,' even though the content of these manifestations is colored by cultural beliefs."[14] Intellectuals are prone to the ailment; counsellors at leading universities sometimes warn psychologists not to use their students as standards for psychological testing because they are skewed towards the schizoid.

The rates of schizophrenia rise with rising indices of social disorganization, according to many studies.[15] One might guess that "wherever anything important is

happening" schizophrenia rates will increase; beware of
a departure from "normal" routines (but we shall have to
explore later on whether "routines" themselves are
"normal"). Beware, too, of the masking of increased schizophrenia when the non-routine and important happens;
war and religion are often ways of containing the increase
in madness by legitimizing them. One percent of the
American population is markedly ill with
"schizophrenia." Since it is a gradient illness, the number may be defined upwards or downwards. Their family
members may reach thrice this number, and are sorely
disturbed and often "infected" by them; the victims of
the disease are outnumbered, so to speak, by their public.

Borderline cases are in the millions. Practically anybody who reads a piece on the subject (and literature on
the subject reaches into the mass media) finds the symptoms uncomfortably close to home.

And, of course, we shall be insisting throughout this
book that everyone who is human is schizoid, that is, a
borderline case. But this requires absorbing all mental
disease into schizophrenia and then reabsorbing all schizophrenia into human nature.

With all this interest, there is a little corresponding
illumination. It is an exasperating mental illness. Its
symptoms are so diverse and irreconcilable that many
savants deny that it exists. They make and unmake classi-
fications often so as to order the mental diseases by some
abiding and knowable principle. Hyperclassification is a
disease of ignorance. When a new family of phenomena
is discovered (or admitted to discussion), be it mental illness or sub-atomic particles or geological strata, a ple-
thora of terms and categories is excreted.

Hundreds of mental events are named. The names are
kept until common causes are found to join their referent
events or some control technique (therapy) compresses
many into one. Six experimenters in a *Science* letter of
April 1979 refer to "a valid clinical classification, be it
Bleulerian or otherwise," as all that can be provided
"considering the arbitrary nature of all presently available diagnostic criteria for schizophrenia."[16] In the end,
Karl Menninger has explained, all attempts at classification have failed, and a single mental disease bordering

upon the concept of "maladjustment" may be the answer.[17] We might call it "holopathy."

Yet other writers are convinced that schizophrenia not only exists but has a genetic basis: they claim that a special inheritance sets the stage. A family, a culture, and "the age of anxiety" can interact to produce a total stress upon the person sufficient to cause schizophrenia only when the genetic component is present. It appears that the disease in its more perverse state involves a person who is likely to be descended from schizoids and who is subsequently helped towards his illness by a set of environmental influences that are well known and generally agreed upon. Such influences include parents or guardians who behave in a schizoid way towards the person. They also include a general breakdown of norms in the near-environment and even the world-*angst* as a whole. These provocative stimuli bombard the person from all sides and continuously over time.

S. Matthysse and K. Kidd speak of a "genetic heterogeneity among schizophrenics;" the same genes may not be involved in all cases; about one in eleven schizophrenics has an extremely high genetic risk, over 99%.[18] Edward Foulks writes that "the predicted incidence in identical twins and in offsprings of dual matings is too low for a single major genetic locus model and too high for a polygenic model. An interactional model involving four alleles is the most likely mode of inheritance."[19]

W.E. Bunney, who directs the National Institute of Mental Health, probably offers the now-established view when he declares that "The issue... is not whether a genetic component exists, but how is the genetic component transmitted, and how do the genetic component and the environment component interact." A colleague who heads the NIMH Laboratory of Psychology and Psychopathology, D. Rosenthal, reports from a study of several thousand Danish adoptees, that the adoptees typically pursue the schizophrenic or non-schizophrenic condition of their natural parents, not of their adoptive ones. "The genetic factor comes through loud and clear." But again the mode of transmission is unclear: "a dominant gene, a partially dominant gene, a recessive gene, or poly genes."[20]

In his admittedly fruitless search for fundamental symptoms, Bleuler once wrote that it is the "accessory" symptoms that usually cause hospitalization, that is, hallucinations, delusions, disturbances of memory, changes in personality, changes in script, speech and physical functions, and catatonic behavior. Problems of "another person" talking in an abrupt, simple and important manner, and of excruciating body sensations in practically all organs, are common.

So all-embracing are the manifestations, that schizophrenia appears to engage all mental ills, as Menninger suggested. And Bleuler said of his work, "It may be that there is only one kind of mental illness; in that case the clinical conditions which we delineate would be artificial creations and there would be no corresponding boundaries in nature... the psychoses may be simple deviations from a norm in varying directions and degrees."[21]

The singularity of mental illness is evidenced in the shifting of symptoms from one named disease to another. What is diagnosed as manic-depression may, at the next examining session, be perceived as schizophrenia. "'Thought disorder' is characteristic of all psychosis and not peculiar to schizophrenia."[22] A certain proportion of schizophrenes are not thought-disordered, while some, perhaps all, mental diseases can display thought-disorders. Thought disorder can be viewed as a problem of self-control, with anxiety or even terror accompanying it.

A pain in the head may transfer its site to the stomach functionally, that is, psychically but with organic consequences. Too, one practitioner suggests that "the basic physiopathology of schizophrenia is a lack of coordination of brain-functions all the way from the cortical cells to the process of feeling and thinking."[23] This idea is rendered more compelling by the congenital relationship between schizophrenia and humanization which is postulated here and developed in *Homo Schizo I*. What seem to be contradictions are resolved when the primitive history of the syndrome is uncovered.

From the beginning, schizotypicality has been the essence of human nature, and schizophrenia has been the thrusting spearhead of human nature. These were established as such when mankind was "quantavoluted." Their existence tends to prove that mankind was created in a leap, and not evolved point by point over millions of years. On one day, in one place, and under knowable conditions, the hominid was transformed into the creature, *homo sapiens*, that perhaps should more properly be called *homo sapiens schizotypus*. Thence, by understandable and logical processes of adaptation, domination and succession, this creature came to represent the human race and still does. Mind, behavior, and institutions veer towards the schizophrenic. Not only is the disease of great importance in society, but actual schizophrenia is only the eminently visible surface of a heavily schizoid world.

SYMPTOMS OF MENTAL ILLNESS

In the address already cited, Paul Meehl offers four sets of behaviors that altogether compose a full illness. One consists of recognized cognitive and perceptive disorders. A second is known to be ambivalence of love-hate, or pro-con, impulses and attitudes toward objects of identification and affect. Third comes the rejection of pleasure in any form (anhedonia). A fourth is aversiveness to other people, even and particularly those near and dear. Negativism and paranoia suffuse the symptomology.

I would expand Meehl's and Bleuler's list of symptoms and regroup them for our own purpose of coming to a focus on the core of human nature. An expanded list would at least contain all of these.

addiction to drugs
ambivalence
amnesia
anhedonia
aphasia
aversion/paranoia
compulsiveness
depression
displacement

epilepsy
mania
multiple personality
negativism/denial
neurasthenia
neurosis
obsession
perception disorders/hallucinations/illusions
    projection/blame
psychosomatic disorders/functional physiopathy
thought disorders/rationalization/delusions

These pathological symptoms will be associated with normal symptoms, and tied together, before this book ends, into the model of *Homo Schizo,* so that they may all be viewed as elements of human nature, emanating from the human core dynamics.

If the list is satisfactorily inclusive, the many facets of mental illness can be reduced to two key parameters, depersonalization or the dissociation of identify, and fears concerning self-control. ("Dissociation," translated from *"desagregation,"* has been in the scientific vocabulary since 1889, when Pierre Janet used the concept.) Both are obviously and strongly connected with self-awareness, the central human trait.

Depersonalization symptoms (episodic) are reported by from one-third to one-half of normal persons aged between 12 and 35. They are usually classified under "dissociative disorders." If self-awareness is uniquely human, depersonaliation must be the most human of all symptoms. Fear is omnipresent, for self-control is the problem of coping with self-awareness, the human trait.

I have already incorporated alcoholism into general insanity. Epilepsy, too, despite its lesser prevalance and exotic history, can be contained in the general syndrome of schizophrenia and *homo schizo.* George Steiner, in *Language and Silence,* writes: "In the early stages of epilepsy there occurs a characteristic dream. Dostoievsky tells of it. One is somehow lifted free of one's body; looking back, one sees oneself and feels a sudden, maddening fear; another presence is entering one's own person, and there is no avenue of return. Feeling this fear, the mind gropes to a sharp awakening."

Epilepsy often involves a double or multiple personality. From ancient times and around the world come reports of the "sacred disease" as it was often called. Seizure by a god or a daemon occurs; a feeling of being beaten by others is common. Certainly epilepsy can be considered a schizophrenic seizure. It is too severe to tolerate and apparently remits until the next occasion.

For another example, the symbolic process in humans is known (perceived and understood) as a map or tracking of salient coded components of oneself. Symbols tie the selves together and connect them with outside affinities. A dissociation and fear of oneself will produce and interact with disorders of signs, symbols, language, speech, writing, and reading.

We shall go much farther in this study, until all of the symptoms or diseases are perceived to generate under conditions of depersonalization and existential fear and theat "normal" behavior, too, can be fitted into both the symptomatic categories, where useful, and into the generating conditions.

RECONCILING THE NORMAL AND ABNORMAL

The symptoms of mental illness generally exhibit a relationship with normalcy in the adjectives that are used in describing them. These adjectives are often of a quantitative and comparative (or relative) kind. Thus Melvin Gray, cited above, says: "A 'healthy' person does not dwell unduly upon his body and his functions." We note the word "unduly." In many places, the textbooks and monographs use words of a similarly undefined character: "inappropriate," "bizarre," "harmful," "preponderant," "unreasonable," "insufficient," "disturbing," "disturbed," "uncontrolled," "unreal," "chronic," "beyond the normal," "interminable," etc.

If these are qualities of parameters of normal behavior, then we should expect the normal behavior to contain the same essential properties. Thus, "a normal person does dwell *duly* upon his body and his functions." Why does he do so? My intent here is to show that mental disease exaggerates, but mirrors, average human behavior. It is as my professor, Earl S. Johnson, told me when I was a 15-year-old freshman. "Crazy people are like you and me, but more so."

Laing, Siirala, Arieti, and many other authorities view schizophrenia as a common sort of sickness shared by the healthy. The paranoid schizophrenic simply responds more to the hostile world than does the ordinary person, says Arieti. In changing his position, as have others, from asserting that the schizophrenic interprets the world as hostile to saying that he sees the world fairly accurately for what it really is, Arieti resembles those, such as myself, who have changed from viewing the original basis of religion and primitive cosmology as grand delusions to arguing that there was, in addition to the nature of man, events that made the world terrifyingly hostile. One type of "normal" then who should be suspect is the incurable optimist who insists that the world is better than it really is. The "normal" says "please excuse the temporary confusion," whereas the "abnormal" says, "If things look confused, that's because they really are."

The issue arises whether normal behavior includes any important operation that is not reflected in insanity. The answer is negative. There is no human characteristic that cannot lend itself to a symptomology of mental disease. When one thinks of the hundreds of human traits, this generalization acquires impressive scope. What is salient, though, is that a definition of mental illness is readily convertible into a definition of human nature. The model of mental illness can be a model of human nature. Is it the only possible model? Is it the most useful model? The answer to the first question is "no," to the second, "yes."

If we list our symptoms of general schizophrenia, the all-human mental disease, we find that they include all of the most important traits of the human being. Opposite each parameter of mental illness we might place a parameter of 'normal' human nature (as in the accompanying chart) and in the course of this book much more of such will be done. This habit, "the great flywheel of progress," in the words of William James, may be shown

SCHIZOPHRENIC AND SCHIZOTYPICAL

Examples from thousands of evident cases of normal and abnormal common mental aberrations from the psychiatric standpoint found in typical human mentation.

Symptom category	Insane non-sectarian	Christian (normal)	Jewish (normal)	Homo Schizo (normal)
Fear	World destruction	Judgement Day	Holocaust or divine Annihilation	Self-destructiveness
Displacement	"I am a kind of god"	Jesus and Mary	Yahweh and Moses	Heroes
Cognitive Disorder (causation)	"If I say so, the building will shake"	When Jesus was born, God sent a star to guide the kings	"If we suffer it is because we do wrong in the eyes of God"	"Humans are metamorphosing into machines"

Hallucination	"They order me to kill and burn"	"God answers my prayers"	"The Lord attends our sacrifices"	"I must listen to my better self"
Human Aversiveness	"Danger is everywhere"	"All people are Incorrigibly sinful"	"Other people are Unclean"	"You can't trust strangers"
Anhedonia	Self-flagellation	"In the footsteps of Jesus"	"To labor condemned after our fall from grace"	"Work is fun"
Obsession	"I must continually wash my hands"	"Pray before eating"	"Dietary rules are to be strictly observed"	"I watch my diet carefully"
Illusion	"People know what I'm thinking"	"God is on our side."	"We are God's chosen people."	Thinking machines
Logic	"The world is black as doom"	"Paradise has no night	"Shoul is dark and dreary"	"Night and day are opposites; like men and women."

to be indistinguishable basically from obsession, which is usually treated as a mental disorder.

Symptoms that are rooted in the same psychological complex take different forms in religious and secular mentalities. I indicate examples of this in the accompanying chart. Any religious sect or political ideology can be placed into the chart, so also any type of individual, varying the clichés, expressions, and attitudes to suit the case. Readers here may test their own self-knowledge.

As many as there are of these symptoms, just as many natural human behaviors can be found to correspond to them. Symptoms resemble the effects of the kaleidoscope; out of several bits of colored cut glass, a great many patterns can emerge when the tube is given a shake. In mental disease all of these patterns are called symptoms, and also often called diseases. The several basic mechanisms — the bits of glass — may not be recognized and known to the person playing with the toy.

Between insane and normal conduct are differences of degree. We can pair off the normal and abnormal, no matter how long the list. If it were not for the fact that many people are convinced that something exists called "reasonable behavior," we would have no problem in looking upon human nature as a set of core symptoms of qualities that are common to both the sane and insane. Then, since the insane facets of the quality seem to fit better to a description of human nature, the nature of man can best be analyzed by means of the concept of the insane. The denomination of the "sane" has been the prisoner of theologians and rationalists. The miasma of wishes, ideologies, ego defenses and rationalizations constitutes itself a schizoid syndrome, a cognitive disorder, to the end that the symptoms of normality are excluded from a formulation that would realistically distinguish human nature. Man does not really want to know himself; most of those who are regarded as specialists in knowing human nature do not want to know man either.

Having said this, we cannot now agree with those who maintain that sharp boundaries separate the well, the nervous, the neurotic, and the psychotic. Thus we have Jeffrey Gray saying that "by and large, quite different tests differentiate normal from neurotics and normals from psychotics; and psychotics do not behave differently from normals on tests sensitive to neuroticism, nor do neurotics behave differently from normals on tests sensitive to psychoticism."[24] The tests involved are, of course, statistical, and therefore the scores must exhibit an overlapping among all three categories.

Now Gray would surely recognize the overlap. He would probably also assert that each category, in verging towards some cluster of responses peculiar to itself, begins to manifest behavior which warrants its being labelled as normal, neurotic, or psychotic. Noone can properly deny this to be the case and this is precisely what we have been saying. For example, he says agreeably that neuroses are "fear gone wrong, either because it is excessive, or because it is inappropriate, or because it has no apparent object." "Fear gone wrong" is out of control. Certainly Gray would not deny that fear plays a major role in psychoses, or, for that matter, in normal behavior. Nor would he totally disagree with Alfred Adler when Adler declares that "the neuroses and psychoses are attempts at compensation, constructive creations of the psyche which result from the accentuated and too highly placed guiding ideal of the child."[25]

Nor perhaps would he deny Carl Jung when Jung writes that, in respect to treatment,

> the schizophrenic patient behaves no differently from the neurotic. He has the same complexes, the same insights and needs, but not the same certainty with regard to his foundations. Whereas the neurotic can rely instinctively on his personality dissociation never losing its systematic character, so that the unity and inner cohesion of the whole are never seriously jeopardized, the latent schizophrenic must always reckon with the possibility that his very foundations will give way somewhere, that an irretrievable disintegration will set in, that his ideas and concepts will lose their cohesion and their connection with other spheres of

association and with the environment.
The dangerousness of his situation often
shows itself in terrifying dreams of cosmic catastrophes, of the end of the world
and such things. Or the ground he stands
on begins to heave, the walls bend and
bulge, the solid earth turns to water, a
storm carries him up into the air, all his
relatives are dead, etc.[26]

We conclude that differences can and must always be
discovered betwen any two groups professing symptoms.
The differences are to be described in whatever way best
contributes to devising a therapy or fitting into a model.
The theory of *homo schizo* regards all behavior as symptoms and all symptoms as issuing from the schizoid core
of human nature. We are still permitted to disclose genetically stronger tendencies in some people than others:
some people are more "human" than others. I doubt that
we can say that some "cultures" are more human than
others unless it is discoverable that some isolated cultures originally branched off with a significantly lesser
component of schizophrenic genes in the make-up of the
group as a whole.

THERAPIES

Intense suffering often accompanies mental illness, a
suffering as agonizing as the worst physical pains, as prolonged as the longest organic illness, more frightening
than the worst tidings from the medical doctor, so hopeless as to lead sometimes to suicide. What of the cures,
then, for insanity? Do they reveal anything of the nature
of man?
I will not speak of cures that are madness twice com-
pounded, a form of direct punishment for the sake of the
punishers — confinement, beatings, ostracism, moral
obloquy, brainwashing. Sebastian de Grazia wrote in two
books of mental illness and therapy.[27] The preventative
against most mental illness he found in love, of the early
attendents for the infant and growing child, and of the

community later on for the person. The latter evolves into
the security afforded by "law and order," by ideology, by
consensus and custom, by authority.

When he came to examine the systems of psychotherapy, he found at their base the idea of authority, often
accompanied by punishment in disguised or sublimated
form. He was not obliged to distinguish sharply between
the shaman of the tribe and the therapeutic psychologist
and psychoanalyst: the main therapeutic message was
nearly always a combination of exorcism by the authority
of the healer and needed practical advice. Primitive,
religious, and psychiatric therapies are successful, up to a
point, because they wittingly or unwittingly treat the diseases of schizophrenia by the therapy of authority.
Authority, as an obsessed compulsive force, is zeroed in
upon the patient, who is comforted, appeased, re-ration-
alized and redirected.

The generally "benign" authority of psychotherapy
stands in contrast to the authority that produces psychosis. In Bruno Bettelheim's words, "the psychotic person
breaks because he has invested significant figures in his
environment with the power to destroy him and his integration."[28] He speaks in this work of concentration
camps and psychological clinics.

If one abstracts the message of Michel Foucault in his
book, *Madness and Civilization,* it says that the mad
inspire madness in others, on a grand scale.[29] Just as the
violence of war brings out the violence on all sides, madness elicits the madness of those who deal with it. Foucault deals principally with the period of the Enlightenment, when rationalization of human relations reached
new heights. Consequently a methodology of therapy
developed. Patients were shocked in order to "awaken"
them. Theatrical performances were encouraged to let
them displace their personalities upon acceptable or controllable roles. The "return to the immediate" was
offered sometimes — work on the land, physical labor, so
that patients might divert themselves by exhausting emu-
lations of the primordial struggle for brute survival.
Travel was promoted — a mobile theatre, after all — to
match internal with external turbulence, to provide cul-
ture-shock therapy. All of this was a gloss on the

underlying punishment for the relief of the observing and suffering punishers, the warders and the public.

Nowadays, the struggle to control the bodies and minds of the mentally obstreperous continues. Besides the punishers, there are the facilitators, one leader being Laing, who grants self-government and "foreign aid" to psychotherapeutic communes, and the denyers, exemplary in Thomas Szasz, who finds in most definitions of insanity a political plot or at least a myth. How does the theory of *homo schizo* stand relative to the popular theories of Szasz, whose brilliant forensics (forensic medicine?) against psychiatry culminated in 1976 with a work called *Schizophrenia.*[30] There he labelled schizophrenia as everything and nothing, a myth, a practical fiction for the elaboration of new prisons, of new professions, of new religions, of new crimes against liberty and creativity, of non-science calling itself social science.

With sympathy for Szasz annd for all the victims of unfeeling, unwise, and self-serving therapy (equally present in "organic" medicine?), I will say this: He believes that there is no disease, and therefore nothing to treat, whereas I say that this is indeed the human disease and we are all patients; he is Aristotelian, Cartesian, an orthodox rationalist and materialist whose sympathy for humans, undoubtedly genuine, is an inversion of Hobbesian materialism on the one hand and Thomistic Catholicism on the other. That is, he is an old-fashioned mind rejecting new fashions (call them "paradigms") in their own terms and disclosing their new contradictions. He has written a dozen volumes to argue that "abnormality" is "normality" but it is also wrong to conclude that "normality" exists in its rational conventional sense. There is no better way to show this than to go on with the theory of *homo schizo*, which I shall proceed to do.

Cure by professional therapy is still far from certain. Bleuler, long ago, wrote that "We do not speak of *cure but of far-reaching improvements*" for schizophrenia; he confesses to have never seen a full recovery.[31] A typical, almost randomly selected follow-up study of psychotherapy for schizophrenia today, this of 88 patients eleven years after a median 80-day hospitalization for therapy in Southern Canada, reports 12 deaths, 2 by suicide, and 51 recoveries (showing "no social or intellectual deficit"). Most had been medicated or readmitted subsequent to release from the hospital. Major tranquillizers and electroconvulsive therapy (ECT) were employed in some cases, heavy tranquilization alone in most. Verbal therapy was not predominant, nor were therapeutic communities organized. Out-patient attention and job-assistance was available. The period covered was one of full employment, economic growth, and general optimism in the area.[32] We are accepting the premise that all patients were diagnosed properly to begin with.

Another type of evaluation, autobiographical, is provided by Werner Mendel, based upon the five hundred patients of his career in psychiatry.[33] He would not score so optimistically his successes, but rather finds that when his patients were sick enough to be very sick, they were most unlikely to be entirely cured. A patient might assume after prolonged intensive psychotherapy a typical social role, such as mother and housekeeper, but would on occasion require counselling and medication. It should be stressed that illness is a form of habit or obsession and that, as you would not expect to turn a life-long blacksmith into a fine ballet dancer, you would not expect to typicalize a life-long deviant.

The situation seems improved, then, since Bleuler's times. Granted that the social setting is not producing the preventative antibodies, affection and authority, of which S. de Grazia writes, the professional therapy and social ambiance of mental illness have attained a cure in perhaps two-thirds of those treated, cure being a fair social and job competence with no more than occasional re-therapy.

Spontaneous remission (which means self-cure if it means anything) occurs in a number of cases. Where therapy has been administered, therapy may take more credit than is due. As the larger studies show, most psychological difficulties are self-treated, with the help or hindrance of whoever happens to be around.

Professional therapy today consists largely of reductionism. Reductionism is discoverable in the authoritative explanations of verbal psychotherapy, in communal security and "nests of toleration," hypnosis, tranquilizers, pain-killers, electroconvulsive therapy, physical restraint, and the less commonly used leucotomy (lobotomy). Surgery, drug, and shock: these all seek to diminish and delimit the psychic energy of the sick, to shrink the ego boundaries, "to get out of Vietnam," so to speak, to "cut your losses." They can be used interchangeably. Usually they must be used interchangeably. In psychotherapy there is scarcely ever a specific, a single shot the bull's eye. Thus electroconvulsive therapy (ECT), which is applied generally by electrical wires to opposite sides of the skull, is certainly punishing: the patient is strapped down so as not to flail at the menace to his well-being. Patients can "feel better" afterwards if only because they have assuaged the guilt of their deviancy from social norms. ECT then arouses the cerebrum generally, drowning out "other voices," and alerting consciousness and arousing self-awareness. It brings temporary and sometimes prolonged amnesia of life experiences: the animal can begin life anew without the nagging of memory, even pleasant memory. The zones of sleep, appetite and sexuality are scoured. Hormones such as prolactine and vasopressine are made to circulate more freely. The cortisol level, which is elevated in 75% of patients suffering from depression, is lowered. The patient usually is relieved from the catatonism and morbidity of depression; he "lets himself live."

Common aims in therapy are to make the patient follow cultural norms, to be peaceful, and to suppress his symptoms: to act less human perhaps. Punishment is often implied, whether in verbal, chemical, or surgical cure. The lesions (wounds) of leucotomy, which removes cerebral tissue, tend to break up the disturbing "character-fix" of the patient; following the trauma, in the course of coping with the injury and reestablishing self-control, the patient often finds a new, more peaceful social character.[34]

It is notable that some schizophrenics incur certain forms of atrophy of the brain. This is expectable, not as showing the organic origins of schizophrenia, but as an instance of self-therapy by psychosomatization. The suffering person performs his own lobotomy. He reduces his

own personality structure. He performs a hysterical tre-
phination. He devises a hysterical paralysis with atten-
dant desuetude and shrinkage of tissue.

Only in certain verbal therapies, as psychoanalysis,
does theory take a rationalist, Socratic position, that if one
knows oneself, one can cope with oneself. It may be
regarded as left-brain-hemisphere therapy, seeking to
restore a person to the status of a thinking mammal, as
contrasted to reducing the patient to a more hominidal
equilibrium. Even here, the psychoanalyst and psychologist find themselves administering authority, willy-
nilly, and relying upon it to cure.

Therapeutic methods, which may hold to distinct con-
ceptions of mental disease, are likely in practice to
become part of a melange. Thus Melvin Gray, arriving at
the treatment of neurasthenia, a vaguely defined hysterical set, says "Multiple forms of treatment — psychotherapy, environmental adjustment, drugs, rest, exercise,
proper nutrition, etc. — were and still are the best
approach."

The general formula for psychotherapy appears to
consist of:

A. Break obnoxious habits of the patient to the point of
   docility (by authority, by uncovering traumas, by
   drugs, electrically, surgically).
B. Re-instinctualize, re-program, re-educate, re-habili-
   tate the patient to a less demanding level of life.
C. Observe the patient's new behavior.
D. Repeat A and B, changing the technique as seems
   indicated.
E. Re-observe as in C.
F. Reinforce prescriptions routinely until therapy is no
   longer demanded, indicated, or affordable.

These regrettably brief passages on psychotherapy
have achieved their intent if they have exposed the prevalance of reductionism in dealing with aberrant human
minds. For the object of reductionism is to get the patient
back into the culture camp. And behind this objective is
the realization that human nature tends to be "irrational
and ungovernable," not knowing naturally "what it really
is," and that it is very frightened at its lack of control of

itself or, may we say, its selves.

A great many traits are inheritable, among them some predisposition to insanity. W.R. Thompson states that "any chromosomal aberration produces a variety of psychological symptoms, including cerebral changes akin to minimal brain damage. This in turn, may result in changes in personality that dispose to many forms of abnormal behavior.[35]

Over one hundred "errors" of metabolism are heritable, most bringing mental disturbances in their wake. The same writer refers to the heritability of sex behavior, musicality, introversion/extraversion, aggression, anxiety, attention to detail, social attachment, level of activity, emotionality, general intelligence (including some specific components such as verbal ability, spatial intelligence, word fluency, and numerical ability), and numerous motor traits affecting skills and athleticism. IQ shows high heritability, 70% to 80% attributable to genetic as opposed to phenotypic variance, and is transmitted via an estimated 100 genes (which may indicate the cloudiness and ethnocentrism of the concept of IQ). It is probably safe to assume that every trait has a heritable variable component; thereby we may be saved much memorizing of lists, disputation, and even research effort. Too, heritability can work with seeming contrariness. "Unaffected offspring of schizophrenic mothers included more conspicuously successful adults than were observed among a control group."[36]

Since mad behavior is variegated, no two madnesses are alike either. We have already alluded to the genetic component in schizophrenia. since Some "one-third of the population suffers from excess anxiety",[37] and perhaps half of normal people suffer symptoms of depersonaliation at times, and, as we have argued, other abnormalities of mind are abundant, and we are normally insane, the whole issue of heritability of insanity may well become a "paper tiger." All symptoms of insanity will have their demonstrable genetic referrents.

The central problem of genetics in psychology may turn out to be the heritability of human nature itself. If our developing theory is correct, and all normal human behavior together with all mental illness descend from a schizoid core in human nature, there arises the question of whether this is a "genetic" trait. Is the peculiar function of the human brain the result of a mutation? If so, then the mutation would have small visible anatomical effect and one would be hard put to distinguish between the human and his immediate ancestor, especially were it to be his very mother.

Now the question of time enters. Has there been enough time since *homo sapiens schizotypus* evolved or quantavoluted to spread the human gene of self-awareness (if there is such) to all persons of the human family? Some persons have blue eyes, denoting a recessive gene. Some genes produce quantitative, not sharply contrasting, qualities, as for example the bone structure favoring high-speed running, or the gene transmitting skin-coloring instructions. Racial genes have not had time to diffuse around the world. Mammalian and other species can spread rapidly around the world; yet some remain isolated. The hominids australopithecus and homo erectus, or their predecessors, diffused through Asia, Africa, and Oceania, but have been conventionally assigned long periods of time to do so. We wonder whether the critical human genes have yet had time to be thoroughly bred into all going under the name of *homo sapiens sapiens*. We may not all be geneticaly prone to insanity. But, if so, this means that we may not all be genetically prone to humanness!

For just as culture can effect, and impose controls upon, insanity, it can govern hominidity. It is distinctly possible that some humans are genetically human — with the schizoid core that we are elucidating — whereas some humans, perhaps even most humans, are culturally produced in their entirety. If this were the case, it would be the greatest irony of all times! Unless a person could prove himself genetically insane, he would need to consider himself a hominid and bow down before the schizoid culture that makes him human!

I do not intend to solve this puzzle in this book, and

indeed there may be no means of doing so. We cannot subject people to the ultimate test, which is to arrange for many small groups to be born and grow up wild, watching for the one group that may be composed entirely of hominids to appear and behave like non-humans, that is, unaware, unanxious, speechless, and uncultured.

chapter two

THE SEARCH FOR LOST INSTINCT

Most babies cry when they are born. If they do not, they are liable to receive their first spanking. This, say their attendants, will clear their lungs; it will circulate their blood; it will exercise their reflexes. It is good for them. This crying may be uniquely human. Calves, for example, do not cry when they are born. They lay stunned for a moment, and then gradually pick themselves up, pull themselves together, receive some licks, and crawl or stumble around. The mothers of apes drop their young almost disdainfully and hardly attend to them at first; the orangutan mother is more considerate, more human.

Perhaps babies cry because they are already more frightened than animals. A famous psychoanalyst, Otto Rank, found the mental state of the baby deplorable, and traced the major behaviors of later life to the trauma of birth. Some conscientious mothers even followed his line of reasoning to the point of giving birth by caesarean operation, thus assisting the baby's birth and relieving its pain of passage from womb to open air. I do not know that the effects of their altruism have ever been reported.

Dr. Rank, passing over the possibly similiar plight of calves, babes of monkeys, and puppies, ascribed the most marvelous effects to the human birthing experience. He sees "in the birth trauma the ultimate biological basis of the psychical." Even the myths of the creation of the world, that are[1] told in many cultures, are regarded by him as a sublime attempt to undo the birth trauma and to deny the separation of the infant from the mother. Although everyone has undergone and many have later witnessed the radical experience of parturition, Rank interpreted myths and fantasies of the end of the world as wishes and efforts of the human individual to be reabsorbed into the great All and Oneness.

Further, "the Flood which initiates a new world period is nothing but a 'universal' reaction to the birth trauma, as the myths of the origin of the earth or the sea also show." Religion, creativity, humanness — all are to be attributed to the tragedy of parturition. No one is exempted. I think that he is reversing the order of nature.

Attacking the perinatal problem by another method, Stanislas Grof employed psychedelic drugs, particularly LSD, in seeking to learn of people's re-experiences of the earliest events of their lives.[2] He could identify four matrices of recollections. One expressed feelings of unbounded ease; another, frightful threat, confinement and torture; a third appeared as a struggle for survival and an ecstatic release; the fourth, a seperation that seemed a kind of death followed by resurrection. These would connect with the physical sequence of natal events and incorporate analogous later effects. This is matrix 2; the unbearable and inescapable situation of the foetus, sensing uterine contractions while confronting a still-closed cervix, would and did engender visions of fear, plague, and natural catastrophe.

Lacking evidence that historical experiences can affect the germ plasma, we must regard these as visions of other life experiences, as secondary or derivative suggestions, and attached to the perinatal process by mental association. We do not deny that they originally occurred. Rather, when they did occur and were experienced and remembered, they reinforced the analogous perinatal feelings. And, if what we have said concerning Rank's thoery is correct, the perinatal experience is a reinforcement of the pre-existing genetic fear of oneself that already begins with the foetus. Hence, a double reinforcement may operate upon the original fear. Every speicies, indeed every individual, has its own pre-existing structure for experiencing; experience is species-specific and organism-specific.

Otto Rank and Stanislas Grof are asking too much of the nasty surprise of birth. Rather, I should say, the baby is crying because, unlike the animals, he already possesses a kind of fear that they do not, and cannot, know. This is his existential fear, an anxiety sensed upon the realization of the existence of himself. He is reacting to a harsh accident, true, but knows already this existential fear and is demanding immediately that he be relieved of it. He already has a frustrated voluntarism, a will that he expects to appease by action. He is terribly frightened because he is already trying to put his head together and to find himself in himself, whereas the animals have merely to compose their circulation and limbs.

The infant already wants more than to fix upon comfort, although this, and food later on, will usually quiet him. Surely, given the option, the baby would prefer to return to the womb. But there, too, he may well have been frightened, not only by jostling and growth pains, but by the sense of the greatest problem of existence, how to form his identity. For his brain has begun to operate in the perculiar human way. He may be already indecisive, unlike the beasts, feeling that there is a decision to be made, and wants to do more than to wait upon the comfort of the nursery. Perhaps it is well to slap him if he does not cry: he should stop dreaming and come to attention.

INSTINCT-DELAY

The baby cannot realize his problem. He does not know that his instinctive mechanisms are blunted, blocked and delayed, and that he will pass his life in a mammalian vehicle, a jalopy that he must tinker with and fix up at every turn of the road. Luckily, he is to be trained immediately as a mechanic. Not for him are the joys of a long life of instinctive behavior, consisting mainly of speedy, replicating responses to specific stimuli.

The delays of instinct, touching upon the whole gammut of behavior, provide the human with a continuous fear. The instincts cause tension in their persistent efforts to complete themselves. At the same time, the person finds himself inundated by the tongues of instinct, lapping upon areas of behavior often little related to the original direction or object of the stimulus-response mechanism. The sexual instinct, for instance, may emerge as oedipal, romantic, homosexual, fetishistic, sadistic, aesthetic and/or aggressive behavior; rarely is it merely the highly relevant "display; hop on; hop off; go away" sequence that even higher animals perform.

The delay of instincts by a possibly genetic blockage is all-important: it permits the chaotic creational flood to rush into all the crevices of the forming human nature. The retardation of his animal instincts is viewed as flexibility in the human's behavior. Human flexibility is both cause and consequence, therefore, because both the "decisions" and the follow-up activity are subject to delays in the central nervous system.

The animal world, by contrast, exists by instinct: events emit stimuli; instinctive reactions succeed or fail; the residuum reassembles amidst the continuing events. Almost never is the process punctuated by pauses to consider a dilemma. If its spasms of calculation fail, the animal surrenders to the inertial process. It falls back upon its collective line of defense, it breeds. The animate world can depend upon exponential reproducibility to render individual choice unnecessary for species survival.

Meanwhile the human creature depends upon what he calls mind or intelligence. He has not chosen to do so. He cannot do anything else. Would that he he could, for his lot is fearful. His reactions blocked at every turn, if only for an instant, he lives in anxiety over the last turn, the present turn, the next turn, and all the ones he can remember or imagine or foresee. Stripped of ready instinct, he confronts an instinct-ready world. He is innately, individually, and culturally anxious, and the world he encounters is too large to cope with non-anxiously.

Terror drives him to act quickly, but not instinctively,

and instinct is the quickest action. Why must he forever fearfully reflect? If, unlike animals, man has to make up his mind, there must be some unique quality in the mind. If two or more options rush into the open question raised by the blocked instinctual response, there is a conflict, an anxiety. Even if there is but a single and obvious solution, a pause to determine so can cause anxiety.

SELF-FEAR AND SELF-CONTROL

When the posing of options is continuous and inevitable, the very existence of a single mind can be doubted. The pervasiveness of choice and anxiety in the actions of the human being must signify that "ordinarily he is of two minds" about everything he experiences. "Two souls within me live, damn!" said Goethe.

Two souls may be too few. The well-known case-study of Sybil documented sixteen different persons in a single human female, each conscious, aware, able, and resting upon the substrata of the other fifteen. Whatever the number, so long as it is more than one, it suggests that a third trait can be allocated to the non-instinctual, fearful creature, which is a multiple personality.

Called by another name, this is self-awareness, a kind of behavior that could never come about were it not for the fact that someone is asking questions of someone else. A self is aware of itself. "I think, therefore I am", wrote Descartes. Not quite, we say. Rather, "I recognize myself; therefore, we are." When, 3000 years before, Moses turned aside to inspect the fiery unburning thornbush, he found there Yahweh who spoke to him saying "I am the I am" and Moses worried (says the Bible) about what people would say when he said to them "I am the voice of the I am that is the I am."

Because our selves share nearly identical anatomical housing and have highly privileged access to each other, for all practical purposes they are considered as "one in body and soul." In fact, the compulsion to be oneself is so suspiciously strong that no matter what the proof to the contrary, the self will always be the irreducible unit of human existence. Like non-Euclidean geometry and warped space, the poly-self will remain a theoretical construct, out of the realm of the common sense. It will help to understand human behavior, however, and have powerful applications in psychological therapy and law. It will, among other things, clarify an idea that is to be found in a many "primitive" and "advanced" cultures, that a person "possessed" is not to be treated as himself. So now we have the human creature, living in a house of fear, governed by a committee, and acting accordingly in non-instinctual ways.

What is the agenda of this committee of egos? The agenda seems infinitely varied; it can contain anything in the whole world, internal, external, from a microbe to the star, unlimited, too, in time or space. But the preamble to every item on the agenda is always the same: "This is a bill to control fear by..." So the human seeks control, first of himself, that is, of the committee: "This house must put itself in order." Then he must seek to control others; he must at the same time, just like a government, govern himself while he governs others. And, besides the others, he must seek to control the world, for he senses that not only these others, but also the whole world, threatens him and needs to be ordered. Something of this conduct of operations seems implied in Anna Freud's idea about the ego's "tendency to synthesis," as opposed to the fear of ego destruction, which she recognizes as an instinctual anxiety.[3] (I say, of course, that the ego was hardly there in the first place.)

Control implies power, the determination of the wills or behaviors of people and events. "Power is an ingredient in the transactions which take place within all object relationships and is thus an ingredient in the interlocking forces which determine personality," so declares Arieti. Veritably we may contemplate now a being that is instinct-delayed, poly-ego, fearful on both counts and power-driven: *ecce homo*.

Control is said to occur when someone determines the behavior of persons or things. The drive to control is a reciprocal of fear. All humans, possessing existential fear and self-fears, must seek control, primarily of the self. Very quickly in all situations the physical self becomes the arena of only a portion of the struggle for control.

External objects and beings are also incorporated into the struggle. The self, others, and the natural world are the triple object of efforts at control.

The total of objects, both inner and outer, operate subjectively without discrimination. Whether a person feels he controls his temper or an empire, by physiological indicators of stress, or by any other tests, he is calmer and more relaxed. If he is insatiable in his wishes to control, the diminution of tension with success will be brief and shallow; his fears will cause him to move immediately to assume control in other spheres. Under no circumstances can the urge to control be satisfied.

Assuming that all humans are basically alike, rather than divided between those who are genetically human and those who are only culturally human (a question already alluded to), the challenge may be offered that women are less interested in control than men. This would imply, by our theory, that they are more instinctive, more unified and stable as persons, and less fearful. More hominidal, therefore? Less instinct-delayed? Such may be the case. There is folklore about "a woman's instinct." This special female capacity is a popular belief today. In the Western European Middle Ages, women were for a time denied a soul, until a Church conference finally decided the issue in their favor. A "soul" translates into the more active madness and suffering often characterizing males.

But it is suggested that for the time being we assume a close similarity of the sexes. We offer, as adequate and at least temporary justification, that women are generally forced out of formal control activities, that they operate "underground" for control purposes, and that, anyhow, an accurate and thorough inventory of control activity would disclose an equality of the sexes.

The absolute renunciation of control-needs and efforts is sometimes attempted. The cosmic indifference of Buddha lets nothing matter save finding nothingness. Once filled with nothingness, one will be at peace. All identifications and attachments are renounced in order to concentrate upon control of the self. With an elaborate strict regimen of diet and exercises, and by abstemious human relations, bolstered by a sophisticated rationale appeasing conventional philosophical demands, a mental balance is achieved that is distinguishable from selfishness, catatonism, or bestiality. Resemblances to autistic trances are present. The discipline remains severe; the drive for control of the world is not abolished.

A more than casual resemblance to the Buddhist outlook is to be perceived in Teilhard de Chardin's attempt to extricate mankind from its dilemma.[4] He sees the remedy as man's reflectiveness, enlarged greatly until the world is co-reflected in his mind in a universe of ultra-reflexion. This is a vague formula, but it takes on greater meaning when we ask what is Chardin's human dilemma. This, it seems, is a state of fear, which he describes abstractly: the great fear of the human species is being closed in and lost in an unfriendly world, condemned to live with himself as a fixed species.

THE SENSE OF "I AM"

Identity and identification begin with the question of the self or ego. "Everyone is to himself that which he calls self," wrote John Locke, in discussing the idea of a person.[5] The self is "an object to itself," said G.H. Mead. The reflexive form reveals "that which can be both subject and object." This is what distiguishes man fom animal, he argued, rather than the alleged possession of a mysteriously endowed soul.[6]

Sommerhoff regards self-awareness as part of consciousness and, in his study of *The Logic of the Living Brain*, says that it is formed of "coherent internal representations of the physical self," hence also of the self's relations to its surroundings. "...The unity of the physical self finds expression in a family of characteristic transformation expectations the brain accumulates during ontogenesis."[7]

Sweeping in more closely toward the concept sought here, Hilgard declares, "The unity of consciousness is illusory. Man does more than one thing at a time — all the time — and the conscious representation of these actions is never complete."[8]

When the personality degrades to "a delusional

chaos," some awareness survives. "Part of that total complex which we call the ego, the 'self', always remains alien to the delusions. This constellation accounts for the fact that the non-affected part of the ego may disbelieve and even criticize the delusions; on the other hand, the incorrigibility and the senselessness of the delusions are precisely due to the fact that many associations contradictory to the delusional are simply not brought into any logical connection with it."

Building one's self is then every person's lifelong occupation. As we have said, he is driven by the fear of not being oneself to begin with. The self is a predisposition, but not a bequest, of nature. Indeed, it is never fully achieved. Man is always an infant in this regard. While apes grow quickly and soon act "self-possessedly", the human can grow in every respect but this, that he never achieves a single self. "The mature person is self-confident," by which is signified that his existential fear is under control and that he egoistically regards himself as one. A total lack of self-confidence results in a kind of vegetative existence, a sickness as grave as any; even the most elementary kinds of self-control disappear into incontinence and catatonism.

Both "identification" and "role-playing" are in the area of the dispersed self. A "role" is behavior according to a social sub-type, which is employed to escape insecurity by virtue of a more secure status. A role may be manifested as casually as a costume for the mardi-gras once a year, or as intensely as a permanent switch in identity accompanied by amnesia. Role changes are common in modern society; they are rare in simple communities, where a fisherman is son of a fisherman, but even there the person goes through life-roles such as adolescence or grandparentage, has a role in a church, and so on. Roles are culturally defined, often assigned, and when fully developed and effective, encapsulate the dispersed self, guarding and maintaining it against dissolution.

Identification can be attested in the assumption of a role, as the boy who identifies with his father, the fisherman, but can more broadly extend to all manner of being and abstraction. Thus one may detach some part of

himself and affix it to an identification with the work-
ingclass movement, or with the Virgin Mary, or with his
family and neighbors, or with a bird. Identification is
associated with the wish to control its object; this may be
difficult, for frequently ambivalence arises out of an
obviously uncontrollable identification.

The self, though it may appear so, is not a social creation, as G.H. Mead and others would have it be. Man
would never have a self, a poly-ego, if he were not struc-
tured genetically to engage in the search for self by a
mind that has to be pulled together. Mead's work is completely intelligible and useful, except on this crucial
point. It is significant that he does not seek to go beyond
society and culture as the determinants. Meanwhile, he
provides us with precisely those kinds of observations
which we need, as, for example: "The phenomenon of
dissociation of personality is caused by a breaking up of
the complete, unitary self into the component selves of
which it is composed, and which respectively correspond
to different aspects of the social process in which the person is involved."[9]

He advanced and stressed the concept of "social
roles," those social housings for the individual selves,
and showed how small children could play games with
their selves, as well as others, being now one kind of person, now then another — father, mother, evil one, good
one, police and bandit, and so on. This author's grand-
child was raised bilingually in Athens, and when playing
with a toy car and policeman, would speak as the policeman in Greek, then reply as the car-driver in English.

Bleuler used the word "schizophrenia" to denote a
split personality, merging the Greek words for "split" and
"brain" or "heart," thus meaning more than brain. Schizophrenia was applied to madness of the disordered personality, and numerous mental illnesses received different names in the early years of psychiatry. Afterwards, it
became fashionable to assert that one should ignore the
etymology of the word, even ignoring Bleuler, for that
matter.

The trend of my work, however, has been to extend
the term in its literal meaning — that is, to introduce the
idea of multiple "splits" — to extend it to cover

practically all mental disturbances not attributable to organic and accidental lesions, whether congenital or post-natal, and to transform the disease into the elements of normal behavior, regarding normal individual and social behavior as specific resultants of certain adjustments to a natural schizophrenia. Thus self-consciousness is what might be termed in the lexicon of psychopathology a form of delusional thought. To be human, then, is to be schizotypical, or schizoid. Not to be so — that is, not to be self-aware — is impossible, or is stupid in the sense of being of the hominidal species of the primates.

Again, all humans, including mad humans, are self-aware. Even in a case of severe catalepsy, self-awareness is evident. Bleuler reports cataleptics who can maintain the same position for months. But, as a patient is moved, his muscles flex and adjust so as to maintain any position in which he is placed. Normal children and hystericals will sometimes do the same, after being punished. Hilgard describes a hypnotised subject who can, as instructed, divide himself into two beings, one who feels no pain upon stimulation and says so, another who feels it and comments upon it.

The source of the phenomena of self-awareness is the dispersed selves. One would not know oneself unless there were at least two of one, the observer and the observed, the knower and the known, or, better, two mutually perceptive observers. In Hilgard's experiment above, he was able to elicit two speaking selves with contrasting points of view regarding a painful stimulus.

Since there is so much of the delusory in human nature, as Bleuler and many other students have shown, it occurred to me at first to regard self-consciousness only as a form of delusion. I think now that it must be reality and that the concept of the single self must be delusory, a kind of megalomania based upon an illusion of the dominating self. Just as the human sees one image with eyes that register bi-focally, so he mentates, especially when asked, as a whole, though his mind be operating eccentrically. Both neurological and psychological evidence of this will be advanced later on.

The ego is not singular. "It" perceives and exists as a poly-self. Any single self in the set is a sensed or perceived claim on an acting and behaving organic system in relation to or in conjunction with claims of others. A person is a system of selves, a polyself system. Ordinarily, people successfully inhibit irrelevant material from enough of their mentation to assure others and cause others to believe that they are acting as a single or at most a self-aware self. Even too much self-awareness is a cause of disturbances, akin to disturbed behavior in the eyes of observers and in the concerns of the subject; suspicions are aroused; rapport is weakened. When persons begin to operate on several levels almost simultaneously, they are accorded various complexes by medical practitioners. Bleuler gave numerous illustrations of such behavior among his schizophrenic patients.

Hilgard's studies of divided consciousness by means of hypnosis expose a "hidden observer" or "co-conscious" as an ordinary concommittant of existence. This self among selves is not a monster, a "beast of the unconscious." "The concealed part sometimes turns out to be healthier than the openly presented self."[10] Expert though he was in hypnosis, Sigmund Freud fashioned his theory of id-ego-superego from classical social psychological theory, from Plato's *Republic* (I argued in a paper of 1949) rather than from experiential materials readily available to him. He thus may have posed the wrong parties in psychic conflicts. The poly-ego concept is structurally and biologically manifest; it can be the subject of experiment; it can be operationally described.

The origins of the poly-ego, the core of human nature, must be in neurological transformations at some time in the past. Here we assume the poly-ego to exist, leaving its ancient origins to be traced in *Homo Schizo I*. Sufficient for the moment is the hypothesis that when this transformation occurred, a number of critical innovations occurred with it, enough so that we can assume a quantavolution of creation, a hologenesis. Human nature came all at once. As the first humans experienced for the first time a poly-ego and have until now repeated the experience with every new person, we look for a massive effect upon the human being and find it in the eternal fear that possesses mankind.

EXISTENTIAL FEAR

Students of fear in humans and animals are rarely satisfied by obvious causes; human fear is not a pie to be cut
up and assigned to wild animals, bad dreams, strict
parents, and the like. It is well to make tallies, thus a
third of the population fears snakes, most of these fear
them intensely; a great many fear heights or being alone
in public places; many fear injury and illness; and nearly
everyone fears an assault at the time that it occurs.[11] But,
perhaps because they are difficult to study and even to
conceive of, "little systematic research has been applied
to the nature of what are sometimes called existential
fears."[12]

As with the concepts of human nature and instinct,
many psychologists would like to rid themselves of the
concept of "fear," believing it to be vague and operationally undefinable. But, as Jeffrey Gray puts it,
"Experimental psychology — as well as common sense —
has been forced to invent the hypothesis of a complex
psychological state, 'fear,' precisely in order to make
sense out of the otherwise shifting and imprecise relationship observed between stimuli and responses."[13]

We do not distinguish here between fear and anxiety.
"Anxiety, the psychological equivalent of pain, is characterized by a feeling of dread.. a vague fear.. not related to
specific situations or objects.. part of the human condition." So says Mendel, abstracting from a lifetime of
administering intensive psychotherapy.[14] Physiologically, insofar as anxiety can be detected, it exhibits the
chemistry and muscular tensions of fear. And fear, when
slight, is indistinguishable from anxiety. And anxiety can
become terror and panic. The common use of the term
"anxiety" has to be attributed to the need to allay people's fear that they may be suffering from fear.

Fear is part of the human and of all that he creates.
The role of fear in religion is large, so that a working out
of fears often has taken place in the arena of the sacred.
Religion approached by faith, says Rudolf Otto, cannot be
the same as religion approached through reason. Central
to faith is *numen*, the specific non-rational religious
apprehension and its object, at all its levels, from the

primitive stirrings to exalted spiritualism. And central to *numen* is dread, for it is the sacred, holy, awful confrontation of man with god or the divine essence.[15]

Fear can be both immediate and existential. Immediate fear erupts upon the encountering of threat to the poly-ego system, a learned and/or sensed emotion that sends an *ad hoc* electro-chemical alarm through the central nervous system. Existential fear, also an electro-chemical effect, is normally at a constant level which we posit to be above some pre-human level.

What evidence is there for a continuous higher level of existential fear in human nature? That man is an anxious animal has been a byword in psychology. This means ordinarily that the human is never at ease with himself. Rare cases of such are a subject of marvelling comment, probally misplaced and incorrect. To suit the needs of *homo schizo*, all neonates are trained to high levels of anxiety.

It is often argued that humans are culturally indoctrinated in fear, and therefore generally exhibit that continuous anxiety which has every conceivable object as its trigger or focus. Cultures are discoverable that train their children not to possess or display fear. Many mothers of modern western culture earnestly try to preserve their children from the sense of fear. The mothers are reinforced by cultural institutions that have special needs. These, where successful, invariably train only an ignorance of or resistance to fear in some respects deemed crucial by the society, such as facing up to an enemy in battle.

Here, in the first place, there is reason to regard the training as retraining, that is, the acquisition of one set of habits to overwhelm a contrary set. The partial training underscores the practically limitless outlets to existential fear; global courage is not hoped for. The brave Spartans were obsessively fearful of their Helotic slaves; fearful of alliances; fearful of women; fearful of their gods; and would turn tail for home even from a battle if an earthquake occurred. The display of fear is culturally determined; the fear itself is universal.

The most persuasive argument against the presence of an existential human fear is that the human is occupied with so many objects over such large spans of memory and futures that one is bound to be always in a state of anxiety over something. If it is not one's health, it is the apparitions of a stormy sky; if not an enemy, it is an institution.

As in so many areas, here too, one must ask first of all if the logic is not reversed, possibly in a type of cognitive disorder: why does the human tend to so many things in the world, not only the infinite now, but the infinite past or future? Is the object pursued or attended to because it serves as an outlet for fear or must one believe that the human is so naturally rational as to fix his concerns upon practically everything, only then to discover a fearful aspect to it all? I think that the answer to this question will emerge from this book.

Briefly, though, a fixation upon a single or very few objects is suspiciously phobiaphilic; the expansion of the scope of objects occupying one does not increase the general fearfulness of one's state, but rather the contrary: it makes the state of fear more bearable. Extraverted, "neurotic" characters typically disperse their attention and, as a result, acquire unusual versatility.

Furthermore, as we shall argue later, fear is not eliminated by therapy. The objects may be changed. Or, by a variety of means, including drugs such as tranquillizers and alcohol, a high level of fear may be reduced even greatly. Fear is controlled by forcing the physiology, not by clearing away impediments to natural courage.

Comparing the occasions for fear it is doubtful that the human lot is beset by more fearful stimuli than engage the attention of animals. Yet we see in man a variety of psycho-pathological tendencies and behaviors — such as merciless aggression and global attentiveness — not present in mammals and apes. Hence we must seek the source of existential fear in a logical and real condition, which we say is the poly-ego. Self-awareness, inevitable in mankind, produces continual anxiety over his inevitably and profusely invented fears.

In 1933, Freud laid down the theme "..that the ego is the only seat of anxiety, and that only the ego can produce anxiety," and "that the three main varieties of anxiety — objective anxiety, neurotic anxiety and moral anxiety — can so easily be related to the three directions in which the ego is dependent, on the external world, on the id and on the super-ego."[16]

This reads, in our terms: on nature, on others, and on the variegated selves. The self is too complex to be divided into id, ego, and superego. There is a pragmatic instinctive principle involved, but there is no reality principle. The self is never a real self, either.

In systematizing psychology, Freud might better have dispensed with external objectivity and relied upon a phenomenological theory of the world as a wholly subjective creation of the mind. The clutch of components of the ego engage themselves in anxiety-reduction operations. The so-called id, ego and superego elements are ancient and misleading ideas of how the mind works, even though they are conventionally handy for political, moral, and hence therapeutic disputation. Certainly, though, Freudian psychology is erected upon the presumption of ever-present anxiety.

Not until we learn how this continuous drizzle of fear and anxiety is precipitated in human life by the delayed instinct and the split self will we understand existential fear. For the moment, we should counsel alertness against assigning to any experience the accountability for generalized fear. This means to avoid any commitment to sweeping theories such as that of Rank's birth trauma, or to presuppositions like Otto's that dread is validated by its divine associations. Or such large categorical explanations as "castration fear," which is undoubtedly of diagnostic utility. Or, for that matter, to any summing up to 100% of fear by adding experiences from the womb to the tomb. Rather, hypothetically at first, and then as certainly as the evidence and logic permit, let us maintain that the human would be fearful and anxious even if he lived a life totally free of frightening experience.

The whole human mental structure appears to be given over to controlling the mind so as to reduce the stress of fear. The poly-self is elected as a governing committee by a central nervous system that was previously under more centralized management. The brain of the hominid loses coordinative ability and in so doing produces the human brain, which imposes a new system of coordination.

The poly-ego, hence self-awareness, would not be present if it were not for the depression and confusion of instincts in humans. What forced the human egos to emerge was the necessity for continuous decision-making and what made this in turn necessary was the delaying of instinctive response. How this happened is to be discussed later on; what it consists of is relevant here.

INSTINCT IN MAN AND ANIMAL

We begin by a comparison. Legions of horseshoe crabs (which are more related to spiders than to other crabs) make their way up the beaches of Cape Cod to breed with precisely the most predictable heavy tide, that which occurs with the full moon nearest to the summer solstice. In the swirling low waters the females discharge their eggs, which are fertilized by the sperm discharged by the males. The adults retire with the tide (save for a few who are trapped in retreating, and bury themselves in sand until the next heavy tide). The fertilized eggs sink into the sand where they develop and wait to hatch upon the occasion of the tide of the next full moon, whereupon they move out to sea.

Instinctively, one may surmise, the horseshoe crab has mastered complex processes that *homo sapiens* would have to learn by pragmatic science. One is the relation of sun and moon to tides, or at least the empirical knowledge of when the heaviest reliable tide of the year occurs. Another is the organization of legions of males and females in rut to congregate at the same place for the purpose of conceiving upon the beach a new generation, which itself develops within the narrow limits of the next lunar month, at which time it can emerge to descend upon the sea.

Thousands of such instinctive processes are possessed by the animal kingdom. In many cases one animal's instincts are aligned to exploit the instincts of other animals. The human, and perhaps the human alone, can make a great many adjustments of his behavior to imitate or relate to and exploit the instinctive behavior of the biosphere. The human's blocked instinctive structure is the basis or take-off point to invent a multitude of instinct-like habits that, for example, would have him waiting upon the beach at the summer solstice to capture the horseshoe crab and sell it for fertilizer and souvenirs. Some animals exploit instincts of other animals, as we have said.

The term "instinct," like "human nature," and "ego," has a suspicious slackness about it. No wonder, given its history. Charles Darwin used it not quite as loosely as he did the idea of "natural selection;" S. Freud used it as a workhorse for one speculative probe after another; Mac-Dougall, the social psychologist, pounded it into mincemeat; Tinbergen managed to use it respectably in his study of animal behavior; and Fletcher recently reconciled its ethological and psychiatric meanings usefully.

N. Tinbergen defined instinct as a hierarchically organized nervous mechanism, suceptible to primary releasing and directing impulses of internal and external origin, which responds to these impulses by coordinated movements.[17] The hierarchy is altered by changes in the intensity or by suppression of other instincts. An influential hierarchical order by Rensch gives as instincts sex, deference, feeding, cleaning, and ultimately hunting and collecting. I doubt, however, that there is any hierarchy of instincts in humans except in a group statistical sense, owing to the human ineptitude for specific instinctive response.

Obviously, all writers have had in mind the large fact that animals and men respond automatically when stimulated in certain ways: they blink quickly when about to be struck in the eye, for instance. (Even so, madmen and small boys can teach themselves to control the blink.) This unrestrained reflex is instinctive, as are a great many chemical and motile reactions of the organs and limbs. In the human bloodstream are to be found leucocytes, cells that hunt infectious bacteria — instinctively? Then where is the instinct: in the whole person or in the leucocyte?

As instincts come to require training (the baby can be toilet-trained) or as the stimulus of the instinct provokes a broader response (when struck, the creature dodges, snarls, and strikes back), they enter an area of science that can ultimately merge with speculative philosophy, as when one speaks of an aesthetic instinct in man. Freud's last thrust in the arena of instinct emerged with a death (thanatos) and a life (eros) instinct.[18] This dualism reminds us of entropy and negative entropy, the universal breaking down of motion and material and the countervailing creativeness of life, which, if given optional conditions of sustained full reproduction would soon cover all the stars and the spaces between with organic matter, and then presumably expand the universe beyond even the dreams of the explosive universe theorists. This thought might be taken as an irrelevant comment on the irrelevancy of Freud's two-fold classification. But neither is the case.

In this very book on the pleasure principle, Freud came as close as he ever did to the theory of *homo schizo*. In the course of denying the domination of pleasure over human mentation, which relates to the anhedonia symptoms adverted to later on, he moves to the question of unpleasure. "Unpleasure corresponds to an *increase* in the quantity of excitation." that is present but unbound in the mind; pleasure is a diminution of excitation.[19] He thus agrees with G.T. Fletcher (1873) who linked pleasure and unpleasure with stability and instability, in between which lay indifference. And he foreshadowed the behavioral conditioning school of today several of whose representatives occupy an honorable place in this book.

Now Freud, typically pushing ideas to their limits of tolerance (and toleration), makes death a pleasure and then an instinct. "Instinct is an urge inherent in organic life to restore an earlier state of things which the living entity has been obliged to abandon under the pressure of external disturbing forces."[20] Instinct: reversion: death.

Freud's "death instinct," so readily misunderstood, can be shown to make sense in the light of the theory of *homo schizo*. For we say that man seeks to revert to the animal in order to recapture the instinctive bliss of the single self. That is, man unconsciously seeks his death as a human, and of the human species. This must be very close to what was gestating in the mind of Freud.

I see confirmation of this thought in a cloudy but weighty remark that relates to the dependent clause of the quoted sentence. For he writes: "In the last resort, what has left its mark on the development of organisms must be the history of the earth we live in and of its relation to the sun. Elementary things do not wish to change but are forced to evolve organically by "external disturbing and diverting influences." My work in *Homo Schizo I* deals heavily with such "influences." What is pertinent here is that, by the theory of *homo schizo*, the evolved thing, man, wants to rid itself of the burden of the very trait that speciates it, that makes it a unique species, and such is the instinct-delay that creates and maintains its perpetual *angst*.

Freud's early preoccupation with the sexual instinct is less pertinent, disclosing, as critics have pointed out, an idealogical attachment to the worries of well-to-do patients in a bourgeois society before World War I. The varieties of sexuality, it rather seems to us, given the cultural accent upon the subject, indicate a dispersed instinct, a conflict of selves, and an employment of sexual displacements to dispose of existential fear. Love consists of identifying an ego element with people and objects (even a 'security blanket') which reassure one against fear. Love is usually deeply involved with control, and control of course is a heavy motive in sexual attraction.

Affection plays so large a part in nurturing and training an infant that it becomes naturally a well-developed area of fixation for many problems of other instinctive zones besides the sexual. One can understand how affection is attached to all manner of "irrelevant" encounters and objects. It can be plucked out and credited with being the basic drive. But we always should refer to the human basic drive as self-control, then to other essential interests such as sex and food, and finally to myriad mixed displays of all of these.

Without enthusiasm and with qualms, a definition of instinct may be put foward: instinctive behavior in a species is present when, in the absence of training, a uniform behavior reliably results following upon a definite stimulus. The number of instincts in mammal species subsumable under this definition must be in the hundreds. An important fact is that for every primate instinctive action, there is a human eqivalent, ontologically recognizable. This fact is relatively easy to argue. However, the near reverse may be also true, as ethologists and sociobiologists increasingly contend: for every type of human action, defined with increasing specificity, there may be a genetically related primate instinct, with allowances made for training in both cases.

The discussion of human instinct centers about the comparative laxness of instinct in the total behavior of man when compared with the behavior of animals most closely resembling him. Compare the separation of the mother bear and her cub, so simple, with the separation of the human female from her child, so complex, so full of woes, the inspiration of thousands of customs and volumes of literature. And include especially the "exceptional" societies such as those in which the mother is trained like the bear mother, who lumbers away leaving her cub whimpering on the limb of a tree, or the societies employing all-male initiation ceremonies to break the maternal grip, or fascist and soviet societies whose nursery schools are intended to abort family influences deemed incompatible with the ideas of the regime, or societies where the tie is broken by taking up one's first job in a distant city. Humans can come close to, or seemingly go very far from, animal practices.

When giving birth, women in comparison with primate females are more agitated and uncertain, and follow practices not observable among the primates, such as engaging attendants. Again, primate females have a defined rut period when they will accept sexual advances, whereas human females frequently are receptive of sexual overtures most of the time. Kinsey found that a mild rut period is present in slightly over half of a human female population. The complications in the life of humans introduced by just these two departures from the instinctive norms of the primates are numerous. On the one hand there are the "unhappy" components in the difference of instincts: confusion, doubt, malaise, anxiety, ignorance, ineptness. On other hand there occur some "happy" elements: flexibility in relating to other environmental demands, such as planning hunting absences; reasonable timing; more frequent opportunities to breed; and the possibility of introducing healthy practices; not to mention luckier males. Here are two behaviors, in primates and humans; they "could be" alike. But some mechanism generalizes and renders indistinct the human behavior. The words used to rate human against non-human instincts are many; observers find in the human instinctive structure "atrophy," "depression," "generalization," "abortion," "diffusion," "disintigration," "vagueness," "blunting," "delay," and "suppression." Obviously we have many words to choose from in denoting the main peculiarity of human instincts.

Pursuing the concepts of poly-identity and fear, and considering that we shall have to provide later on an operational and etiological system for whatever word we choose, we settle upon "delay," instinct delay. This can be postulated as a general suppression of brain-mediated responses to stimulus such that an instruction can intervene to make unreliable any response. Among instructions can be included decisions, so that one can imagine the delay as automatized, unconscious, or deliberate. Culture, that is, training and education, can affect both instructions and decisions.

POLY-EGO VERSUS INSTINCT

The basic product of the instinct delay is the poly-self. Assuming that several centers of the brain can become seats of an "ego," the delay of instinctive response will cause these centers to develop and exercise influence. The instinct delay produces mille-seconds of "hesitation" and "doubt." This is enough for the several centers to sense a problem, that is, non-fulfillment of the instinctive loop of stimulus-response-extinction of impulse, and to react. The general consciousness is supplemented by a superior and dominating special brain center and several inferior but rival ones.

The dominant consciousness now perceives its rivals and the "problem." It casts a pall of fear over the central nervous system, including itself. The problem of non-immediate fulfillment of the instinct impulse is complicated by the sense of competitive decision-making or instruction-giving centers associated with it. Hence the external fear of ourselves is established. Physiologically a low-level of Cannon's fear-flight effect, involving the adrenals, is produced.

Now we have in operation: instinct delay, poly-ego, and existential fear. The person behaves accordingly. He seeks control of the laggard instincts and their wayward derivatives. He seeks to organize his poly-ego into an effective and more comfortable relationship. He tries to abolish his fear, which, after all, is nothing but a continuous play of the fear sensations of animal life and which, mistakenly, he treats as nothing more than an interminable chain of immediate fears.

Man can and would like to fill infinity with his control activities. "...The overriding purpose of the behavior is an attempt to achieve some security and certainty for the person who feels threatened and insecure in an uncertain world. The possibility of controlling oneself and the forces outside oneself by assuming omniscience and omnipotence can give one a false illusion of certainty. Therefore the main ingredient is one of control." So writes L. Salzman on *The Obsessive Personality*.[21]

Time and space concepts are great instruments for control. Man in effect enlarges the world by imposing more and more of a *time* frame behaviorally upon it. He obsessively connects himself with natural instruments of time-passage, hence time-reckoning. The same occurs in the *space* world. This is part of an irresistible expansion of Man's will to control, which is of course dependent only upon his insatiable need to control his head which in turn depends upon the unquenchable fear that fills his head (and total body libido). And the fear comes from his inability to execute promptly and certainly the numerous and varied, often contradictory, orders of the incoming stimuli; He is more agitated in civilized than in less complex, calmer societies, and more in rapidly changing than in "stagnant" cultures. And the inability is fostered by the blocking and diversion (displacement) and echoing of incoming orders. The brainwork involved is discussed in the next chapter.

Control by evolutionary reversion is impossible. Man is unable to reestablish the instinctual basis of existence. He cannot speed up his responses and eradicate their derivatives, except that his attempts at doing so produce the astonishing phenomenon of culture. Nor can he put aside his centers in favor of "one king, one throne, one people." Nor finally can he do away with his fear. The failure to complete automatically his instinctual urges, the dissipation of these urges into bizarre forms, and the conflicts of his "split brain" guarantee a level of fear that would approach panic if it were not channelled into new worlds of activity and location.

"YOU CAN'T GO HOME AGAIN"

Animals possess analogues, structurally and functionally, to human compulsions, obsessions, displacements, identifications, and other human mechanisms. Further they can be trained and experienced so as to approach in limited ways the enormous human ability to alter behavior by training and experiencing.

Chimpanzees use sticks to hit the ground, throw at predators, poke for termites (breaking off awkward projections), and choose the more suitable from a set of sticks. They can invent. Their females (and the gorillas') anticipate and protect their infants from potentially dangerous situations. They use sign-words and hover on the brink of making symbols of them. A mother rhesus monkey, whose young male has approached a female and aroused the leader, will divert the leader from chasing him by suddenly assuming an attentive position towards a remote point; this alerts him to his duties in foreign affairs and allows the rascal to escape. And so on.[22]

What must be stressed is the unique human dependence upon these mechanisms. Humans are absolutely helpless without constructing these mechanisms. We can picture the situation as a trade-off. In return for losing a huge number of instinctive reactions, the human acquires an ability to reconstruct reactions quickly and in manifold forms.

As loss of control occurs, fear erupts. The human seeks

to return to the hominid and restore the animal mechanisms, but in marvelous ways. By continuously searching to retrieve his nature, man provides himself with thousands of behaviors of the same categories but inestimably greater in appearances and consequences. He even creates robots, near to absolutely instinctive "animals."

Seen from one perspective, the human behavior is homologous to the animals. Seen from another, the human behavior is only analogous. Whether one opts for the former or the latter view is simply a question of whether to regard as important the phases that intervene between stimulus and response: instinct delay — loss of control — existential fear — diffused or diverted reaction. Since these phases create the human, we prefer the view that human behavior as a whole is only analogous to animal behavior, but that man and primate share homologous infrastructure and functions. The human adds a special neural loop to the stimulus-response cycle.

Identification is strictly constrained among animals, for instance. The animal self is monolithic. An evanescent mother love of the bitch for her cub will only temporarily crack the stone of self. Yet one may not ignore the dog who anticipates the feelings and command of the master, and who may die in mourning upon his demise, a strong but narrow identification, possibly of human-like physiological origins.

Fletcher, in his work on instincts, classified affection as instinctive in both animal and man. Affection consists of the satisfactions brought by a sense of identity, with sexual and control overtones, but, again, often exists side by side with resentment and hostility as ambivalence, depending upon the apparent effectiveness of the controls being sought through identification. However, not only abundance and variety distinguish human from animal affections, but also self-consciousness. Insofar as a person is self-aware, his self-awareness will travel with his identifications and affections.

But even in self-awareness, we should preserve the useful hypothesis, as put by Lashley, that "the rudiments of every human behavioral mechanism will be found far down in the evolutionary scale and also represented even in primitive activities of the nervous system."[23] Conflict and self-destructive behavior can be trained into a rat.

Most ethologists seem presently to agree that the differences between man and other species, while apparently wide, are still differences in degree rather than in kind. This view may be correct on a phenotypical level; as stated, analogous behaviors can be extracted from man and beast. But this is not the crux of the matter. If the human utilizes a mechanism that duplicates animal behaviors but this mechanism is implicated at the same time in other functions which do not accompany the animal behavior, even though in some cases the animal uses other mechanisms for the implicated functions, we have an important structual difference.

Phenotypically the behaviors may be alike; genotypically thay operate differently. A bird may be musical, and so a man, but a bird can compose music rarely and perhaps never invents an instrument like a violin. This may have to do with such findings as that animals seem not to possess cerebral specialization in any manner like humans. No double dissociations, for example, have been reported in animals.[24]

Even if it can be proven that "animals have an ability for perceiving rules, incorporating them, and then applying them to appropriate situations" it is not correct to add "whether or not this ability is learned or innate is not important.."[25] The vast role of training in human behavior is a proof of instinct delay. I cannot think of a more significant distinction on which to base a separation of species. Man is condemned to a life-work of completing his instincts. If he were not so proud of himself as a species, he would perhaps say that the transition from hominid to man offers a splendid example of regressive evolution.

The individual is constitutionally unable to reinstinctivize himself. It is commonly imagined that humans can revert to the beast. Not if it is *homo sapiens schizotypus* whom we are discussing. Mental disease (i.e., schizophrenia) cannot cause such a reversion and does not in fact do so. A person is not genetically capable of becoming (by mental illness or otherwise) a healthy (or even unhealthy) mammal. Such a person can commit every imaginable perculiar or abnormal act, but it will be a human act. One should not be misled by the multitude of instances in which sometimes, in cults, ceremonies and mental illness, a person will play the role of a pig, bear, horse, etc., or for that matter, identify with clouds, angels, chairs, and rocks.

This inherent incapacity to re-mammalize is one of the most persuasive proofs that a genetic mutation occurred in the final transition from hominid to human. For, even if human behavior had changed from the hominid to a new fixed behavior owing to a permanent change in environment, such as we shall later discuss, it would be possible to retreat from mental illness in the direction of mammalianism. That is, a way would be found to psychosomatize and build up a new chemico-electrical combination to supply a new type of person. It may be noted that when a mammal is driven into "insanity", it seems to become self-aware, that is, human, and when it is cured it reverts usually to its normal un-self-awareness.

De-instinctivization is accompanied by another important development in the human, namely, individuation. A social group is forced to tolerate deviations, if only because its totalitarian intentions must founder upon the rocks of its inabilities. The individual must fail, as well, in his desperate attempts to control himself, that is, his alter ego. Much less can he attune himself perfectly to the modal group behaviors. Under such circumstances, the ideal of individualism evolves and prospers in the very presence of the ideal of group conformity. The person becomes ultimately aware that he is different from others; the gaps between the various demi-instincts and the required definite response in actions and habits become filled with his unique character. Each human can be different — and comes to think of himself as different — because he has a unique set of habits or activities to fill the gap between demi-instinctual response and definite practices as the norm.

As with other animal-human analogues, the observations of Eihl-Eihesfeldt and Lorenz are illuminating but theoretically inconclusive. Their explanation of aggression comes down to the following: two things cannot occupy the same space at the same time. In the case of animals, two cannot eat the same morsel, couple with the same female, hide in the same small hole. When, infected by the same desire at the same moment for the same object-use, they lack (permanently or temporarily) a sense of indirect consequences — which is to say, a sense of plan or of future — or they conceive of no other known solution, or when there are "actually" no consequences, beyond the encounter, that matter subjectively to all participants and the group, then a specific violent (or implicitly violent) exchange may occur.

Next, animals that behave in groups have codes about their aggressive and other behavior. These codes both limit and enlarge the scope of dominating and violent behavior that may be expected in any representative set of encounters.

In the case of man, the limits are so broad and the impulses so complicated that so far as we can tell, any innate tendency can be converted into a type of encounter that everyone concerned would regard as "non-aggressive" and, of course, "aggressive."

We conclude that *homo schizo* produces more behavioral effects than any species, as many as a great many species put together. When operating with a perceived challenge and under scientific rules, he can imitate or reproduce almost every animal behavior. He can reproduce his logical apparatus by computers. He can outwhistle birds, and decoy ducks. He can cut his birth fertility to nil, or stimulate multiple births by chemicals. He is the most flexible animal, the most individually varied, a virtuoso, a polymath, and so on. Prod his brain electrically and an endless flow of free associations and a stream of consciousness is verbalized, though it is neither free nor conscious. And what is in his mind is potentially in his behavior. Considering that his physiology is almost identical with certain primates and that the apparatus used for being human has been hitherto practically indistinguishable from them, we much seek the origins of his uniquely broad and sophisticated outputs in a freedom from instinctive binding. The search is just begun. We go on with it now, in the operations of the brain.

chapter three

BRAINWORK

The human skull is an impressive work of natural architecture, especially when bald. It seem to be an apt crown for a creature of will and decision. But look inside this formidable bone casing and see what a disappointing glob of ooze is the master of thought. Undifferentiated, it has a pasty white stuff over a grey matter, spangled with fibrils and fibers, the whole suffused with a pink from countless blood vessels, and, if it could be dug into, it would reveal firmer membranes, and a chunky stem that connects to the long spinal chord.

The differentiation of large areas is so vague that some surgical operations are couched in how many grams (of the 2000 or so) are removed or how many millimeters of depth one may safely penetrate.

Unlike other organs in the body, the brain does not usually reject tissue transplants. This feature not only suggests that the chemistry of the brain is generalized but also why specific functions can locate here and there and relocate, too.

Brain operations are delicate partly because we do not know what to be delicate about. Still, successful brain operations must be as old as the oldest settlements of mankind, because a number of ancient skulls exhibit trephinations, penetrations by bores and saws, and a subsequent healing and continued life. What came out is unknown or perhaps the aim was to relieve pressure; there is, after all, little reason to believe that the atmospheric pressure on earth, or the electrical pressure for that matter, have remained conveniently the same. Anyone who has confused brains with "sweetbreads" at a butcher shop will agree that "the brain has many characteristics of a gland." And R. Bergland and R. Page go on to say: "it contains hormones, it is bathed in hormones, it has hormone receptors, hormones may serve as its synaptic neurotransmitters, and hormones modify the brain's main function, behavior...Endorphin and other hormones may be produced in small quantities locally within the brain but transported in larger quantities from the pituitary to the brain on demand."[1] We see one reason for the brain's innocuous appearance now: its innumerable cells are like a massive inelegant hotel, in and out of which hordes of tourists flit. It houses a great many transactions.

This grand hotel is well lit. It is completely electrified. Every neuron is an electrical capacitator. The hormones could not move so readily otherwise. For the brain lacks muscle to lever the hormones about, and it is insulting slang to call a man a "musclebrain." The blood capillaries of the brain are very numerous and carry around the food of the cells and remove their excrement. They also transport hormones to their work sites. If the mechanical pumping system is out of order, even for a few minutes, and the hormones do not get to work, many brain cells asphyxiate and the lights go out forever. The capillaries may burst, too, from time to time; the larger the rupture, the greater the damage, but the location of the stroke is more important; vital faculties may be impaired. Although the brain can switch many functions around its inchoate mass, there is a limit to its versatility.

Its liability to asphyxiations and strokes does not mean that the brain is overworked. A persuasive case can be made for the belief that humans have far more brain matter, especially of the highly touted "grey matter," than is needed for normal functions. J. Lorber found a "socially completely normal" young man with a large cranium, a 126 I.Q., and a first class honors degree in mathematics, but with cerebrospinal fluid taking the place of at least nine-tenths of the normal complement of cerebral tissue.

Highly excited and continually enraged characters are sometimes subjected to leucotomies in which, perhaps emulating unknowingly the ancestral practice, some material of the frontal lobe is cut or burned away like a malignant tumor, leaving the patient afterwards somewhat dulled but relaxed. One wonders whether there is a disproportion between the storage capacity and the practical facilities, among other problems, so that the active behavioral outlets are technologically backward. Perhaps this might account for the displeasurable unsatisfied agitation of people, who sense too much, undergo spasmodic muscular urges, and want to express an impossible number and variety of thoughts.

Suppose infants were to be typically relieved of some of their cerebral matter, in a practice like circumcision. (Frantically crying small children have been experimentally leucotomized, in fact.) How would they develop? Would they be nicer to their parents: then Bleuler would not have to laugh at those who, he said, attributed insanity to the lack of family discipline.

They might even be relieved of one of the two hemispheres of the brain, preferably not the left hemisphere, which seems to have some rational qualities. One would hardly know the difference — after all, who knows that a person is going about with a kidney removed? — and, as we shall see, some difficult human problems might be solved. For one thing, everyone, without exception, would be right-handed; this would represent a considerable social gain and relieve many people's anxieties. But it might handicap the ten per cent or so of genetic left-handers whose left brain is on the right, and they would lose some of their more "rational" faculties. This could be prevented by waiting until the handedness of the infant is proven, but would leave society with its left-handers.

Still, the government might wish to allow another ten per cent or some percentage to lose their left hemisphere, as a low-budget method of supporting arts and culture; we would have an anatomically generated group inclined to be musicians, poets, and artists who will be right-handed, but in other major respects distinct from the rest of the population; they would probably not understand fully the joys of mathematics, logic and spelling; the caste system, sought for thousands of years in India and elsewhere, would become a fact.

THE ANIMAL BASEMENT

Little is known of brainwork, but what is known can carry us surprisingly far in our conception of human nature. It is well, first, to remind ourselves of how the human brain and central nervous system relate to their lower class relatives of the animal kingdom, and how much of human activity begins, and ends, in the basement. Then we can suggest where to look in the central nervous system, especially in the brain, for the source of those operations that are peculiarly human: the activations and transmission system, the electric and chemical processes, and the proneness to specializatiion of functions found in the cerebrum. With this knowledge, we may venture such hypotheses as appear plausible on the dozen or so aspects of human nature that are the hallmarks of this book: the poly-selves, control, anxiety, instinct-delay, displacements and projections, memory, obsessions, habits, language and symbols, pragmatism and sublimation.

Animals sense their surroundings — smells, chemicals, sights, temperatures and so on. Their sensitivity can be more varied, greater, subjectively "more ingenious" than the human's, or less. Like man, "an animal does not react to all the changes in the environment which its sense organs can receive, but only to a small part of them."[2] (A carnivorous water beetle does not attack and devour a tadpole simply if it sees one, but it will attack any solid object, tadpole or not, if a kind of "smell of meat" arouses it.) Internal operations of the nervous system must contribute "motive" in animals.

Thus Tinbergen goes on to say:

> There is a mutual relationship between internal and external factors in the sense of an additive influence on the motor

response. A high intensity of one factor lowers the threshold for the other factors. A high hormone level increases the responsiveness to external stimulation ; if the hormone level is low, very intensive external stimulation is required to bring the total of causal factors above threshold value.

Automatic centers of the Central Nervous System maintain a continuous flow of impulses to central nervous motor mechanisms; but some kind of block prevents an uncontrolled and chaotic discharge of muscles. The discharge requires adequate stimulation by signs typical to the species, whereupon an innate releasing mechanism removes the blockage.

All of this about the CNS and instincts of animals apply to humans. Rigidity of instincts and behaviors, and the restriction of choice and decision, in animals, generally are more than among most humans but are not to be exaggerated. That food cannot divert animals from sex and *vice versa* is of course incorrect, and so on to the confusion of decision-making, that is, the selection of what drive to pursue and how far, which is vulgarly considered to be a human problem alone. Any animal can take a long time to make up its mind — too long, in many cases, and disaster or failure or good fortune may result.

In the thirty years since Tinbergen wrote his book on animal instincts, ethology has run wild and is pressing upon the sacred functions of the human mind. We need to be most cautious in our defense, consequently. The cerebrum of higher animals directs the hypothalamus to cause the pituitary gland to stimulate by an "adrenocorticotrophic" hormone the adrenal medula to exude catacholamines and the adrenal cortex to emit corticosteroids that plague the motor and nervous system from the brain to the toes for action. The hypothalamus governs the pituitary gland, controls the clocks of the brain, alerts the body to changes soon to occur, and synchronizes the performance of the endocrines throughout the body.

The hypothalamus, buried deep in the brain, is so

widespread among animal species that it is unlikely to be the source of distinctive human behavior or to have changed to become so. The fact that it is responsive to cerebral signals suggests that the "human-disease", when it affects the whole system just described, originates in the cerebrum.

The human anatomy offers essentially three brains, it is true — four, if the cerebral hemispheres are accorded autonomous status. One is reptilian (the archicortex), one from the lower animals (the mesocortex), and one from the higher animals (the neocortex). A. Koestler has argued that grave problems arise for humans because of "insufficient co-ordination between archicortex and neocortex.[3] He ascribes intellectual operations to the new brain, and emotional behavior to the lower, older systems. MacLean refers also the "schizophysiology" of the limbic, as the older is called, and the neocortical system, saying that the old brain provides a crude and confused, animalistic and nonsymbolic picture of the other world.[4] Koestler proceeds to the theory that rational behavior, housed in the neocortex, is interrupted, disorganized and overwhelmed often by the activity and responses of the older systems.

I cannot follow this reasoning. For one thing, it could take no account of the late splurge of research into interhemispheric differences and of late electrochemical research. More significantly, the theory seems to be based upon an old thory of human nature, the mind and body distinction, the reasons-and-emotions duality, the rational-irrational distinction, that has led psychological theory nowhere. The human can be viewed as fully nonrational, or as rational, but so can the earthworm. H.J. Morowitz has gone the limit and asks sypathetically, "Can Bacteria Think?" They are human-like in tissue, functions, and genetic coding. They respond to varied stimuli, exhibiting sensing, bio-clocks, memory, and aimed organic mobilization (decision). The human is, of course, very different on traits that humans deem important.

The cerebral cortex or neocortex activates intensely and overall when stimulated by pain or strong anxiety. Blood flow, metabolism, and electrical fields and discharges increase. The person becomes alert to the self and the world around him. There is no question that the pragmatic philosphers were correct in assigning to anxiety, to the sense of problems, the major role in problem-solving efforts, hence intelligence. Man would like to solve his problems by automatic reflexes but he must feel pain and anxiety, both specifically and generally before he can perceive the problem, and while he works upon it and resolves it.

The cerebral cortex, for all the noble brow it presents and the most important tasks assigned to it, results from a slap-dash design. Surprisingly, when the subject is at rest and awake, in a comfortable supine position with eyes closed in a silent laboratory and neither spoken to or touched, the pattern of flow throughout the cortex is not uniform. On the contrary, the flow is always substantially higher in the front part of the cortex than in the central or rear parts.[5] The density of blood vessels is the same, hence "the remarkable difference in flow rate suggests that the overall activity level of the front part of the resting brain is about 50 percent higher than that of the rear parts."[6]

Apparently, as expected, the aware human is spending his quiet time "getting his head together." The phrases are "busy planning and selecting" behaviors; "focused on inner thoughts, particularly on reflections on one's own situation;" "simulation of behavior." Notable is the fact that the perennially excited frontal region of the brain seems to suffer from poor evolutionary logistics, a merely ordinary blood circulatory system. It is as if Washington, D.C., had the same postal system as Detroit, but the employees worked longer hours. The situation suggests that the evolutionary saltation or quantavolution which precipitated mankind, in order to evade helpless confusion, may have selected large frontal brain mass, but that this expansion in volume did not result in all-around equalized work assignments in coping with the problems presented.

Widespread among animals and working to all intents and purposes as it does in man, is the neuro-transmission system. In humans, neural impulses are passed from one neuron or nerve cell to another; 10 billion neurons, these

with their projecting fibriles — an axon to emit a message, dendrites to receive them — are half in the brain
and half elsewhere in the body. No two neurons are
chemically the same, because, said Polyak once, "All
neurons have different *shapes*."[7] And they carry differently shaped muscles along their dendrites, too, according to Crick. Between any two neurons exists a gap, a
synapse, where chemical neurotransmitters wait like
boats to ferry messages among the neurons. There may
be a dozen types of boats; a few pick up a message merely
to dump it, while the others transmit their messages duti-
fully.

An increased electrical potential of a neuron, relative
to an adjacent neuron, makes it emit a charge which rides
a chemical molecule, the neurotransmitter, across the
synapse gap to hand it over to the adjacent neuron. The
neurotransmitter then breaks down like the exhausted
messenger in King Lear. It seems a great waste to lose
these myriad molecules when they might be left to ferry
many another charge between neurons; perhaps it is to
keep the hormone factories humming.

This island-hopping path may be considered "slow"
or "fast" depending upon what kind of speculation one is
indulging in. Speeds of a mile a minute are common.
Delays here may be significant in letting messages go
elsewhere. Also the messages may not get through
because of the insufficiency of neurotransmitters to carry
them and because of sabotage by other boatsmen.

The neurons are exercised to do their part. They beat
electrically in the nervous system's rhythm of perhaps
ten times a second. "Neurons... have electrical beats, and
large numbers of them beat in place, as armies marching
in step. When impulses come in, from the eyes particularly, the neurones begin to scintillate, to get out of step
with each other, and the brain wave rhythm breaks up."
So says Ralph Gerard.[8] Too much synchronisation gives
tubular vision, too strict an attention to one thing. Too
weak a sychronisation would promote inattention and
flightiness. Perhaps, thinks Gerard, the strictness would
depress attention and be a cause of mental depression;
perhaps slackness would elicit anxiety, mania, even epilepsy.

We say, yes, this is an old and common system, but we can see in it some possiblities of human pecularities. Gerard gives us more food for thought: the thresholds for messages crossing the gaps fluctuate; electron movement, Brownian movement, and other factors vary at any given synapse. If this were not the case, every input would excite exactly the same output. Innovation would be as minimal as with spinal and emotional reflexes. With threshold fluctuations the same stimulus may vary the paths of its impulses and thus favor innovation. Of course, he suggests, in this case there would be less coherence and more flights of ideas.

THE LOCATION OF INSTINCT DELAY

We wonder whether the synapse may be the location of the instinct-delay that we regard as the basic glory and problem of humans. Gerard points out that

> The synapse can only be present because it is important **not** to have a message go through on an express track from one receptor to one effector. Otherwise, why break the nerve path and cause slowing, the chance of confusion, and all the rest? The synapse permits chageability, allows the units to connect now this way, now that way... Every synapse is thus, in effect, a decision point. A message comes to it from the pre-synaptic fiber; does it go out over the post-synaptic one or doesn't it go out? That is the decision the nervous system makes — at a near infinity of places and times.[9]

Many animals have the same system, indistinguishable in detail from the human. Let us grant that here may be the source of animal decision-making, for instance the determination to hunt rather than rest, or simply to rest rather than move. With this, I see two possibilities for the "Human Difference."

We may have a pollution problem: the human system
may be dumping so many neurotransmitters and neuro-
inhibitors into the synaptic canals that messages cannot
pass or cannot pass clean. This would occur, say, if the
human endocrine glands were overbusy at a constant
rate, whether from mutation or some physiological constant, environmentally induced. Suppose that dopa-
mines, which are neurotransmitters, generally clutter the
passages: the results would be a universal set of schizophrenic behaviors. Remove a large proportion of them
and we revert to the hominid.

The present interest in dopamine receptors in the
brain and elsewhere highlights the electro-chemical
complexity of the human being. Dopamine neurorecep-
tors are more numerous in the brains of diagnosed schizophrenics, especially in the limbic area and the candat
nucleus. Depressing the receptors suppresses schizophrenic symptoms. The energizers of the dopamine
receptors are numerous drugs, some of which exist naturally in the body. Does a particular diet or food do so?
Does an atmospheric gas do so? A particle? An ion as
attached, for example, to oxygen? Does ambiant stress
level? Does climate? (hot, cold, damp...?) Winds? Could
a combination of these stress the hominid to the point of
humanness? And persist permanently?

The body absorbs a continuous supply of small negative ions, negatively charged molecules. There are some
1000 to 2000 ions per cubic centimeter of air over open
land, in a ratio of five positive to four negative, according
to Soyka and Edmonds.[10] Many reports declare over-
doses of positive ions are unhealthy, inducing overpro-
duction of serotonin and emotional imbalance and list-
lessness. A.P. Dubrov has assembled a volume of studies,
many of them from the Soviet Union, on the effects that
the geomagnetic field has upon the biosphere, including
humans.[11] The two effects — the ion and geomagnetic —
are related, and both are implicated in brain activity. At
today's levels, they condition the anxiety level of
humans, and the behavior of plants and animals. Whether
the present rates were established in the course of human
evolution is important for explaining human nature
today, but is consigned to the volumes on *Homo Schizo I*

and *The Lately Tortured Earth* for discussion. How these phenomena affect the speed of mental operations and memory recall is unknown.

Like people, who pollute their own environments, the brain is frequently its own poisoner. For, in a *coup d'etat* which may have occurred at the time of humanization, the "higher center" of the brain seized most of the power to requisition the drug supplies of the body and to order the manufacture of more. Even though a hemo-encephalic barrier exists to protect cerebral tissues from most of the drugs going though the body tissues, the barrier can be breached by concussions, intoxication, and "affective storms" which result from the sudden flushing of the brain with certain hormones. The storm could originate from traumatic fear — accident, rape, battle, etc.

Acute states of anxiety ensue. If "continuous and successive, they might weaken the hemo-encephalic barrier, causing an increase in permeability, and, consequently, the affective ability of the individual."[12]

The instability of the cortex is rendered more possible by its separation by other barriers from the midbrain extra-pyramidal apparatus. Cortical agitation may itself promote increased stress on itself, also, and on the central nervous system if it breaks up, as for example happens temporarily in hypnosis; its transactions with the midbrain and limbic system through the extra- pyramidal apparatus are destabilized.

A baffling problem is presented in that no single substance seems to control any given behavior of the human or his brainwork. The brain has a great many endorphins and peptides, which are identical with hormones found throughout the body. What instructions do they convey? Are they coded or merely combined in their associatiion with other substances and electrical charges? The flow of adrenalin from the adrenal medulla, a neural tissue atop the kidneys, is excited by nerve fibers which can ultimately be excited by the cerebral cortex. Electroconvulsive therapy, for example, applied to the brain, activates the adrenal medulla. Drugs can motivate cerebral activity but also distort it. Since enhanced motivation always presents the problem of its control, the distorted attitude is most likely out of control.

The pituitary gland is associated with the brain, part of it being composed of brain tissues. It emits perhaps a dozen hormones. These affect growth; they stimulate thyroid gland activity, the sexual organs, pigmentation; they influence blood pressure; and so on. These processes and many others in endocrinology are not well understood yet. Substances come from several sources; they may have specific or general inhibitors. They may affect several organs, their quantities do not have well-measured effects. When later we speak of displacements, the multi-functional overlap in behavior affecting endocrinology becomes a factor of importance; it invites confusion (including perversions) in the absence of intense directiveness toward a goal.

If one also asks only which gland or organ is the most important determinant of human nature, one would have to give the traditional answer: the brain, and particularly the cerebral cortex. All else is almost indistinguishably animal and no peculiar human operations have been noted for any function or secretions. We cannot discount the possibility of a constant change of a quantitative nature in the total endocrinal system or even in the adrenals that would place the human in a distinctive drug environment, compelling him to behave differently — to think, to talk, to make war, to have gods. However, if this has happened, it is because of a "decision," a forced and involuntary command, of the cerebral cortex. It orders its own drugs, its own blood supply, its own electrical currents and charges. It can both reduce and increase its orders: that is the vital point. It may appear, all too early, that I am coming to the idea of the World as Will, to use Hegel's expression, so I must say that I am exceedingly aware of the complex interaction occurring inside the human and between the human and his environment. *Homo sapiens schizotypus* is not at all the traditional idea of cerebral *homo sapiens sapiens*.

The human cerebrum, we hypnotically repeat to ourselves, is much larger than the primates', even if exceeded by the elephants'. If the human central nervous system, including the endocrine glands, is not proportionately increased in size, we have a situation where electrical and chemical supplies have to be generated or, if not generated, then rationed among a vastly greater number of neurones and synapses.

This, although working against the first mechanism of Human Difference — pollution and excess — would yet have the same effect, of confusion, dispersion and delay by frequent non-achievement of synaptic threshold requirements, overworking feedback signals for more supplies. Far more displacements would occur. The most "ridiculous" and "irrelevant" behaviors and thoughts would be normal. A chronic general anxiety would be present: justified fears of failure coupled with continuous interference in the completion of tasks. This begins to look like the Human Difference.

That the speed of neural activity accounts for differences among species is unquestionable. Alexander von Muralt has called "saltatory conduction" a great advance in evolution.[13] The speed with which nerve impulses are transmitted is lowest in primitive forms and highest in mammals. It is 25 meters per second at 20°C in myelinated (sheathed) frog nerves to 100 meters in mammals. The velocity depends upon the conducting mechanism, the diameter of the fibre, the myelinisation of the fibre, and the ambiant temperature. The cephalopod nerve must carry a far heavier bulk of fibre and consume much more oxygen to carry the same message as a frog nerve. The frog nerve relies upon tubular sheaths of high-resistant protein, myelin, to concentrate the passing electrical impulse, and upon feeding the impulse at nodal intervals between sheaths with ions and dyes to accelerate it by leaps from one sheathed interval to the next. Mammals have evidently a more efficient system than the amphibious frog.

Experimentation is in too early a stage to distinguish between man and primates with respect to their relative efficiencies in saltatory conduction. That man's conduction velocity may be less, or may put strains on the supply of charges and accelerators is conceivable; humiliating though it might be to possess a "regressive" evolution, this could promote a generally higher level of nervous tension, hence "intelligence."

Holding neural speed constant in all "higher" animals, there would still exist a speed problem with humans. We should inquire whether the human brain expanded coincidently with humanization or "long before." If the two happened together, humanization might be the effect of slowed responses owing to greater synaptic distances. In the simplest model, two types of distances are involved in a stimulus response. Thus: the left hand transmits a feeling through the central nervous system to the right brain hemisphere, which feels "hot" but must transmit the information through the intervening fibers of the corpus callosum to the language center of the left brain, which then forms the words "It's hot!" for the voicing apparatus to exclaim. First, does the large size of the right cerebral hemisphere make any difference to the speed of the impulse of the heat signal? Second, does the distance traversed within the brain to inform the left brain mean another delay? Third, does the distance from the language center to the exclamation center and then the voice muscles add more delay? The answer in all three cases is probably "yes."

Unfortunately, we are not in a position today to know these three speeds, nor those of a primate with which we would compare them. The interhemispheric transfer time has been studied and times of from 3 to 28.5 milliseconds have been obtained for fairly comparable tests. R. Puccetti, calculating that a flash of light through the left visual field to the right hemisphere, thence to the left hemisphere for conscious reporting, would take 9.75 msec for a certain subject, reasons that perhaps twice this time, 19.50 msec, would be required for the right hemisphere to 'know' that the signal had been completed; that is, only after 19.5 msec would the transaction be fully perceived. He believes the delay must be unconsciously perceived but suppressed, "fudged over", to use the vernacular.[14]

Swanson and Kinsbourne found interhemispheric transfer times of from 2 msec to 21 msec depending upon the degree of uncertainty and displacement of location with which the subjects were presented the stimulus; the findings led them to doubt that the interhemispheric delay was significant.[15] The difference between 21 and 2 was assigned to the searching process. The authors grant the simplicity of the test. Even a minimal difference would be greatly enlarged if the brainwork had to zig-zag many times across the corpus collosum. (An experiment with a cat showed a first interhemispheric crossing of under 10 msec velocity and a second interhemispheric delayed response to occur 40 to 50 msec after the initial response.)

Swanson, Ledlow and Kinsbourne conclude that "crossing the structural link does take time, but the time is short and is overshadowed by other factors that involve how the subject distributes attention before stimulus presentation and how the stimulus directs attention after presentation."[16] This generalizes from tests so simple that ordinary animal behavior must involve many times the interhemispheric delay. And only in the case of humans is there a significant specialization that would necessitate interhemispheric transfer and coordination in a large proportion of brainwork and behavior. The human exercises many of his important qualities through myriad transfers.

When a hemisphere is performing one of its special functions, high electrical measures register, by contrast with the opposing hemisphere. The activity is evidenced in high average evoked potentials (AEP) and in electroencephalogram beta waves.[17] These results confirm that the experiencing which is taking place in one hemisphere is not occuring strongly in the other.[18] Under such circumstances, there must ensue over time a great many contradictions between the left and right brains, in memory, method, and predispositions of attitudes and behavior. Every new experience therefore requires more preparatory transfers for coordination and planning.

The "ever restless human mind" thus must be more than a metaphor and more than an abnormality of some people. To behave as a whole unity, decisively, with both hemispheres, requires continuous trade-offs of impressions. If enough cannot be done while awake, dreamwork must go on apace. Here, too, is a source of obsession. Transfer dyssymmetry of several types occurs analogous to coordinating two allied armies on a battle front; one can never be sure that all are agreeable, informed, supplied, and prepared for action, and the action carries its own nasty surprises.

But, before going further with the potentialities of the bicameral brain for producing human nature, a brief statement of the situation may be in order. Many studies have appeared in the past few years.[19] An impetus was provided by the availability of persons who had undergone a commissurectomy in which the cord of fibres constituting that giant commissure, the corpus callosum, was severed. With this, the great part of all direct connections between the two cerebral hemispheres is broken. The left side of the brain is not privy to new information or signals presented to the right brain, and *vice versa*.

The patient is not apparently abnormal; indeed, if the operation were performed to block epileptic seizures, he feels better, because the electric storming of the right hemisphere cannot cross the chasm of severance so as to storm the left hemisphere. Sperry wrote: "Everything we have seen so far indicates that the surgery has left each of these people with two separate minds, that is, with two separate spheres of consciousness,"[20] — together, we would add, with the general consciousness discussed above.

The gist of the studies, whether carried out upon normal brain structures or commissurectomized ones, is that the brainwork of the two hemispheres differs. Although either hemisphere can carry on all known mental operations alone, when the two sides are coordinated in the normal manner, each has its special functions and "superiorities." "Asymmetries are in general present at birth or in early childhood or even in utero.. very probably genetically determined.. not absolute, but are distributed along the spectrum.."[21]

The left hemisphere, which, contrastingly, connects with the right side of the body, is called dominant (except that in true left-handers the right hemisphere is dominant), not so much because it specializes in the logical and analytic processes, and verbal and mathematical functions, as because it controls the right hand. The right hemisphere specializes in spatial orientation, arts and crafts, recognitions of whole images, and music and acoustics, including vowels but not consonants. Generally the left brain is more localized, the right more diffuse and prehuman.[22]

Yet something of all of these occurs in both hemispheres. Some of it is culturally induced; fluent Japanese speakers carry their vowels on the left, westerners on the right.[23] The right hemisphere (until the Japanese case came along) was described by some students as feminine, the seat of intuition and artistic taste, whereas the left was labelled rational and correct.

Memory is notably diffused throughout the brain, although a single hemisphere or less could store more memories than one could ever recall. A hemisphere is insensitive to its sources. It does not footnote a datum as coming from outside or from across the corpus callosum.

In fact the brain receives, recognizes and stores information and sensory bits without discrimination. They all become electrochemical transmissions whether they begin as caviar or cacophony. Once they reach the brain the transmissions generate resonances in a number of cells, sometimes widespread, sometimes localized. If they are intensive experiences, they resonate thousands of times on top of the electrical rhythms already present in the cell. They dig in especially where similar circuits already are patterned, and both reinforce, refer to, and learn from (are modified by) the preexisting patterns. Discriminations of sight, hearing, touch, smell and taste are created in the brain. A taste of nectar is a gang of electrically resonating cells with experiences of sweet things from the mouth. A mild electrical stimulation of related cells in the brain might provide an even sweeter taste.

The latest model of the brain — and there have been many before — views it as a repository of holograms. A hologram is a global representation of an object produced by two laser beams, one focused on the object prior to interfering with the other beam, and the interference pattern can record itself on a photographic plate with what our brains regard as verisimilitude.

Karl Pribram hs illustrated the holographic process by a tennis novice watching an expert play. As he observes, his brain makes transformations of the whole configuration, activating and impressing the appropriate motor patterns. That is, the brain resonates to the watched behavior and is reminiscent of the gestalt theory of learning and problem solution.[24]

In his treatise on the brain, Pribram points out that any piece of an artificial hologram film reproduces the whole of the figure, which, if analogous in the brain, means that every cell or a great many clusters of cells might contain total images of much that enters the brain. This may be why, in so many instances, a lesion of the cerebrum is compensated for, the brain being in this regard one of the most dispensable tissues of the body.

In addition, the hologram concept lets one explain better one of the two basic types of logic engaged in by the brain to simulate the recapture of primate instinct, the analogue and the digital logics. Without reliance upon the calculating modes of the left hemisphere or of speech, the righthanded person can employ his left hemisphere on a parity basis with his right in accomplishing instant intuitions of the connections between all manner of distantly related objects, memories, and ideas by superimposing new holograms upon old and reacting to the new experiences in the light of the old.

The brain is perhaps receiving and storing prior holograms in the millions, and is recognizing its own when its ordinary feat is duplicated outside, as artificial holography. Animal brains must make holograms too. The point is that humans may be making two sets for each hemisphere. Such a situation may have grave consequences, because the two hemispheres are not identical and add different resources to the process.

The division of holograms, together with the specialization found in each hemisphere, and even adding the delays occurring in interhemispheric transmission, cannot overcome the centralization forced by the pragmatic needs of the one body, the shared limbic and midbrain elements, and the central nervous system and musculature otherwise. There exists a sensation of consciousness pervading the whole brain down to the stem.

For example, a concussion will usually act to depress generally all electrical activity; the localized blow is referred generally. Again, in a 15-year-old right-handed boy, callosally sectioned, the right hemisphere could not initiate speech, but could understand nouns and verbs, could carry out oral commands and could write with the left hand.[25]

S.J. Diamond describes a circuit that spans the whole brain from the parietal lobe on one side to the opposite parietal lobe, and which encounters the corpus callosum in passing.[26] Giraud describes a global sensory psychic experiencing, common to man and animals, that arises out of the sympathetic nervous system, glandular secretions and muscular tone.[27] Jerison warns against over-emphasizing localization and specialization, which may be useful to isolate parts of the system in order to study them more easily: "recent evidence points to the waking brain as being a complex interactive system in which truly isolated functional systems probably never occur."[28]

Sommerhoff, who ignores the "split brain" entirely in his large treatise on the *Logic of the Mind*, writes: "In terms of internal representations the unity of the physical self finds expression in a family of characteristic transformation expectations the brain assimilates during ontogenesis." The unity of the whole self requires the additional inner representations where the object is seen by the observer who knows he is observing. Thus the self comes from experiencing, and is the record of experiences and expectations of further experiencing.

The source of consciousness appears to be still in the brain stem. From there, even in commissurectomized subjects, some alternative — that is both left and right side — operations are controlled. Such operations "are capable of exercising a metacontrol over the higher processes of consciousness."[29] This would be the animal consciousness, not self-awareness.

How vulnerable the unity of the self is, and yet how adamant everyone is, including ourselves, about the self being an absolute unity. The analogy of a social organization comes to mind. It is in a perennial conflict between the division of labor and centralization. As Kinsbourne has pointed out, bilateralism, by which he means a highly coordinated dualism of the hemispheres (for learning, perception, memory, and volition, as his own effective investigations have shown, are independently able in each hemisphere), is not needed for linear information processing, hence specialization.[30] This is a matter of dispute. And a certain amount of information *is* dualistic.

It must be stressed that specialization in the brain is not complete in any respect, no more than the division of labor in society is ever absolute (there is always a shoemaker or tailor at work despite the great factories). Brain specialization is limited to a dominant ganging or bunching of cells such that they alone respond (or do not respond) unless they are excised, in which event the minor gangs take over their functions, on a reduced level at first, then increasingly so, and sometimes with full capacitation. The union shop, when on strike, so to speak, finds its work taken on by less skilled scabs.

We can assume that even the very minor specialized bunches here and there are active all the time. It may be these which are responsible for some of the competitive mutual inhibitions, as well as collaboration, between the hemispheres that Kinsbourne has noted.[31] Hoppe speaks of the quantitative and qualitative impoverishment of the dreams, fantasies, and symbols of commissurotomized patients, laying it to an interrupted preconscious interhemispheric stream. stream.[32] He suggested that a "functional commissurotomy" may be present in some severe psychoses. That the hemispheres can pull themselves apart functionally seems no more absurd than the known cases of total hysterical paralysis or catatonism.

J. Levy argues that differentiation of functions which are lateralized is a result of competition whereby speech and language, e.g., develop in the dominant hemisphere and displace less elaborate psychic processes such as patterning images into the opposite sphere.[33] The source of this pushy competitiveness must be humanly genetic. Anatomical and physiological differences between cerebral hemispheres develop in the human foetus.[34] "Non-human animals have not been demonstrated to possess cerebral specialization in any manner similar to humans; that is, no double dissociations have been reported in nonhuman mammals."[35] The genetic impetus may have originated in a mutation to the large cerebrum, with a neural "weakness for data collection and transfer" in one hemisphere, which required continuous orderly attention.

That these minor locales may be disaffected is not an extreme view; the researchers, perhaps in their exuberance, speak of contradictions. When callossally sectioned, one hemisphere can be led to think and act angrily against the other. Are we to believe that there is no tension between left and right brains in the presence of specialism, when the corpus callosum is exchanging not only sensory infromation — albeit sometimes traumatic — but novel commands to change itself, give up its habits. Hence sensations of hesitation, doubt, reflection, disobedience may be part of interhemispheric relations; since a hemisphere does not know the source of a message, it cannot be declared that doubt and disobedience and fear are "external" sensations, incapable of being incited from a source within, namely the opposing hemisphere.

Nor should we ignore another reciprocating effect of specialization. In society as a whole, a tendency to specialize intensifies efforts at coordination. The same logic may apply to interhemispheric relations. A great many more messages will flow as the brain specializes. This may occur in a given lifetime and be more cultural than genetic. The civilized capabilities are left-brain and may be at the basis of the larger everpresent anxiety of the civilized person.

HANDEDNESS

Handedness, usually to the right, may itself be an important factor in precipitating humanization. It is genetically predisposed. For example, newly born infants turn four times more to the right than to the left. It seems quantitative in its intensity; it can be ranked by how much it dominates a person's relevant activity. It can be altered and reinforced by training. Injury to the dominant hemisphere can of course affect it partly or totally.

Handedness is observable in some mammals, for instance lions[36] and various monkeys. It may have been elicited and stressed because human activity was being stymied by conflict and hesitation in the brain. A hand, and the right one was potentiated, had to be given preference. The novel decisions (calculating, symbolizing) were being made by the left brain; perhaps it could not count upon the right brain passing the commands to the left hand without blocking or censorship. Otherwise why would not the left brain have resigned the extra quantum of dextrousness to the left hand under the control of the right brain? And passed its share of manual tasks to the right brain to execute, as the right brain does now do it?

The latter "choice" makes it appear that either the dominant brain by its peculiar specialization otherwise makes for dexterity, or that dexterity induces specialization in one hemisphere. But what do language, abstraction, logic, and symbolism have to do with dexterity? Is it sheerly genetic coincidence that the two are enclosed in the same hemisphere? The right brain could use dexterity, or bilateralism, as well. Music, sounds, spatialism, images: these need a right hand also. Nonetheless, a right-hander is left-brained altogether. And the brains of mammals, including primates, are only slightly asymmetrical, and behave, with clumsy hands, more like two right-brain human hemispheres.

The apparent solution for the human effect is to introduce a third factor, the fear of loss of control owing to the onset of left-brain specialization. Owing to a pressing need to specialize, whether genetic or electrochemical, a leadership or dominance problem is presented. "Somebody has to be boss" in the face of increased inputs of unresolved differential impulses, attention and decisions between the two hemispheres. "The wheel that squeaks gets the grease." Let the left brain, which is causing the new problems and is even physically enlarged to a degree, take the initiatives and give it the baton, the hand, the already most developed instrument for dealing with the world.

Sperry reported that monkeys with sectioned commisures accept either of two contradictory solutions to a problem, one solution coming from the left, the other from the right. Not so man. For matters in the right-handed domain, the left brain insists upon its solution even if wrong and forces the left hand to give in, if necessary. In its few manual competences, the right hemisphere does the same. It must be one hand, not two, else the problem will be sent "back to the drawing boards."

Species changes are rarely neat. A solution is piled

upon unresolved problems. New tissue is made of old. A new task is given to an old bone. Two holes become a nose, two feet a fishtail. In cats and monkeys, personality, temperament, coordination, internal functions, alertness, activity, achievement of learning, and responses — all remain the same after the corpus callosum is severed.[37] Bilateral symmetry persists, rather uselessly, in the brain. The hominid surrendered bilaterality and gained a human mind. Human nature begins with an unbalanced brain and a determined hand.

Dexterity by its very existence reinforces poly-egoism. Apart from what may be happening in the brain (though never separated from it), the full anatomical laterality, manifest in a thousand ways, makes itself felt as a division between major and minor modes, dominance and subordination, ruler and ruled. The dominant body side is even sensed as heavier, Ornstein has pointed out. When someone slaps his own forehead guiltily (usually with his dominant hand) and says "I could kick myself," it would probably be with his dominant foot.

The brain as soma is an insensitive organ, so we feel no contradiction of the left brain dominating the right side of the body. Hence the right (though representing the left brain in action) is obviously authoritative in legend, custom, law, politics work, and other practice.[38] The right is morally right. Right-sided behavior and authority are connected. Since the right side is authoritative, the opposite of authoritative is antiauthoritarian. Often it is "leftist." We may surmise that also in the individual the left-side is anti-authoritarian. The basic polyego is of a ruler and ruled, but the ruled is frequently anti-authoritarian, a leftist. In authoritarian cultures, the left-handed are said to use the "wrong" hand (e.g. Alsace, France). In administering a pretest of a national survey questionnaire, employing the occasion of an all-female meeting of Planned Parenthood, a birth control group appealing to independent-minded women, I observed that the baker's dozen of members present were all left-handed. I received incredulous and suspicious reactions when I remarked about it afterwards.

An experiment may be presumed that would demonstrate that persons protesting an imagined "capture" by another party (paranoia) will reveal the resentment against the offense by uncoordinated hand behavior when compared with authority-accepting subjects. Perhaps even the enduring conflict between "science" and "humanism", the "Two Worlds" of Professor Snow, can be construed as an interhemispheric conflict situation.

The specialization of the left brain encompasses speech, grammar, figures, signs, abstract solutions, classical logic, and the dominant right hand movements. These are products, not the *Ding in sich*, the underlying drive of the brain. They must refer to a more basic concept, and I find it in the term "order." "Order" contains nuances of "Truth," authority, goal-setting, completion, instrumental and linear progression. This is all that we would expect from human nature. (of course, the left brain simultaneously contains its mammalian routines of half the body." We need only turn over the final card: the opposite of order; what prompts order: confusion, delays, fear, disorder. We need not be amazed and then suspicious at the stupendous analogy with society and social thought, where right and order fight together against anti-authoritarianism and disorder.

It may be that the more the asymmetry the greater the disorder of the brain, the greater the perception of fear and of the need to control the self and the world. Sex differences may be salient in this regard. Lionel Tiger reports: "The single fact, that some part of the brain is characteristically different in males and females, is one of the most significant findings in neuroendocrinology."[39]

Perhaps the hormonal variation is related to brain asymmetry, for we discover in the research of Jerry Levy proof of the greater symmetry (bilaterality, hominidity?) of the female brain. The right hemisphere of a woman has greater verbal capacity than the male's and her left brain can handle perceptual information better than a man's. This confirms older psychological tests comparing boys and girls on spatial and language tasks.

It does not obviate the possibility of total cultural determination of the difference, but this is not likely. The differences collate also with the insistant, though disputed, claim that men are more dominant and power-seeking than women. Again, it would be important to have intensive research done on the correlation between the gamut of asymmetries and the range of control demands with regard to the self and others.

In much mental illness and in personal and collective disaster, as Deikman and Parry have indicated,[40] there occurs a takeover of behavior by right hemisphere religious, aesthetic, ecstatic, imagistic thinking and intuitive irrational action. The reader may be reminded of an expression from World War II: "There are no atheists in foxholes." According to A. Shimkunas, in schizophrenia the left hemisphere is overactivated and overloaded, and is accompanied by a highly arousable right hemisphere. Interhemispheric transfers are defective and cannot be processed in the commonly organized manner.[41]

ORDER AND DISUNITY

If there is a fear of oneself, where does the presence and fear of several selves and of ego dissolution originate? The split brain is obvious but whence the multisplit? As ventured above, the minor locales of specialization in both hemispheres may, in handling events, offer different solutions than the dominant solution, no matter in which sphere. I am tempted to suggest that the resisting major hemisphere may enlist minor special spheres as allies. For instance speech can be interrupted by a blockage of imagery from the right hemisphere. The blocked imagery can go to vague speech centers in the right brain or spread to motor centers that refer back to the major speech center as compulsive vocalization. Bleuler (359f) described how patients were observed to operate on as many levels of identities as they had "complexes," whereas normal people inhibited irrelevant material.

Although certain human operations generate from a bicameral brain and the problems of its coordination, we must not regard these two cerebral chambers as the two centers of *homo schizo*. The conditions resulting from the brain discoordination can include not only a sense of several identities and no identity at all, but also an interplay of elements, messages, responses, and directions

within a single hemisphere. As a by-product, and ultimately a possibly great achievement (or defect), of the
lack of phase coupling between the two hemispheres,
elements of a single hemisphere may develop embarrassing or inspiring contradictions.

A one-hemisphere person can maintain as many
mind-sets and behaviors, perhaps, as a two-hemisphere
person can. These would include neurotic and psychotic
and all other types of behavior. This thesis stands yet
unproven. Perhaps it cannot be proven, like the feral
man, the hypothetical human who from birth has not
known humans. Infants are on occasion born without
corpus collosa and other commissures, but this condition
is accompanied by abnormalities that render general
judgements difficult. Persons with extensive one-sided
brain damage are studied under similar limitations. The
origins of human behavior *in utero* and its rapid extension outwards from birth, make even the meaning of
post-callosolectomy behavior in a young child unreliable.
His lack of basal anxiety, or excess, or typicality in
respect to it, can hardly be laid to the sectioning of his
corpus callosum.

The reasons why psychosis and neurosis may be possible in persons with severed callosa are several: observers and experiments practically all agree that such persons are surprisingly "normal," which for us means to
possess the nature of "*homo schizo*" and the potential for
mental disturbance. Second, the two hemispheres still
retain rich connections with the limbic system through
the brain stem, and through this indirectly with each
other; both the direct and indirect connections can produce typical and atypical behavior. Third, within itself,
each hemisphere carries thousands of well-trodden
neural pathways, including atypical ones, so that each
can maintain its own peculiar behaviors; it does not matter absolutely that these paths drive off the cliff, so to
speak, when they arrive at the sectioned callosum.

If a living person is discoverable who by mutation or
accident has always subsisted upon one hemisphere, we
would have to argue that he or she is not quite human. He
should reveal a defect on the basic parameters of *homo
schizo* that we have laid down. That he would not be

devoid of human qualities and would be generally human might be surmised; the heavy acculturation that would discipline his mind and behavior from birth onwards would earn him membership in the human race.

Pursuing this line of reasoning leads to the possibility that humanization occurred in one place, at one time, to one person and with sufficient systematic force to account for a left-brain/right brain difference plus an endocrinal or electrical potential, say, that conferred what we call "human nature" soon upon a small number of persons and then later upon a larger number. (Yet once more we reserve the possibility that only a minority of humans have possessed the dominant genetic structure peculiar to the species, which was necessary to establish the constitution and behavior of the species.)

MEMORY AND REPETITION

We have fixed upon hormonal and cerebral imbalances as the probable source of human delayed-instinct behavior. Humans are prone to hormonal and electrical irregularities in the processes of neural transmission. They also convert a phylogenetic bilateralism into a species-specific division of labor and heavy-handedness. There is enough "wobble" and "conflict" in message transmission and brainwork to delay all instinctive behavior requiring cerebral references, to the point of genetically predisposing self-awareness or a poly-self, a general fear or anxiety, and a grasping for control wherever the attention may settle, in order to assuage fear and gain self-control.

The remaining concepts that were introduced in order to explain human nature in the first chapter can be explained readily in terms of the brainwork already described; these would be memory and obsession; habit and compulsiveness, to which I now append psychosomatism; and displacement, utilizing language and symbols. Memory consists of electro-chemical gestalts or holograms diffused around the brain with some asymmetry: so much we have said. A recent theory, not to be dismissed, even argues that every neuron contains all memories. The deeper the imprinting, or the more active the electrochemical gestalt, the more obsessive it becomes, prone to compete with other experiencing for attention and volition; by these last terms — attention and volition — we mean connecting with general consciousness and pushing past or suppressing all other gestalts of the moment with a heavier charge, "beating them to the punch."

Presumably, unlike animals, the human develops his memory by continual brainwork; that is, memorizing is itself an obsession, transferring and reinforcing memories is part of the overtime behavior of the human mind. The desire to forget is in competition with the fear of forgetting. Who is to judge when memorizing has become obsession, and should cease? Decisions of what to forget and what to remember are "policies" of the "highest" importance to the person and to society. I shall have more to say of this in the next chapter.

Enough has been said earlier on habit and compulsion to carry us forward into the subsequent chapters. Memory, obsession, habit, and compulsion all reduce to a single basic operation in the brain: that of repetitiveness. It is for the ameliorators of undesirable symptoms and for ethical philosophers and politicians to make innumerable distinctions of practical conduct. People and cultures can be graded and scored, encouraged and deprecated, in hundreds of ways. Within the brain, sometimes dealing with itself, at other times transacting with the outer world, a constant busyness occurs which a) experiences by internal and external sensing, b) imprints neurons electrochemically, c) distributes and redistributes charges, and d) emits commands, many to be aborted, to change some internal function or external relation.

Homo schizo's aim in life is to recover his instincts so as to reduce fear. In a roundabout way, the being seeks to control all the ultimately uncontrollable operations to reestablish the tranquility of conscience-less, instinctive behavior. Even when unsuccessful and painful, he persists. Given the options of a blow from outside or an unending succession of self-blows, what creature would choose the way of man and rest content with it? What blow can equal the premeditation of death — a thousand blows to a coward and who is a hero, except the animal, while man suffers the inevitable consequences of identification with the dead, poignant recall, projections into the future and anticipations thereof?

All brain operations instigating somatic change are psychosomatic conversions. This is obvious, upon reflection: the sight of food stimulates the appetite, which sets the guts to "growling." Indeed, it is no quibble to say that all brainwork is somatic, hence psychosomatic; every thought leaves its trace. But even psychiatrists say "psychosomatic," meaning some physical abnormality that they will track to its psychic lair and despatch by psychotherapy. At the same time, if possible, they will be applying medicine and surgery to the physical wound. They are materialists, as is this book. In what we are saying, there appears to be no need to introduce a new kind of psychic essence. Going along this route, our ignorance, too, is assumed to be materialistic.

Many observers, even, or should I say, especially, medical men, incompletely realize the full "harmony" (to use a perjorative term paradoxically and with malice aforethought) of psychosomatism and "purely" mental aberration. So we find, for instance, Hoskins accepting the common idea that schizophrenics are frustrated, inadequate, lacking in robustness, and unable to face the stresses of life.[42]

The same can be said of infantry soldiers being withdrawn from the front lines. The losing battle of control has been fought in the inner and in the outer systems, in the tissues and in the conventional expressive apparatus of voice and conduct. Not only this — crowds of schizoid "draft-dodgers" have escaped the line of battle and carry on in politics, the stage, in all walks of life — not least at the dinner table.

"If anything can go wrong, it will," is more than a joke in psychosomatism. There seems to be no limit to where the brain can reach in its flights from fear. It is not only a matter of being tired in the morning, but also of paralysis, of being covered with open sores, of a stomach digesting itself, of fingers like claws, of heart attacks, of impotence, of deathly coma. The brain, and it must be the "higher centers," dealing with the "lower centers" in lieu of dealing with the outside world, exercises its obsessions and compulsions. "The stomach doesn't need more acids? Give it acids anyway." "I've already ejaculated a holy word? I'll repeat it a hundred times."

The brain's decision to do one of these seems to be based upon a victory, a pyhrric victory, of course, of one lively gestalt over another, both sides unleashed to battle upon the breakdown of the ego order. Both have their "traditions" or habits behind them, their memories and training, their proneness, so that whether a person psychosomatizes or bays at the moon is predictable to a degree, this despite the fact the that both tendencies are rooted in the dense thicket of same-seeming cerebral neurons.

If all psychic phenomena are somatic and have somatic effect, is the reverse also true, that all somatic disease is psychic? If a skier breaks her leg in a fall, does she have a psychic wound? Medically, it may be irrelevant to say so: an ambulance, a hospital, a bolt, a cast, and in several months she will be skiing again. Psychologically, her case may have so many aspects as to defy analysis in a few lines; to quote her mother, "She's crazy to take chances like that, just to be with the others."

Perhaps further study might arrive at the conclusion that the only facet of the whole affair that was not psychic was the breaking of the bones. Then it is like a duodenal ulcer; the only facet that is not psychic is the ulcer. Or the heart attack of the manic depressive; only the cardiomuscular erraticism is not psychic. It is probably significant that most people, in explaining a personal accident, find themselves at fault; we suspect that the source of the guilt feelings may be not only their religious training, but a private knowledge that they were psychically not in command of themselves.

"Civil conflict" within the brain, because of specialization and the larger regionalization, must be far more frequent than observed, even continuous. It is the monitor and censor from the dominant section that gives out regular bulletins that "All is quiet on the western front" — until the front collapses.

Migraine (megrem, ultimately from the Greek and Latin hemicrania, half-skull) may provide significant testimony of inter-hemispheric conflict. Migraine is a common severe headache of one side of the head, occurring more frequently among women. Since no apparent organic cause can be assigned that does not merely reiterate the symptom, and bacause psychic distress often precedes a migraine, it may be heavily psychosomatic, more specifically an ego conflict engaging the left and right cerebral hemispheres.

The preference of the disease for women may be attributed to their more eccentric endocrinal secretions, and indicates that the chosen weapons of battle are hormonal, and the crux of the battle the resistance to an equilibrated flow in the handling of material that requires smooth inter-hemispheric cooperation. That women are less brain-lateralized than men would appear to excite less hemispheric conflict, however, unless the psychic cause of the conflict was not in a prominent aspect of laterality, that is, not in speech or handedness. I have noted that a mother and daughter suffering migraine were, respectively, rigidly conscientious and slackly rebellious, opposites in temperament. Perhaps the source, then, is in a general neurasthenia, a question-begging word, but at least meaning a genetic lability with respect to brain-transfer under stress and hence a potential responsiveness to fear-reduction therapy. To the genetic lability is added the ambiance, the mother in the case cited, who demonstrated the model and earned emulation by identification.[43]

Homo schizo does not possess psychic command of himself. It is rare that a person will acquire a strong, united selves-image amd be able to play the game of countering one anxiety with another, each in a positively desireable guise, and come to do this so habitually that one's whole character appears to be instinctively balanced. Whereupon, if anything goes wrong, one may correctly say "It's not my fault," and "Bad luck;" or a bacterium, or a structural genetic effect is a sufficient explanation of the evil. As for the brain tissue, it is a "no-fault" system. It moves in remorseless neutrality. Sensory data, whether endocorporeal or exocorporeal, turn on and off the same kinds of gestalts, stimulate the same score of hormones. The body system is more passive; it carries on, by means of a skin, the animal distinction between an inner and outer world, but the human has in his nature to evade this skin-deep difference, to shame the snake and shed his skin a thousand times a season.

chapter four

DISPLACEMENT AND OBSESSION

We have come to view the human as a poly-ego casting forth throngs of displacements, paradoxically in order
to recapture instinctive certainty and so reduce the level
of one's anxiety. "Paradoxically," I say, because there is a
heavy return flow of displacement; they are in the mind
and hence cannot simply be cast off, but are to be
regarded as transactions: what goes out must come back.

From this elementary state of human nature, the morphology of thought emerges. It begins like a person who
seeks to build a crude dam across a brook. He seizes and
places rocks in the path of the flood, intending to embed
enough of them to block the flow, and, after a time, he
does, but there is leakage, and there are diversions of the
water, and anyhow the flow must continue by some
means. But still he has a structure. In the mind these
would be obsessions. And the rocks of obsessions are also
of different forms, which we call compulsion, habit,
attention, and memory, all of which we shall define here.

Before confronting the ideas of displacement and
obsession, an aside may be permitted, an apology. For it
seems that I am culpable for using metaphoric language
in describing a neurological and behavioral world, as
with the analogy of bridging a stream. But not only this,
which may be excused if the metaphor does not beg the
question; further, I may seem to choose terms too often

out of the jargon of psychopathology, as with
"displacement" and "obsession," perhaps even preferring them to terms describing normal behavior.

I have found, however, that the terms most useful in
describing mental operations are technical words tinged
with reproach, as if a person should not ordinarily engage
in such an activity. In the very first chapter, it will have
been noticed, I took the step of distinguishing human
nature largely by what would be considered a fault in
animal behavior and hardly sounds nice when attached to
people — an instinct-delay. And then "schizo" itself. I
must warn that this verbal situation may become worse.

But names come out of attention and identities. A family will love a dog and whiles away many an hour talking
about "what old Shep is thinking of now. Look at him! He
knows a lot more about us than we think he does. Too bad
he can't speak." I should hardly wish to challenge such a
statement, which would arouse a united family against
me, but what word would we use for the process going on
in the people if not "projection," the ascription to "old
Shep" of ideas that are our own. Much more could be
made out of the simple remarks quoted, too, but we must
move along.

The qualities of humans that one cherishes are aspects
of the qualities one dislikes. And, because the empirical
science of psychology has been built upon what is pro-
blematical and evident, the most helpful terms may be
those conferred upon disliked qualities. The "good"
comes out of "bad," so to speak. One takes what one gets,
as in evolution where the marvellous eye comes out of a
"damaged" skin, the tongue from the endoderm, the leg
from a fin, the cerebral cortex itself called a successful
tumor, etc.

If it were not for the throngs of displacements, we
would be able to attend to very little of what we are
pleased to attend to as humans. And without projection, a
delusion certainly, we could not "know" the world. The
"sick" propensity to displace and project in uncontrollable quantity is the fundamental basis for human behavior
and its competences. To speak of "cures" for these mechanisms is like asking how we may best perform cerebra-
lectomy. The most clever humans are those whose

displacements and projections are the most varied, free, abundant in hypothesis, while stupidity can be readily associated with an inability to perform these operations, whether because of blockage or hominidalism.

Some words I might otherwise use would belong to a defunct theology and philosophy that prospered for 2000 years from Aristotle to Descartes, which, as will be described in another chapter, employed ideas of man as a rational being, much of whose behavior would be termed irrational. In that vein, savants spoke of "reason against faith," and argued interminably but inoperationally over the conflict between the two faculties.

Most people still use the language of, and tackle problems of human nature in the manner of, Aristotle and Saint Thomas Aquinas, so that we have an additional task set for ourselves, namely, to show that one does not get very far in understanding human nature by this traditional route. But again, the analysis of reason is for Chapter Seven.

In this chapter, stress is placed upon the major mental strategy that the human mind employs to exist and ply through life. I employ the word "strategy" realizing that it is teleological and that things without purpose should not be granted purposes. (But not such usages as: "The strategy of the French generals in World War II was obsessed with the Maginot Line complex." That is, strategy can be both conscious and unconscious.) I can also use the word "mechanism" leaving to some demiurge the purpose of constructing this "mechanism." I mean by "strategy" or "mechanism," of course, a system by which the human operates, but again one must beware of the word "system" because that implies an order, and again an author or a demiurge or a will to operate systematically. Shall we say that by these words we mean: "It happens that a pattern (or gestalt) is evident when a human acts"? And, given the operational pattern, typical consequences follow." Thus we can rationalize some suspicious terms here, and also in the chapters to come and in the past chapter, where we talked of the urge to re-instinctivize, a pattern of behavior that is largely unconscious, uncontrolled, and un-willed.

Upon the elementary state of human nature, the

morphology of thought is erected. It hardly matters that
some of its aspects are regarded as "normal" and others as
"abnormal." It is like a mountain, that is a precipice when
viewed from the north, and a slope when seen from the
south; the core can be of the same mineral substances.
The basic shape of thought occurs by displacement and
obsession.

DISPLACEMENT

Personal histology and history cast their images
against the screen of instinct delay. A major effect is the
human displacement complex. Animals displace, but
humans do so with a plenitude and magnificence that lets
us be astonished at ourselves.

N. Tinbergen, an authority on the stickleback fish,
unsurprisingly took examples from the animal in his general treatise on instincts. A male stickleback cannot ejacu-
late sperm until he seduces a female into depositing eggs
in the nest that he has built. If two males are forced to
nest closely together, they dig nests continuously "and
the result is that their territories are littered with pits, or
even become one huge pit." Their nest-digging activity
here is part of their fighting repertoire. Similarly,
"herring gulls, while engaged in deadly combat, may all
at once pluck nesting material..." American television
seems at times to follow only one plot: "Sex and Violence: guess which is which?"

Tinbergen writes, "The motivation of an instinct
when prevented from discharging through its own motor
pattern finds an outlet by discharge through the centre of
another instinct." Further, "the fact that a displacement
activity is an expression, not of its 'own' drive..but of a
'strange' drive.., makes it possible for it to act as a signal
to fellow members of the same species, provided it can
be distinguished from the 'genuine' activity, activated by
its 'own' drive." As I've heard boys jeer at truculent com-
rades, "Are you tough or hungry?"

Every action involves an emotion, which is the sensing of action, therefore an experience. And every other
experience involves an emotion. Every experience

invites a response, an experience feedback of some affect. Both the experience and the feedback cross the neural synapses and are in the human manner delayed at the crossing. Wherever they may wander, while waiting for their vaguely denominated neurotransmitters, they inspire a new activity, a new experiencing, which is a displacement.

The human has all the instinctive foundations of the animal. But once unleashed, human instinctive behavior can rarely reach its target, if such can be discerned, but expresses itself all over the cerebrum in a splatter of displacements. Tough *and* hungry *and* devout, the Aztecs cannibalized their enemies. The Hebrews of *Leviticus* devised fulsome logic to accompany the slaughter and eating of a beast.

It is a basic proposition of anthropology that in a "pure" culture, all practices and artifacts are interrelated. Human culture is one grand intermeshing of displacements. The result, working backwards, is to defeat the blind workings of the brain. Everyone is given to know, and to see it proven, that displacements, no matter how remotely scattered among the recesses of the central nervous system, are logical and under control. "Hold onto your mind! Nothing happens but that it is all of a piece."

The stickleback and the seagull have relatively so few displacements (although even these were hard to discover and label), that Tinbergen can readily assert that they are genetic. I think that only the infinite variety of human displacements lets *homo schizo* congratulate himself on his large imagination, splendid lucubrations, ingenious associations, and poetic invention. It is important, all-important, "what we live for," etc., but who says so is ourselves — judges in our own trial. The human is sufficiently depressed instinctively, and thereupon anxious enough, and has enough continuously active positive and negative feedback operating, amidst ample gray matter, to support a world of delusions, no two of them alike.

We can appreciate then how absurd it is to attempt physiological distinctions between good and bad (healthy and unhealthy) displacements and projections, just as it is to divide good from bad (healthy from unhealthy) psychosomatism. Nor can we even speak of true and false displacements and projections. Once the brain casts its affect upon the external world, that world is physiologically real. When a god suffuses the starry heavens and a lover glances covetously at a stranger, what happens to the brain is as real as what happens when one drinks a wine or receives a blow in the stomach. All are *real* experiences.

Displacement might be conceived very broadly as one's sensing of anything as having effects upon one. Surely it is animal, yet the concept is the same in ethology and psychoanalysis.[1] Thanks to displacements, a great world exists that has no "excuse" to exist. But it is a virtual cornucopia in humans. "Anything" means just that; no mater is ineligible as an object of human displacement. Attempting to segregate logically or empirically those things — an enemy, a swamp — that will surely affect one, and other things — a sound, a shape — that will most certainly not affect one is largely useless. We merely say, an animal displaces little, while a human displaces much.

PROJECTION AND PEDAGOGY

So it is with projection, which is a common feature of displacement; anything can be a subject of projection. Projection is the animation of the universe. Everything potentially is sensed to have a will with regard to oneself. The breeze sings to one, the birds call one, the volcanos command one, one's automobile refuses to run, the enemy possesss one's thought. Displacement and projections operate in the thousands in the human mind. While the mammal tends to a few things, the human extends almost unlimited attention to the world, an attention containing affect, that is, psychic involvement.

Displacement is accompanied by affect or emotion. The human, and for that matter the animal, does not pay attention to anything unless it invests the thing with emotion and anxiety. This process seems predictable, inasmuch as the reason for the displacement in the first place is to test the capacity of the displacement object to receive a neural load that is not being fully unburdened by an instinctive reaction to a stimulus.

The displaced affect being unloaded may be called positive or negative depending upon the instant state of the discharge. The perception of hovering vultures in the distance is a cultivated interest, with an ambivalent response, to which a new positive or negative affect is added, depending upon whether one imagines them to be focused upon a foreign body or a body with which one is identified. It is clear, too, that ambivalence accompanies attention to a great many displacements, even gods and spirits whose presence has signified both benefits and deprivations in times past. Indulgence and deprivation become forever related to the identification-affection nodes.

The central nervous system is laced with interconnections of affection. Once the larger world opens to the baby, he must begin to accept those displacements that his attendants point out as the true sources of indulgences and deprivations. His teachers, while pointing to certain nearby objects with a cause-and-consequence nexus fairly obvious even to the inexperienced human, are especially interested in indicating to him some very great abstractions as ultimate causes of his well-being or ill-being; they are not at all scrupulous, even if they could be, in pursuing cause-and-consequence in such cases.

For most teachers, logic has an authoritative meaning. The myriad names of gods and spirits are short-hand vulgar logic. So it happens that their obsessions with gods and laws and great natural forces are imprinted early upon the young. A consensus of obsessions is achieved, along with some disrespect for necessary causal connections between the objects of identification and the actual production of benefits and evils.

To inculcate in a child the determination to use only a special pot for his toilet needs can be, depending upon the age of the child and criteria of correct performance, a massive exercise in the transfer of obsessive behavior from adult to child. The displacement of toilet-training obsessions upon many other objects occurs readily, whether the object is an administrative routine (a "clean

desk") or the traits of god, so the the Judaeo-Christian
god is not imagined to have an alimentary canal, but
many other cultures dwell upon the excretions of their
gods, the very word "urine," for instance, being originally from the god "Uranus," who rained many things
upon the Earth.

TIME AND REMEMBERING

Man practices displacement and projection in creating
space and time. The space dimension is little more than
the scope of displacements, to begin with. Measure the
area of displacement and one has the boundaries of
space. The poly-ego can fill infinite space; put another
way, all space can be internalized so that a most remote
object - a star, say - or a thought or an hallucination can
vie with an insect bite for his attention, even affecting the
way in which he scratches the bite. A person, and not
necessarily a savage, feeling guilt before his god, may
scratch himself roughly.

There is a need to sense time, one more empire for the
mind to conquer. Memory is of the animal, too, and so is
the ability to reach back for the pattern of experiences to
relate to an immediate or approaching experience. The
distinction of human memory arises from its flexible control of recall. Since man's experience is rich, his memory
impressions are richly patterned. It is one more great area
to which he can resort for the resources of control. He can
play one film against another, like a curator of a hologram
museum, until he selects one or imagines a new one that
will cope with an ongoing experience. Once more, fear
drives him over the stubble field of instincts.

The delayed impulses that are aroused by experiencing flow out electrochemically in all directions through
the mind and back and forth between the hemispheres of
the brain. They excite the glandular and muscular system. The feedback of "flowback" is voluminous, too. The
irrelevance of much of the activity does not embarrass the
brain. It highly stimulates it. Some twenty percent of the
typical person's oxygen intake is consumed by the brain.

What effect does this have upon the level of fear? It

makes the universe fearful; for owing to projection, now the fear which is displaced upon others returns, relevant, and reinforced. But, at the same time, the fear is probably thus rendered more bearable, at the price of weakened identity and a great many unnecessary involvements.

What, then, happens to the need to control? *"Divide et impera":* the more one's displacements are scattered, the more the selves feel secure. The need to control, already strongly felt respecting the alter egos, is also pointed towards the outer world, other people, things, notions, the sky, the phantoms out there. The great power-seeker of the universe is *homo schizo*. He seeks to control everything onto which he displaces and projects. Where his fear is sensed to lie, there he will seek control.

Time is an expansible contoured travelling bag to carry displacements, indexed by the pockets they occupy. Old memories rest as imprints that become expectations in present action. The present is a developing succession of snapshots upon used film, especially film containing analogous memories from the file. Andrew Jackson at the Battle of New Orleans thinks: "We can expect the British troops to attack us in rows and frontally, as they always do," and they did and were mowed down. An hallucinator says: "Members of my family were across the football field yesterday and that made it easier for me to talk to the crowd on the other side;" and he asked his family really to attend the following week, to lend further aid. Time's veritable meaning in any person's life is almost entirely a plastic envelopment of shapeless experiences, erratically related.

Cultures take over the obsession with time that the individual cannot avoid and *pro bono publico* define the intervals of time that must be mastered. This requires certain schizoid distortions of time. "Pure time," or "absolute time," does not exist save as another delusion; yet one of the greatest of all cultural drives since the beginning has been to find absolute time. Lunar time is a mass of obsessive behaviors — rites, lore, and scientific study — surrounding a fairly expectable cycle. Past bad experiences and their anticipated reoccurrences are probably the chief factors in the choice of time clocks and the ways of using them. Disputes over time-reckoning and calendars have precipitated many bitter struggles in human history.

The "rational" student protests: "See the big pay-off from marking time: planting, hunting, saving resources, warfare, rendezvous." No doubt, these are the pragmatic effects (gains) from partially restoring animal instinctive capacities. And they can only come when a cultures's people succeed in frightening themselves into observances of certain obsessions. As an *aide de peur*, gods and suns and terrible memories are called upon to assist as *aides-memoires*. In consequence the obsessed biologist and gourmet can calculate exactly the time to arrive at Cape Cod when the instinctively driven horseshoe crabs arrive to breed.

Time is also a way of watching oneself, hence watching the world of one's displacements. The sky-watcher is fascinated in part because he can see how "absolute time" is up there and controlling his destiny. As Immanuel Kant once said: "Two things fill the mind with ever-increasing wonder and awe, the more and the more intensely the mind of thought is drawn to them: the starry heavens above me and the moral law within me."[2] There ensue the obsessions of mental discipline, the routines by which life is conducted so as effectively to generate, in individuals and groups, those technologies, artifacts, and means of subsistence that so exceed the capabilities of other species.

The rules of memory and the rules of forgetting are the two sides of the same coin. Who says remember, says select. Who names memory, names forgetting. In the earliest human, memory was a desperate structuring of current events to retain on the surface of the mind what was necessary to be human — that is, a sense of time, a manipulation of symbols and projections, and the practical means of ordering the environment — while relinquishing to the subconscious the impressions so intense that they would catatonize or panic the organism.

The sharpness, detail, and durability (in conscious and subconscious form) of remembering is proportional to the gravity of a trauma, that is, to the deepness and adverseness of its effect upon one or all areas of life. Forgetting speeds up with the intensity of the trauma. Thus a

severe memory and its forgetting in all or part go hand-in-
hand, and they follow upon the heels of the traumatic
event.

The most intense memories occur without being
willed. They emerge encased in dreams and myths. The
less intense memories ride upon and cover over the more
intense ones. Disorders of recall, of forgetting, otherwise
unexplainable, can be interpreted as the effects of what is
memorable having become willy-nilly attached to the
unrememberable, and often relate to the symbols and
affects of the repression of the great disaster, that is, the
primal conditions that established the rules of the conscious human.

Memory and forgetting operate like a bookkeeping
system to keep the mind in balance. Little is forgotten,
and therefore the balance will continue to show a profit
or increase throughout life. Like many bookkeeping systems in commerce, memorial bookkeeping has numerous
ways of casting a balance. With the forgotten material, the
mind works to create myth and art, even scientific
hypothesis. By storing and recategorizing forgetfulness,
the mind achieves its ability to maintain consciousness
and behave with instrumental rationality (that is, with a
cause and effect logic in relation to practical goals).

Memory, in the specifically human sense of ability to
recall at will, is inseparable from the sense of time. One
can bring back the past in part voluntarily. This past can
be shared with others through signs, symbols, and language. It can also be cast into the future, just as other current and past experiences are cast forwards in time.

The future-thought is born and partakes of the delusional quality of human nature in general. For time is a
concept whose only existence is that given it by the
time-keeper. Yet its implantation in humans gives them a
tool for mental expansion and environmental control (as
well as for suffering), not otherwise recognizable in the
plant and animal kingdoms.

Culture institutes furious rites to make people
remember something that they are forbidden to remember in all of its detail. Saturnalias, the prototype of all
anniversaries, famous scenes of joy and orgy, are mas-
querades literally of the end of the world. They must be

compulsively celebrated in order, by aggressive joy and
wantonness, to cover up, to ensure the amnesia, of events
that cannot be forgotten. People create an elaborate
mnemotechnology, to use Friedrich Nietzsche's term, to
assure that they do not forget whatever it is that they have
forgotten, that is, suppressed. In this same sense, a great
paradox emerges: we remember most emotionally what
we forget most determinedly.

Memory of animals is set into "naturally" occurring
categories by the predictability of instinctive response.
"As I respond, so must the world be," would be a fancied
animal or plant cosmological formula. The information
storage and retrieval system are automatically coordinated for the most part. The human has the unique problem of determining what data to store and in what forms
to retrieve it.

He is very much helped by instinct, of course. Like
the beginnings of most modern computer data banks, the
material going in is predetermined — bank cheques,
social security accounts, tax records. Thereupon, however, the human stores immense amounts of material that
an animal computer technician would call "garbage."

The vast weird human universe of displacements is
duly punched into the memory bank. When the experience is recalled, it emerges not in the pristine sharpness
of the original experience, nor even in a dulled image of
it, but as a new thing, like a raised rusty anchor encrusted
with weeds and shells. It entails various distortions, sup-
pressions and reinforcements.

OBSESSIONS, COMPULSIONS, HABITS

Lorenz tells of a goose that at daybreak habitually
climbed a flight of stairs, stretched herself and was
greeted, thereupon taking up her daily activities in good
temper. This day she was prevented from climbing the
stairs. She was in a wretched humor. Finally, the source
of her distraction and depression was surmised,; she was
given a chance to perform her morning ritual. Thereupon
her good humor was restored and she behaved as usual.

Obsession, not habit, we say, was involved. To specify

the occurrence of an abnormal resistance to change in routine is not proper language when referring to a goose. But no clear line is to be drawn. Many a person is silly as a goose. In "normal" humans, we expect an acceptance of the frustration and an adaptation to the new condition. Why do we accept this? Because we appreciate that "normal" people are aware of what they are doing habitually and hence are capable of letting a frustration flow over into "irrelevant" spheres of activity. No sooner do we claim this, though, than we realize how few people are without severe reaction to a break to some of their routines. That is, most people are more or less obsessed. If they cannot find their shoes in the morning, they will behave strangely for a long time, until somehow they find the shoes, find substitutes, are given "reasons," or develop a new lifestyle for spending the morning without shoes.

Stern memories, pathologically called obsessions, are an important part of human memory. Obsession is "excessive," "unstopable" attention to something (by which, as usual, we mean "anything"). An animal can be trained to "extra" obsessions. Humans are naturally obsessive. They can be obsessed with a pair of shoes, a piece of cow dung, an inner voice or pain, the Second Coming of Christ, or a line of poetry. This "obsession with obsessions" determines what is remembered, what is recallable from memory, what the person will spend his time on, where the important things of life are in his estimation to be found. Moreover, it will give him an enormous capability. A person will be able to abandon all other thoughts and temptations and stick to a task through thick and thin. With this one (or two) abilities, he reconstructs animal instincts with some embellishments. That is, provided that he is compulsive as well as obsessive. Freud speaks of "the compulsion to repeat — something that seems more primitive, more elementary, more instinctual that the pleasure principle which it overrides...the pleasure principle — to which, after all, we have hitherto ascribed dominance in mental life."

A simple example of compulsion is the patient who insists upon playing the same chord a thousand times in succession. Or the repetition of nonsense syllables unendingly, which reminds one of religious liturgies that depend for effect upon an obsessive idea and the compulsion to repeat, which in turn must be related to the catatonic wish to stay as one is, forever in place. This again connects with the obsessive compulsive return to origins, to a recollected and imagined primordial set of events, *illud tempus* (that primordial time when ...) which M. Eliade has so well abstracted from primitive ceremonies.

The terms "obsession" and "compulsion" are separate but confused in the psychiatric lexicon. No special neurology is assigned to one or the other. Each can be tied to both behavior and thoughts. Obsession is of the family of memory, planning, and habit. It is a compulsion to repeat. Compulsion is the kind of driven act which is likely to become an obsession. Insofar as all major problems associated with the terms are internalized, they are indistinguishable. Furthermore, they may originate together and act together.

Existential fear, and the need to control it, pursue the logical line of reestablishing the human as an effective mammal. It is not our choice whether to vary from it. We have no recourse; if we seek to follow the smithereens of our explosion of attachments, we shall go to pieces ourselves, psychologically and shortly afterwards as living organisms. We must stay at home while our displacements travel adventurously, and here recompose the hominidal character as best one may: hence, obsession and compulsion, or obsessed compulsiveness.

Obsessions are linked to habit. They are deemed "bad habits". Compulsion may be an urge to shout obscenities upon entering a church. Obsession may be an agonizing repetitive recall of an embarrassing scene, like the time one uttered a string of obscenities in a church. The relation of obsession to habit is clear in this case. The relation of compulsion is not, as in many compulsive behaviors the thought has preceded the deed and has occurred obsessively prior to the occasion when the act is finally committed. then it is a habit of thought converted to a deed.

Obsession can be viewed as a form of deeply imprinted memory, which repeatedly calls the attention of the self to its selves. If a person suffers a fearful accident, the memory of it may occur with or without volition and despite a will to the contrary. At the same time, an obsession (and even faint memory is in a sense an obsession) is a repetitive trained behavior. Therefore it is a habit. It is also a compulsion, for one is compelled to recall.

Compulsions as acts are distinguishable from habit only by intensity. A drug habit becomes a compulsion, or addiction, when the behavior that is represented in the mind forces itself upon the organism, consciously or unconsciously. It is impossible physiologically to distinguish between a compulsive tic of the eyelid and a compulsion to step on the brake when a deer surprisingly leaps out ahead of one's speeding automobile.

Furthermore, a great many compulsions are consummated repeatedly, especially when uninterrupted by the forces of law, the community, the family, another person, or by destructive reaction or nature of the objects, or by self-destruction as in the compulsion to commit suicide.

We have two further cases where a compulsive element is present: one when the act is singular in its nature, but lacks a history of obsession with it, and springs forth compulsively as an invention. Such would be an impulse out of nowhere, as a model worker for twenty years is seized by the idea of walking out of his office immediately, forever, and does so. We would surmise that the thought had been formulating in an obsessive form but unconsciously, for a long time. This contrasts with a case in which, after a decade of concentration upon a mathematical problem, a solution offers itself to a professor abruptly, and the obsession is extinguished. The place of habit in both cases, despite the compulsion and extinction upon their conclusions, is manifest. In this second case a compulsion might be exercised upon the completion of the compelled act. The professor might insist upon the correctness of his solution, despite all proof and urgings to the contrary, and then proclaim it, marking the close of his prolonged studies.

Habit and obsession are distinguishable in two ways, one misleading, the other appropriate. In Aristotelian terms, a good person is one of good habits, and habits are what are rationally accepted by the free will of man. In modern and preferable terms, habit is an obsession that is governed by awareness and instrumentalism; a habit can be broken or strengthened; conversely, an obsession is a rigid habit. A controllable obsession is then a habit. The habit can be generated, moderated, and extinguished, according to the consequences sought from its practice.

Only when the obsessive foundations of habit are understood, however, can the distinction be made. The human "naturally" is prone to obsession. This is because "the cheapest way to run the works" is to concentrate energy upon the most forceful options and derive security and profit from them. The infant gains all he can by means of affection, so his whole life becomes colored by the exercise of and the memory of the affection he achieved in the beginning. All his other values are supplied *via* this one value which of course in its turn is not only a way to food and warmth but a way to reduce existential and immediate fear.

One ought not slip into half-way explanation, the sophistry of "Which came first, the chicken or the egg?" Toilet training is an obsession that is culture-bound, varying widely. To be instituted it had to be preceded by an obsession for obsessions. The question is: "What generated the master strategy obsession?" And, once more, we revert to the theory of a disordered poly-ego that welcomes order and repetition as a substitute for instinctive reaction.

People speak of animal habits, though not of animal obsessions. It would appear that an animal habit is already an obsession. If a human trains an animal, too, the animal's habit is more obsessional, in our terms, then habitual. The same difficulties are encountered with the two words, in the animal and human settings, and we had better abandon any distinction here and regard the two concepts as interchangeable in the physiological context.

The human is obsessive-habitual because he cannot otherwise cope with existence. His obsession-habits are infinitely variable. They succeed, not precede — although the organic structure is partly in place — the basal human disorder and are the human method of correcting the disorder, with all due limitations and difficulties.

In the illumination provided by psychopathology, habit is more readily understandable as an obsession under some degree of control, but at all events as a repeated practice, the regularity of and insistence upon which makes it obsessive, and the social judgement of which makes it reasonable as opposed to pathological. So it goes with compulsiveness very often. One might say that all obsessions are compulsive, but not all compulsions are obsessive; these latter are better called impulsive acts. Still, it would be rare that an impulsive act does not proceed from unconscious obsession, or from an impulsive character, typically given to such actions.

Examining behaviors known as memorizing, commemorative (as with the need to celebrate collective anniversaries), obsessive, bureaucratic, conventional, compulsive, and ritualistic, we find in them the essence of habit. Habit originates in the need to control exploded behavior and unruliness. Fear or anxiety reduces in the presence of habit, increases in its absence. If fear diminishes, one can claim that instinctual behavior has been in some sense restored and the reduction of fear was anticipated in the creation of the habit.

chapter five

COPING WITH FEAR

"First of all, the gods created fear in the world." So goes an old Latin saying. The expression can be reversed, for it was also said, as by Statius, "In the beginning, fear created the gods." Let us suggest the primordial condition: human fear and holy dread. The fear is the existential fear of which we speak in this book. It remains, when immediate causes of fear are absent. So it is incorrect to blame ravages of ordinary life, as did the philosopher Thomas Hobbes (1588-1679), for mankind's fearful state. Regarding primeval man occur several famous lines of his *Leviathan:*

> Whatsoever therefore is consequent to a time of war, where every man is enemy to every man; the same is consequent to the time, wherein men live without other security, than what their own strength, and their own invention shall furnish them withal. In such condition, there is no place for industry; because the fruit thereof is uncertain: and consequently no culture of the earth; no navigation, nor use of the commodities that may be imported by sea; no commodious building; no instruments of moving, and

removing, such things as require much force; no knowledge of the face of the earth; no account of time; no arts; no letters; no society; and which is worst of all, continual fear, and danger of violent death; and the life of man, solitary, poor, nasty, brutish, and short.

Hobbes, by our theory, is incorrect in two important regards. He explained "progress" as a result of "order" whereas, in *Homo Schizo I*, order and progress are seen to have always and necessarily been mixed; man is by nature bent upon order. The twentieth century, and Hobbes' own times even more, provide "poor, nasty, brutish, and short" lives in large numbers. Hobbes also conceived of human life as originally solitary. From his birth, *homo schizo* was individuated, it is true, by his human character, but he still required the group, actually demanding a larger group to work out his insatiable appetite for controls.

Further, as we have been saying, man was very much more dependent upon psychological "income" in comparison with material subsistence. However, fear accompanied him on his widest and wildest searches. Contrary to the speculations of Hobbes and markedly against John Locke, writing in the same period, man's mind was no "blank tablet" *(tabula rasa)* upon which experience alone might write. By origin, ever since, and at present, man's mind is congenitally inscribed with an existential fear that inspires his most important human operations.

Closer to our concept of existential fear were the ancient philosophers Epicurus and Lucretius. They understood such fear, even in "good times." Lucretius (96?-55 B.C.), who sought a scientific account *Of the Nature of Things* in order to allay human fears of death and of the gods, presented the universe as an essentially neutral and natural order. Significantly, in view of Chapter Seven to come, *ratio* whence "rational," is the synonym for order.

Time to Lucretius was an infinite succession of cycles of creation and destruction, fashioned out of eternal atoms. Mankind should come to see death and disintegration as the work of nature; "to be able to regard all that is with a mind at peace," wrote Lucian (V, 1203). To no avail. Philosophers and theologians can pile all of their wishes for mankind Ossa upon Pelion without his ever attaining the heights of the peaceful mind.

OMNIPRESENT FEAR

People will agree with the observation that life is spent largely on the problem of feeding themselves. The comparable idea that life is spent largely in coping with fear is met, by contrast, with disbelief. That fear should be central, dominant, and universal in humans is hard to believe, and harder to accept. Indeed one may propose, to begin with, that a cloak of denial is spread over the idea. We are afraid to admit what is forever present and all-determining because the admission, we fear, will simply worsen the condition.

No amount of testimony by heroes as to their frequent fears, no expositions of how humor erupts as a safety-valve to fears, nor all the case studies and historical treatises on fear and anxiety available for affirmation, can dispel the will to believe in a life without fear. How can fear be so all-pervasive, it is objected, when our lives are crowded with details of thought and behavior from which fear is usually absent, as when tying a shoelace, eating a dessert, digging a ditch, reciting prayers, or reading a romantic novel? Once more, to reply, the very fact of crowding our existence with details arouses suspicion that a mechanism of avoidance and adaptation is operative, avoidance of and adaption to fear.

To convince oneself of pandemic fearfulness, one ought to consider the total life-ways of all people in all cultures in all times. One checks off the major portions of life clearly beset by fear: infancy, childhood, dreams, religion, war service, competitive sports, risks of all kinds, old age. Then note the component of fear in all conscious mental illness and normal "neurotic" feelings. Then recall all the fear one seeks to impose upon others — intimidation, command, coercion, and so forth: is this not one's own fear projected (and milder) and is one not

the victim, too, in one's own turn? Further, are not all
those behaviors that are included in the paradigm of leg-
endary creation, primeval stories and fairy tales emergent
from fear? And, as Hobbes declared, does not man live in
fear of violence when he is not engaged in it — just as
foul weather affects not only the days when it happens
but also the times when it might occur?

Still, where is the fear in apple pie a la mode? Dietary,
to be sure, whether fear or defiance of overweight. But
the lusty appetite of the twelve year old boy: where is the
fear there? In the mother-figure looming over the culi-
nary transaction? In showing fathers how mothers love
their sons? The apple and Eve? In the haste to gobble the
pie and get away from the table? Why must one explain?
This is all trivia; but it is in explanation of the trivial that
science shows its muscle. Here is an instinct to eat a
sugary carbohydrate, a culturally defined concoction,
with ramifications into the habitual cuisine, the family
table, with "Mom" and the "sweet tooth."

If it were a cannibal feast — then noone would doubt
that terror is at the diner's elbows. Instead we have a
most generalized, sublimated human activity, but still
human, and hence suffused — even if remotely and joy-
fully — by fear. For the history of this particular feeding
is incomprehensible (indeed there is no history to tell)
without, like the Last Supper of Jesus, its carrying along
the most ancient determinants of human species behavior. The trivium is generalized into a multitude.

This line of reasoning is no different than that so well
employed in sociology and economics when we say casually that "Joe is one of the army of the unemployed."
Whatever the special circumstances of Joe's case, he is
part of a large statistical aggregate responsive to general
causes. He is part of an army of fear. Or should we choose
some stumbling, famished French soldier in the retreat of
Napoleon's army from Moscow in 1812?

PHYSIOLOGY OF FEAR

In terms of the psychology of conditioning, existential
fear is to be regarded as continuous self-punition,

whether it is called fear, anxiety, frustration, or depression. (Depression, writes J. Gray, is "a state induced by sudden loss of important sources of reward.")[1] The punishment takes the form of inhibiting rewards, the most basic of which is probably the surcease from existential fear itself. According to Neal Miller and his associates, in a conflict between approach and avoidance the animal will come to rest at that point where the forces favoring the simultaneously feared and desired goal equal each other. The "decision" is to come to rest. Then the human, by our theory, cannot come to rest, nor does the wild animal completely, in the presence of the effective extinction of the stimulus. The human continues to live in a heavily displaced world where the avoidance-fear sensation will always find some home and sustenance.

The physiology of existential fear, apart from the brainwork of cerebral conflict, is not structurally or electro-chemically much different from that of mechanical fear (in the presence of accident, blows, threats of punishment, aggression of divine wrath). Nor is it distinguishable from the long-term fear of death. It is clear that it does not constitute a major structural leap in evolution, though its actual effects are quantavolutionary. Hence it operates much like the animal mechanisms.

Especially *apropos* is the "fight or flight" system, about which we can say, with Tepperman,[2]

> Although people who are disturbed by teleologically 'impure' thinking in biology are sometimes made uncomfortable by Cannon's 'fight-flight' characterization of the sympathoadrenomedullary discharge, the fact is that the over-all effect of such a discharge is to mobilize the individual to meet an emergency.

Hans Selye elaborated a model of the fight/flight mechanism, as well as Cannon, generalizing it into a "General-Adaptation-Syndrome" or G-A-S.[3] So much of total human activity implicates the G-A-S, that one is compelled to view it as the dominating action determinant, which by the theory of *homo schizo,* means that once the G-A-S comes into play, once the Central Nervous System is operative, the essence of the response to stress is also functioning. One does not flick off the G-A-S when one is thinking about the rings of Saturn or washing dishes. And Jeffrey Gray employs in his own theory of fear essentially the Cannon-Selye model, "a single fight-flight mechanism which receives information about all punishment, and then issues commands *either* to fight *or* for flight depending on the total stimulus context in which punishment is received."[4]

The enhanced release of the adrenomedullary hormones, epinephrine and norepinephrine, denotes that a fight-flight signal has been passed to the central nervous system. In humans, the signal (I would argue) is incessant, or at least intermittent and rapid, and comes from a high level of excitation of the cerebral cortex, which is continually dealing with conflicts — past, present, and future. For a precise description of the body's response, we may best refer to Tepperman:

> The over-all response to the effects of simultaneous sympathetic discharge and adrenomedullary secretion involves cardiocirculatory responses which are qualitatively similar to those seen at the beginning of exercise—an increase in cardiac output, increase in pulse rate, rise in blood pressure. In addition, after a brief initial period of apnea, there is an increased minute volume of respiration. Splanchnic vascular constriction (including a reduction in renal blood flow) and dilation of the skeletal muscle vessels produce a redistribution of the enlarged cardiac output which anticipates muscle work. The central nervous system arousal effect of the catecholamine substances results in alertness and quick responsiveness. Hepatic glycogenolysis, its attendant hyperglycemia, and the mobilization from the fat depots of a large supply of free fatty acids (FFA), all collaborate to

provide a quick charge of readily available energy to muscles that may be called
on. Chemical changes in the muscles
themselves increase their capacity for
work and possibly diminish the generation of a fatigue signal by the muscle. The
central nervous system effects of the substances may, at the same time, diminish
central perception of fatigue. As if in
anticipation of blood loss, the spleen contracts while the coagulability of the blood
increases. If a committee of expert physi-
ologists were appointed to draw up specifications for a set of physiological responses that would meet emergency needs it
would be difficult for them to devise a
more interesting or effective set than that
described here.[5]

Notable is the cyclical effect, for the brain, arousing
itself to signal a fancied or real threat, is immersed in the
products of the responses to the signal, and hence can be
forced to continue the signalling. Fight and flight tend
never to end, save out of exhaustion. And human thresholds of exhaustion — of will and of muscle — tend to be
forced to farther limits than those of animals. Horses and
dogs reach their limits because men drive them. Whether
in sex, sports, eating, warfare, prayer, business, or art,
humans frequently test their limits.

Anxiety is moderate and continual fear and, were we
dissatisfied with the mechanisms of fear in producing
human nature, we should seek the mechanisms of anxiety. But they are the same as those described already.
The dozens of physical and mental symptoms of anxiety,[6]
if they are not subsumable under the fear/flight system in
operation, are by-products or effects of the system.

The explanations of anxiety are significantly related to
the theory of homo schizo. M. Gray mentions five types of
hypothesis. That anxiety is a catastrophic response of the
organism to stress is advanced by Goldstein. That anxiety
is a threat to one's concept of the self is advocated by
Rogers. That anxiety arises out of unassimilated percepts

is put forward by McReynolds. That it is related to commitment and awareness is Kirkegaard's notion. And that
it signifies perceived threat to existence as a personality
is conceived by May.[7]

All can related to the poly-self problem. Going
beyond Gray to the sources, one can synthesize from
them a concept of anxiety as an unending (because not
quite exhausting) flight from oneself occasioned by
defeat in containing emotional stress and by inability to
face up to the everyday world. These opponents would
be never a sufficient cause, however, were there not the
everpresent existential fear that the self is not itself, but
rather a dissociated confederacy.

And the outer world *per se* is a source of fear because,
with this discordant confederacy, who can be sure that
the world is real and fixed? One need not be a philosopher to sense this fear, but it helps in expressing it. As
Schopenhauer wrote, "The uneasiness which keeps the
never-resting clock of metaphysics in motion, is the consciousness that the non-existence of this world is just as
possible as its existence."

Is anxiety normal? Yes, endemic. Is anxiety part of the
fear-flight syndrome? Yes. But for the "flight" part of the
syndrome, we must investigate other behavior, beginning with punishment.

GUILT AND PUNISHMENT

A taboo forbids some relationship of a group's members to an object or being. It functions as an obsessive
phobia. It can also be regarded as an unconscious plan by
a social group to proscribe an activity in general but to
grant that the prohibition will be violated by "sinners."
Despite the score of theories as to the nature of taboos,
there seems to be no significant difference between a
taboo and the process of law in rationalized societies
except in the degree of analytic awareness accorded to
the two types of phenomena.

Both condemn a transaction; elicit guilt for its performance; excite reliably the "satanic" impulse of individuals to violate the proscription; thereby exciting

impulses in the satanist and, by identification, the society, to feel guilty; punish the guilty and give thereby a sado-masochistic bonus to the group members; and then conclude with the expectation that the cycle will repeat itself. So the taboo, and the law, are techniques of varying awareness for producing routine behaviors, with exceptional cases providing a leavening of guilt and punition.

A taboo and a law that are never violated are not only unnecessary, but undesirable, and a contradiction in terms. It is for the group consensus that the law or taboo is needed, for "reasons" and "consequences" that are more or less clear but in any event affirmed, if only in order to exercise the ritual guilt and punishment that the human uses to assure that his psyche is under governance and can control its aberrations, both internal and external.

Punishment of the self and of others has the same etiology. Humans who could punish others but not themselves, or vice versa, are structurally impossible. That observers have been misled to believe that people exist who are capable of one but not the other attests to the deluding permutations that are possible in the essential need to deal with the punitive aspects of the gods.

Guilt is an obsession with the conceived need to punish some part of oneself.

> I am the wound and the knife!
> I am the slap and the cheek!
> I am the limbs and the wrack,
> And the victim and the torturer.

Thus Baudelaire.[8] Guilt and punishment are both "moral" activities, meaning by moral that their processing in the central nervous system is associated with compulsive identifications with symbols or beings of authority. The wish for, or condoning of, such authority is a wish to control oneself and others, thence ultimately existential fear. The origin of morality is frequently the perceived behavior of the gods, whether based on some reality or hallucinatory. The behavior of the gods is an effective instrument for inculcating fear because of their actual behavior as perceived by the delusory and projective apparatus of the primeval human mind.

The gods, as perceived, commit wanton injury, cease to commit injury, and commit benefits more infrequently. They do so ostensibly in all the combinations and permutations of the high-energy natural forces — lightning, seismism, volcanoes, hurricanes, meteoritic phenomena. They also do so by facile penetrations of the minds of people — demanding, exhorting, frightening, and promising.

The individual split-self, comparing itself with others, works to discover a pattern of actions that distinguishes his behavior from that of others, and one category of others from another category. Driven by extreme anxiety, his hypotheses become obsessions. He discovers what he thinks to be such patterns and the relation of such patterns to the response of the gods.

He proposes and follows with obsessive subjectivity and paranoid zeal the line of conduct that appears to promise the greatest benefits and the lightest treatment from the gods (and their representatives — men, animals, plants). He projects his own correlations into the motives of the gods. Depending upon his charisma and the degree to which the god's behavior actually has a consistent appearance to others as well as himself, he makes a consensus of believers, a religious sect.

To strengthen his own self-restrictive behavior and to bargain for control over others, he transfers his authority to the sect. He finds thereby an accommodation that far exceeds, in the security and satisfactions that it brings, even the great benefits being experienced by group cooperation in hunting, farming, and manufacturing. Indeed, this basic security is so beneficial, that it causes the great development of these latter activities, and of art, sex and procreativity. All of these activities, affecting all life, became then suffused with and dependent upon the origination of guilt and punishment.

Punishment takes many forms — of the self and of others, of the world and of the thought, of the body and of the mind, of deliberate action and of subconsciously driven behavior, of mildness and extremeness. All emanate from self-awareness and the reservoir of primeval fear filled by it.

The need to punish is always independent of the demonstrable effects of the punishment. Fear finds its nexus whenever it encounters the obstacle of its own illogic. To sacrifice one's own child to a demanding god is by its own extremity of pain and sorrow the proof that the punishment must be effective. Moreover, the persistent and universal presence of human sacrifice is the mere outcropping of self-destructive and destructive activity, both deliberately and subconsciously conducted, which masses itself beneath the innumerable different cultures that have evolved since mankind originated.

The kind of punition that asks first for the logical connection between offense and punishment, and seeks to follow the crime with correction in the future, has only occasionally and especially in recent times had some impact upon deliberate punishment. Even then, though faced with psychiatric theories attacking primeval guilt and punishment, the urge to punish has tended to go underground into the subconscious, there to expand upwards once again in destructive behaviors that are handled in a context of fear in which punishment occurs as an ever-present instrument of relief and discharge.

Basic patterns of behavior are infused with appropriate modes of punition — catatonism with paralysis for having moved, and by moving, moved the world order to destruction; obsession with numerous rules to proceed in fixed ways on pain of a variety of punishments ranging from mild social disapproval to the most horrifying extirpation that can be devised; sublimation with the torturing of thought, art, and institutional behavior, generally playing out the eternal drama of the sin of being human; orgasm with displays of violence, sacrifice and ecstasy.

The common need for authority, especially one who can punish and forgive, is plain, for punition tends to unite the self, whether it be by the self or by the authority, and a god is therefore much needed. So is the god needed in external relations, interpersonal affairs, where as Martin Buber, the theologian, says, God, the Great Thou, enables human I - Thou relations between one person and another to subsist.[9]

It is plain what an important role the gods play in

holding the self together, and why gods are assigned the tasks of punishment. The tenuous self, striving for integrity, for self-rule or selves-government, invites a third party, the god, to intervene, who, by definition rather then logico-empirical proof, restores order in the self by punishing one or more of its components; it matters not which, and matters not why. What matters is that the punished being feels whole, feels "better" afterwards. Such is probably the essential dynamic of masochism.

The transfer of godlike qualities to the rulers of the state — kings, judges, and generals — and of institutions (presidents) and families (parents) lends these real beings authority, which hoi polloi can disregard only at the risk of punishment, whether self-inflicted or imposed by the rulers.

Witness today, for instance, a typical sequence of problems and behavior in the "educated" family, pictured through the mind of the father: 'My children have no conscience... They discovered that I was not obeying a third party... they don't obey me... they feel free to attack me... they should have been given a party [abstract and delusional] to which both I and hence they would refer judgements... I could have dominated them [paradoxically] much more if I showed them that I was submissive to a third party... then they would join me in reltion to the third party and I would not be the target of their hostility..."

Every life activity displays guilt and punishment — sexuality, food production, tool-making, war and justice, death. The peculiarly human aura of sexuality, like that of other human life areas, is owing to the architectonics of fear, with its archinstruments of guilt and punitiveness, working its way through the continuous mind-exploding mechanisms of the split self (selective memory, symbolization, control-seeking).

As M. Gray has mentioned, fright in man is more complex than in animals because "the new dimension that is reached in man can be viewed as symbolic fear."[10] Sex and fear systems are tied together in endocrinal secretions, so that there is little need in psychology to devise a logico-rational explanation of how, beginning with fear, the human mind runs to sex, or *vice versa*. The fight-flight system is basically the fear system, and is "ubiquitous," using Tepperman's word.

Bleuler discovered early that "the idea of intercourse is often expressed by that of murder," that "wars and duels are symbols of cohabitation," and that the idea of being burned is tied up with murder and sex.[11] Often we observe that peacetime anxieties or fear produce sexual impotency, whereas wartime fears, where violence is pervasive, produce lust and rape. Men going about looking for jobs develop impotence; men infiltrating an enemy town or abandoning it seek sexual outlets. Unleashed violence uses sex as a screen for and release of fear. However, regarding murder, say, sex is not the originator. The life areas are intertwined, as are all others.

The human does not compartmentalize, especially when under stressed fear, nor do many animals, but the human has a lower threshold of compartmentalization than the animal and must endure, indeed often enjoys, the confusion and mingling of life activities. Strange, because the human is the greatest analyst of mixtures, and can separate, in his mind and by scientific tests, the life areas so that pure categories of sex and aggression and work, etc. are educed.

A wide range of "normal" and abnormal" behaviors are developed in man, reflecting every known special sex behavior of every species, even at least up to the point of zoological impossibility as in divine and mythical hermaphroditism. (In rare cases, as today, and in perhaps a flurry of mutational cases in primordial natural disaster, hermaphrodites may have provided the grain of truth to the common myths of divine hermaphroditism.) Man's mind certainly dwells upon hermaphroditism. Resistance, obsession, sublimation and orgiasm, in turn and in combination, emit a host of various sex behaviors, individual and group.

What the mental strategies do to characterize the sex instincts of humans is also done in the other areas of life. Consequently, if one were to eliminate, in each successive area of life, the generic holistic mechanism working upon continuously renewed and stored fear, one would discover at the end of each process of elimination a root element, the sexual, the grower, the maker, the fighter, the dying person. Although no more complex than the fullness *in toto* of animal behavior, these areas are elaborated in an exceedingly rich manner within humans by the basic mechanism operating out of fear in unending supply.

AVERSION AND PARANOIA

A common element in schizophrenic symptomology is an aversiveness to humans. This includes social distrust, desire for privacy, fear and dislike of others, expectation of being rejected, and the conviction that one is unlovable — all on an intense level. A strong rejection to being helped is common. It is a mutual rejection of the body-selves and a separation from the world and others of the poly-self. It is self-conscious — not animal awareness, but a delusory standing off from oneself, with the whole world (inner and outer) thus revealed, expanded by the sense of time — of recall, memory, and forgetting — and of space.

The "paranoia" comes from the Greek where, anciently, to be "out of one's mind," that is *para* (beside) and *nous* (mind), denoted insanity in general; in American vernacular one would say "I was beside myself with worry." Now, narrowly, paranoia is restricted to projections of threat. The paranoic aspects of primordial ad existential fear are well known. Fear fathers destructiveness. Whenever the skies darkened, or certain stars approached, or the Earth trembled, paranoia was stirred up. Legends often openly assert that "because" the gods were destroying the world, men took up arms against each other. Even voices out of highly civilized cultures, such as Alsatian peasant culture, will assure one that wars follow upon great meteoritic showers, as in 1914.

What the gods are intending, as projected, is retrojected back to oneself, to one's group members, and to outside humans. *In extenso*, it often happens that the gods instruct men to destroy each other. Official psychiatric reports of the great Alaskan earthquake of 1964 describe how blame for the disaster, often couched in terms of an Act of God, was expressed in guilt-feelings and in accusations against others, such as "I changed by church," or "He changed his church."

The inventive aspects of paranoia are considerable. The paranoid is highly energized. He stresses symbolism. He acutely discerns remote analogies as he searches for conspiracies. He prospers upon the unknown and unintelligible. He is obsessive, confident where others falter; he has answers, and insists that others adopt his answers. The dominating role of the paranoid in the origins and history of civilization becomes understandable. His "sickness" was no sickness in primordial times.

Nor, properly rationalized in the language and procedures of existing culture, is the paranoid "sick" in the world of today. For every provable connection of effect with cause, humans resort to hundreds of paranoic assertions. The reason, when experts are asked why, is usually given as "ignorance." But is it not as easy to apply a simple logic on what is known, or to confess ignorance, as it is to learn or invent false accusations continually? The primary ego is compelled to assert its omniscience and, since the function of "knowing" is really to reduce internal fears, accusatory explanations are in heavy demand.

A paranoid is usually beset by ambivalence, the love-hate double face and double mind of the schizophrenic, the abrupt turn from one to the other make relations between schizophrenics and others often more terrifying than consistent hostility.

AMBIVALENCE

But ambivalence, we should argue, if we are set to follow *homo schizo* theory, must be universal in man and culture. And so it is. it is the good and the bad of everything. it is "the two sides to every question" that underlies the judicial systems and many cultures. It is manifest in the fact that people and cultures "choose" to differ in every way that they can, from one another and within themselves. The alter egos must emerge. Cannibals can be divided into those who eat their enemies and those who eat their friends.

Levi-Strauss says that the incest prohibition is the only universal culture trait, a bold and learned claim. But a moment's consideration will put the claim into a revealing context. The scope of incest rules differs: some stop with parents, other with nuclear families, others with uncles and aunts, other with clans and so on in various combinations. By their existence and limitations, the rules implicate contrary wishes, hence ambivalence.

Furthermore, societies have rules about everything that can be the subject of rules; incest is no more specific a concept than murder, and all societies have rules about murder; further, all societies "by right" are totalitarian, implicitly if not explicitly endorsing the old army saying that "there is a right way and a wrong way to do everything in this Army." (There is an alternative rendering which is, "There is the right way, and there is the Army way; you do it the Army way!") Finally "rules are made to be broken;" without infractions there would be no rules, which means, more subtly, that it is desirable to have infractions, if only to gratify the punishers, but, more than that, in order to let what is right be known.

Today the gods are less frankly present in the operations of the "normal" mind and institutions; but the schizoid meaning of the primordial gods is clear. It is not enough to say that the first human mind could imagine the gods and imitate their imaginings (projection and retrojection). It actually did so on the basis of more reality than is fashionable to admit nowadays. The human mind was born with the gods, that is, with those terrible entities of the sky that are said to have wrecked the world, and that were hovering above and swooping down over a period of thousands of years, ever refreshing the reservoir of fear in the human mind.

The animation was imagined, or so our modern logic insists. No matter, for every symbol stood for a memorable sign, every myth represented an event, then came imitation — prompt, unquestioning, and illogical. Above all other relationships in the world was the identification with bodies that both hated and loved humans on a massive scale; these were the gods who turned upon another, castrating (Saturn-Uranus, Jupiter-Typhon, etc.), maiming, tearing off heads and limbs, hurling mountains and cosmic discharges at each other and at men. "Black magic" sees a hand in everything that happens. The paranoid often sees the same. Comets and meteors readily simulate the hand. The prehistoric caves contain the hand in great numbers. The "Hand of God" is frequently reported stretching out from the heavens to the agonized populace. At one and the same time, it is the image of terror, of inevitability (the hand finally grasps), of help and of punishment.

But the hand is only a part of the rich assemblage of forms that natural bodies can assume, all of which contributes to the original and continued reification and anthropomorphizing of the gods. Schizophrenics, more commonly than controlled normal schizoids, reify the outer world. Insofar as the schizotypical human has been in the forefront of human development, the gods as "humans writ large on the skies" are unending.

What they did to men was beyond modern belief and was deeply suppressed. But it was never truly forgotten. The myths of old, the dreams of the normal, and the autistic reveries of the schizophrene are basically alike in structure and purpose: to manage the unmanageable. Whoever survived had to believe that they were the chosen people of the gods. Further, all the new aspects of their environment (like the manna and the ambrosia from heaven) that helped them to survive, kill enemies, give birth, and carry on creatively (arts and crafts) made them believe in the love of god. It is the famous "double bind," which social environmentalists attribute often to a mother who works out a hate-love relationship with her child, and which makes the child schizophrenic. But going back generation-to-generation to the earliest times, the mother, and her mother, and so on, can only deal in hate-love ambivalence, because they were so dealt with by the primeval divinities.

ANHEDONICS

After ambivalence comes the pleasure-phobia, the symptom of anhedonia, which Meehl has called "one of the most consistent and dramatic behavioral signs of the disease" of schizophrenia. It is a "marked, widespread, and refractory defect in pleasure capacity." Man has been mistakenly called a hedonistic or pleasure-seeking animal. The psychiatrist would say that this is correct only if self-destructive and other anhedonistic behaviors can be termed pleasurable. If whatever the organism seeks becomes, by definition, pleasurable, then it is hedonistic.

The hedonistic theory is inherited from the Benthamite school of early nineteenth century England. The psychology of hedonism had taken over a commanding position in Western societies in the guise of democracy and socialism. Certain philosophers — ancient Epicurus for instance — certain societies, not many — the United States for example — take up the idea enthusiastically. Or, at least, so imply the advertisers. But, say the critics of American civilization, the attempt at hedonism fails miserably.

In reality, the pursuit of hedonism is always a secondary social aim. No society has ever been founded upon the pleasure principle. All societies are ideologically committed to the principles of anheonia: pleasure is evil; pleasure is impossible; pleasure brings punishment; suffering is good; pleasure is a release from disciplined suffering; pleasure is to be tolerated only upon the celebration of a disastrous anniversary, as an orgy inviting repentance. The orgy is a complex of smile and snarl — as in dogs we have known, and in humans we should wish to investigate.

It is from the human person that society is constructed, and where anhedonia is born. To prove this, one may begin with deduction. Pleasure-phobia is logically implied in the theory of the fearful polyego. The mental construction of the human is fundamentally unsettled. The frustrations of existence — to satisfy needs and evade the blows of nature — write an undulating pattern over the basic unsettlement.

Now if one is permitted the irony, is it not strange that pleasure should be regarded as natural and in this day people who are anhedonic should be regarded as mad, when it is the hedonist who perhaps should more naturally be taken to be mad? It is significant therefore that the definition of pleasure itself is the greatest weakness of hedonism as a philosophy. The hedonist begins by thinking of pleasure as a commonplace idea: "eat, drink, and be merry," "a car for every family," "peace and plenty," "a chicken in every pot," "free love," etc. That is, the hedonist turns out to be a superficial psychologist who has a rationalist uni-dimensional view of people.

However, most people seem intent upon rejecting this kind of pleasure in part or whole. As soon as one asks of the hedonist, "What gives people pleasure?" he must reply: "People get pleasure from whatever they wish to do or have done to them." Pleasure, then, in a word, is "voluntarism," as in the old-fashioned expression, found in several European languages as a mode of address to superiors, e.g. "What is the gentleman's pleasure?" Under the *Ancien Regime* in France, the King signed all of his promulgations with the phrase, *"Car tel est mon bon plaisir,"* which phrase would be related upon every reading of a law or judgement, as when a man was condemned to death, "For such is my good pleasure."

But of what does voluntarism consist in primeval humanity? Assuredly it is in fulfilling those devices that are animal in kind: feeding, fornication, fighting and fleeing danger. More than that? Yes, hanging around where one can feed and fornicate and feel free from danger the next time on each cycle.

What else, that is typically human? To refuse food, to refuse sex, to fight instead of flee. Even more, to do all that can possibly be imagined to use these elemental desires in ways that will establish and secure the most wanted triple-control of the self, others and the gods.

Let us look at the earliest legends of mankind. What do they have him doing in these regards? A great many unpleasurable things. He sets up a host of taboos against the most plausible kinds of enjoyment.

He eats only certain food, and at only certain times. He eats what is bad to eat when good foods are available. He eats in certain way, giving a portion of the best of his food to the gods, as hungry and insecure as he may be. He fasts. He eats his gods and his enemies. He builds a great oral literature on what to avoid eating and subsidizes priests to tell him what not to eat, when, and how to prepare what he does eat, ulcer or not. Would it be permissible to suggest that two out of every ten humans who have ever lived have died prematurely from pursuing irrational eating habits? (Meaning by irrational: ingesting or avoiding because of non-dietary reasons what is severely prescribed or proscribed.

Sexual behavior, too, is thoroughly permeated by restrictions and impositions. Name an animal that lingers in coition. Other than man, of course. That exults in creating a female orgasm. Whose orgasms are compared with death itself? Not "I am born," but "I am dying" is the sometimes climactic ejaculation by the sexual partner, with subsequent relief and relaxation from having met with death and survived. And again creates a philosophy, as the Hindu, for one instance, that explains how you weaken yourself unto death by sexuality.

So, too, conflict. To defend is "natural;" to flee is natural; but not to attack deliberately with one's guts roiling, in row upon row with bayonets fixed, with death ahead, yet death from behind upon whoever falters. Whence the awards go to those who have suffered most joyously, doggedly, "without questioning why, but to do or die." Verily who seeks pleasure seeks its own reward; who seeks pain and suffering is exalted before oneself, before man, and before god.

The earliest glyphs and scripts of mankind are pleasure-phobic to the degree to which they are sacred. Coming from the Egyptians, Hebrews, Sumerians, Mayans, Chinese, Icelanders, Myceneans and Greeks, these coherent patches of history and morality stress without exeption that the pains of existence must be and should be, hardly ever do they set up mammalian or sublimated pleasures as a human ideal.

The anhedonism of primordial and schizophrenic humans is understandable: existential fear demands not pleasure, but relief. And this relief results from a broad spectrum of activities that are hardly pleasurable: self-mutilation, sacrifice, cannibalism and exhausting ritual. The ambivalence of the gods and of the self, too, warn against pleasure.

T. Reik has argued that the original sin was not sexual but rather of *hubris,* the imitation of the god's power, such as the seizing of the God's fire.[12] It was alright for the Homeric heroes to address the gods as "blessed and happy;" but being themselves happy was an invitation to disaster.

Far more institutions have been created in ancient and modern times for the suppression of pleasure than for its enjoyment. But as Freud intimated in his *Civilization and Its Discontents*, without suppression of the instincts there would be no civilization. Herbert Marcuse has more recently elaborated upon the thesis in *Eros and Civilization*. Even these trenchant criticisms for culture now seem superficial. They have but carried forward another version of "the noble savage" of eighteenth century philosophy. One cannot discover, nor properly induce from pre-history, a human culture that sought to provide pleasure except as it might be incidental to relief and escape. Anhedonism is imprinted upon human nature; the individual schizoid psyche, which is pleasure-phobic more than pleasure-prone, abets and invents the anhedonistic institutions. And institutions "hate pleasure," whereas they cultivate suffering.

Usually, pleasure-phobia is an aversion to interpersonal and "animal" pleasure rather than to cognitive and aesthetic pleasure. The schizo-type can evince aesthetic and intellectual hypercathexis without the fears and guilt of interpersonal pleasures (i.e., human pleasures). Anhedonia is not apathy, but is pseudoapathy, a tense and anxious state; its final form is catatonism, which is really "playing possum" with the gods.

CATATONICS

Manu, the Noah of the Hindus, "practiced severe and great self-mortification." Wearing a bark shirt, his hair matted, "while he stood on one foor with his arms raised, with bent head and eyes unblinking, he performed awesome austerities for 10,000 years." He was chosen by order of the gods to recreate all creatures after the Deluge. "By virtue of his very severe self-mortifications the manner shall be manifest to him."[13] So the model of man is taught the greatest knowledge by the greatest suffering.

Freud in one place quotes Kaempfer on the taboos governing the Japanese Emperor of old:

> In ancient times he was obliged to sit on the throne for some hours every morning, with the imperial crown on his head, but to sit altogether like a statue, without stirring either hands or feet, head or eyes, nor indeed any part of his body, because, by this means, it was thought that he could preserve peace and tranquility in his empire; for if, unfortunately, he turned himself on one side or the other, or if he looked a good while towards any part of his dominions, it was apprehended that war, famine, fire, or some other great misfortune was near at hand to desolate the country.[14]

Gurdjieff reports an experience from Central Asia. There in a village a religious sect was playing games of magic circles. A girl was frozen in the circle that other children had drawn around her. She could not move out, nor could adults from the sect drag her out. Persons who entered and left the circle remained in a catatonic state for many hours. It seems that one entering the circle grants her vital force over to an outside being as a bribe to prevent harm to oneself. Thus emptied of vitality, one cannot move.

There is more than an analogy with some psychological problems in a rigid bureaucracy. The incubant at his desk gives over his life forces to an outside being — in this case the inanimate collective representation that is the agency or bureau. Whereupon the employee becomes inert, immobile, and cannot direct the very forces he is employed to manage.

Workers concerned with disaster assistance comment frequently upon the fatalism and denial of the victims; often the outsiders are baffled and become angry. In one of the few honest reports ever written on this question, a transport expert working intimately with the truck drivers bringing food in the recent Sahelian drought and

having substantial contact with the rural population
reported that at first none of the local population seemed
ever to have heard of the drought; later he concluded that
they felt it deeply and were taking rational steps to min-
imize the hurt in ways they had known all their lives. In
much of the savannah and desert of Africa, people take
drought to be a necessary divine warning that religions
and moral standards are slipping and that a revival is due.
The harm done to them must actually be received in a
sacred mood. It is notable that this report is of rare hon-
esty. Ordinarily the nervous givers of alms must be reas-
sured that the recipients are responding "logically" and
"rationally," and reporters generally supply such news
upon demand.

What is the fear of change of habits, customs, society
and human relationships, even of aging? Is it based upon
some pragmatic calculus of cause-consequence; that is, is
it based upon the experience of change, discovering that
change is always for the worse? And why does the feeling
vary so greatly, then, among individuals, so that, for
example, a social psychologist such as Lowell could
divide politicians and public opinion into two categories:
the optimistic and the pessimistic?

The fear of change derives from the anxiety over the
potential loss of an ego stability, which is markedly worse
the less the poly-ego is stabilized to begin with. May this
not explain the phenomena of personal and social con-
servatism and stagnation? The process in society, as in
the person, is self-aggravating. As a society destabilizes
in revolution, whether social, industrial, or political, far
from people becoming habituated to the change, they
become more desperate. Even though the change may be
rationalized as beneficial, any material improvement and
a formal lift in dignity become inadequate consolations
for the failures of individuals to compose new poly-selves
for the new times. This should constitute a lesson for
non-Marxian revolutionaries.

A catatonic patient, like Manu, is far from
"despairing" of control of the world. He may hold a position for months, but if moved, flex and adjust so as to
maintain the assumed position.[15] His ability is unconscious in that it far exceeds any normal ability. Other

patients (Bleuler called them "waxy cataleptics") were
without spontaneous movement but maintained any position in which they were placed. Another type went on
repeating motions that were supposed to have begun and
stopped. Often the cataleptic exercises himself in an
"affirmation of negativism" that requires great muscular
energy and coordination.

Here is what other mental patients say: "I can't move
if I am distracted by too much noise. I can't help stopping
to listen. That's what happens when I am lying in bed. If
there is too much noise going on I can't move." Another
says, "I get stuck, almost as if I am paralyzed at times."
They are driven sometimes to losing their subjectivity.
They become objects and, as one patient said, "Objects
don't have feelings."[16]

Catatonism tells the gods or other authorities: "I do
not move, lest when I move I am noticed, and the world,
too, will move." Catatonism is a common response to the
shocks of primeval and historical disasters. It is seen in
every accident ward and expecially in military hospitals.
In a great disaster, such as Hiroshima, catatonism is a
major behavioral response.

Non-rationalized cultures (mistakenly termed
"primitive")) simulate catatonism when reenacting the
earliest days of creation. Members of a certain Jewish
sect must remain throughout the Sabbath in the same
posture that they were assuming when the Sabbath
began. Children present during traditional religious ceremonies are warned to be particularly silent and immobile while the priest reenacts the primordial end of one
world and beginning of the next. Wherever the authority
of religion has descended upon secular institutions — be
it a library or the mausoleum of Lenin — a "respectful"
silence is maintained. Gestures become restrained.
Clothing becomes "appropriately" sombre, unobtrusive.
All that is individually outward is suppressed, and it all
"happens naturally."

Short of catatonism and beyond anhedonia exists the
realm of apathy. Schizophrenics, the psychiatrists say, are
so contradictory: sometimes excessively voluble, hyper-
active, frenzied, and then again and for prolonged periods apathetic. Nothing interests or excites them. They

may be occasionally aroused, and then retreat dramatically into torpor of manner, posture, and speech. They are imposssible to arouse. No one knows what stimulus will once more perhaps excite them. Meanwhile no indignity inflicted upon themselves or others, no injustice, no deprivation seems to matter. Electric shock treatment is resorted to, a horrible experience, a repetition of primeval bolts of Jove. Occasionally, a cure of apathy results, but note that it is a worse pain, a greater fear of the lightning discharge, that arouses the patient, not a pleasure; no pleasure will ever do the job. Pain, not pleasure, is the route to resuscitation, a recovery of a status as a punished one, a way to please the self, others and the gods.

Self-deception of anhedonia and catatonics can be carried to the expected extreme of self-destruction by suicide, just as with the other delusions of man. Karl Meninger sees in all mental illness a core of self-destructiveness. Freud's last paradigm had "Thanatos," the death instinct, juxtaposed to "Eros," the life instinct. There is no use in trying to draw a line to include only the mentally ill. Self-destruction in its most obvious forms, leading to death, is an extreme anhedonism, by definition, which is to say that other self-destructive behaviors that are not so obviously leading out of anhedonia are tied into anhedonia for the simple reason that man seeks self-control holistically and hologramatically; the symptoms are interrelated. Oblivion in catatonism and death is the ultimate control of the self by surrender; the self is no longer divided or in disarray or scattered.

ORGIES AND HOLOCAUSTS

But a place must be made for orgiastic behavior. Whereas one kind of violence emerges from the discipline and sacrifices of "law and order" or obsessive social forms and institutions, a second kind of violence entails the tearing down of structures and institutions. Sometimes this occurs in Saturnalian orgies where deliberately, for the nonce, all social forms are turned upside down; masters serve slaves, equality reigns, contracts are broken, wealth is burned or otherwise wasted. Amidst the Assyrian terror, Isaiah cries out: "Let us eat and drink, for tomorrow we shall die." *(Is* 22;13) *Ecclesiastes* do him one better: "Eat, drink, and be merry..." At other times, orgiastic violence becomes warfare and social purges, such as witch hunts and political reigns of terror.

"The conscience for which [Hitler] stands," wrote Lasswell in 1933, "is full of obsessional doubts, repetitive affirmations, resounding negations, and stern compulsions."[17] Mass death followed. The obsessional and the orgiastic work hand in glove. Human sacrifices, an ancient Pharoah inscribed, will purge you to the satisfaction of the gods. Warfare, for the Aztecs, was continuously needed to provide prisoners whose sacrifice was demanded to keep the world orderly and the sun regular.

Sizemore and Myers have connected schizophrenia, fear of world destruction, and ancient catastrophes.[18] Eissler calls Leonardo da Vinci's drawings of the end of the world by flood, fire, hurricane, and explosive seismism his last and greatest works.[19] The orgiastic event commemorates the end of the world or of one world. "Better a terrible end than an endless terror," said the Nazi slogan. Again, it is a replay of the primeval times of disaster, a carrying out of the will of the indignant or new god. Political force represents phylogenetically the force that overturns the earth; therefore, necessarily often, political force is adored, is not to be restrained, and when abused, remains still genealogically right. There are many analogies in the human mind between natural and political violence; Shakespeare, as Irving Wolfe demonstrates, interchanges social, personal and nature's language in a shower of metaphors. Holocausets are demanded. "The beast within us" is called forth. But, of course, it is not a beast; no beast acts so; it is the human within us that is called out.

A common phrase in writngs about repulsive practices is "Even as late as..," as if mankind has been on an upward track of moral conduct. "Even as late as the Roman Empire, infant sacrifices to Saturn occurred...etc." "Not until the Spaniard arrived, did the Aztecs cease their regular cannibal sacrifices of thousands of persons," or "the Jews of Czarist Russia and the Armenians of the Ottoman Empire were not freed from the dread of pogrom and massacre until 1920," or "As late as the 1880's the Shawnee Indians sacrificed a maiden upon the near approach of planet Venus."

However, relief is not in sight. Progress is a matter of a few years. Somewhere, at any given time, a massacre or deadly persecution is probably taking place. The human "holocausts" of the German Nazis, Russian communists, Chinese communists and nationalists and of the lesser Balinese military, Cambodia communists and other groups of the past half-century took perhaps one hundred million lives. Wars and starvation by neglect killed another hundred millions. And the world arms, while it talks in terms of killing more hundreds of millions of people.

It is not difficult to prove that *homo schizo* is nearly as far from "killing only to eat" as he ever was. Nor has any social invention appeared that might promise a definite end to such catastrophic behavior. This, more than anything else, ought to motivate the study of human nature. We know, do we not, that the historical modes and inventions of systems of social cooperation have failed all critical tests?

There is an automatic anhedonia about modern holocausts. The pleasure-phobia sacrifices others to reassure itself: "The only good Indian is a dead one." But the phobia then goes farther to hide the emotionality of the deed by bureaucratizing (routinizing) it. The self-suffering (which is not rationalizable to others) is translated into sublimated self-suffering that makes sense to others. In cultures where religion provides infinite legitimated anhedonia, this is an easy matter; every impulse to suffering can be indulged.

SUBLIMATION OF FEAR

Nevertheless, older religions (theocracies specifically) set up channels of suffering that lead to astonishing aesthetic and intellectual products. Especially in cultures deviating from heavy religious norms, self-suffering by sublimated activity is given an individual or scientific-bureaucratic base, and it is here that the schizophrenic is identified; since he is not incorporated into bureaucracy and rituals, his activity is exposed as psychopathic; then wonder is expressed at the great aesthetic and intellectual product that emerges from his suffering mental state as in the case of the composer Schuman, the sociologist Max Weber, the novelist Kafka, and so on.

Aesthetics and invention are displacements and trans-substantiations of interpersonal suffering, conveyed in ideas and symbols. Thus frequently the schizoid patient surprises his keepers by contrasting behaviors, on the one hand completely uncoordinated and erratic where people are concerned, but on the other hand competent, cool, logical in the pursuit of music, mathematics, and zoology.

In such pursuits, the schizoid leaps over his uncontrollable anxieties of the other self, the other person, the living nature and gods. Then he or she doubles back upon the percepts and cognitions left behind, purging them until they form a colorless fabric of abstractions which he drapes comfortably over himself.

In movies, novels, and journalism people (normal) express surprise and anger at how many institutions of love and priests of love behave contrarily; these are unfeeling, inhuman, interested mostly in abstracted aspects of people and things. Such frequent behavior of "welfare officials" is partly their anhedonism and partly their personal aversiveness, whether expressed by them characterologically or as typical representations of institutions.

A climactic case of a love instituion built upon a great fear and hatred is afforded by the American Jonestown community of Guyana, South America, where several years ago some 900 people living in a community of love were suddenly transformed by their leadership into a community of suicides and killers, to the end that within a few hours almost no one was left alive. In the interviews and reports issuing upon the disaster, the phrases of terror and doom dominate.

Man cannot lift himself by his own bootstraps. The human has been and is always in some combined state, varying cyclically in intensity, of self-punition, aversive-ness, anhedonia, ambivalence, paranoia, catatonism, and orgiasm, as well as obsession. The social structures are but an extension to help him control these embodiments of anxiety. It may be hopeless to seek exceptions *via* cultural anthropology or special religious sects.

Fear phenomena can be manipulated, handled, understood, balanced, but not erased. Otherwise we should have a vegetable or simple animal, for the animals closest to man have also a problem of eternal *angst*. A normal scientist (and to be a scientist implies an abnormality), admittedly a superman of rationalized controls, is *ipso facto* allowed and trained to mistrust his senses, to mistrust the word of others, to regard everything as important (that is, engage in the most remote displacements), to check and recheck anxiously, to be obsessive about his subject, to avoid personal identifications and emotions, and to suffer self-punition over extended periods of times. What is science, indeed, but a capitalization of instinct-delay and the heavy anxiety-alert to explore and exploit their very products?

chapter six

SYMBOLS AND SPEECH

Speech is the favorite among the traits said to mark the human being. "The chain of nucleosynthetic evolution.. breaks over the derivation of language," T.A. Wertime writes. To speak and understand "marks the crucial breach in the symbiosis of primate and nature, the onset of contrivance and 'sin'."[1] Language breaks the instinctive bond between man and nature and sets man free in a maelstrom of delusions. Other species are outdistanced in the race to set up communication systems, but still their achievements limit the human claims.

Speech is systematic symbolism. Symbolism characterizes all outputs and effects of human behavior. Whether we grow crops, organize business, or sell books, what we do has symbolic origins and is conducted by and amidst symbols, and deals with symbolized things. The final form of much human output is largely symbolic, as with scientific, technical, and ordinary discourse, also with art, some myth, and a part of religion and magic. Ernst Dichter, a well-known human relations consultant, produced for the use of manufacturers and advertisers an encyclopedia devoted to the psychological connotations of a great many industrial designs.[2]

Human speech, language, the 'vox humana' does not consist of written words. The

> written word is merely a representation of speech in another (and more constraining) medium — a further level of symbolism, since language itself is a set of symbols for concepts which themselves correspond but poorly to external reality. Language is a code of a code; writing is a code of this code of a code.[3]

I quote this out of a personal letter from the linguist Malcolm Lowery.

SILENT SYMBOLISM

Not to be excluded from symbolism are graphic codes, signs, marks on trees and stones, sacred paths and benchmarks, routes among the stars, and very many other human productions. All are sent and received as symbols. Illusions are symbols inasmuch as non-existent objects or facets of objects present themselves significantly to the brain, standing for something else.

Studies of American Sign Language, a system imparted to the deaf and employed by the deaf, sometimes by the deaf to the deaf, establish "the fact that to be a medium capable of expressing the full range of human intentions language need not be spoken. It is the human brain, not the mouth or the larynx that makes language possible. ASL is a complete language."[4] Wit, humor, poetry and song are within the capabilities of sign language.

Hence, language without speech is possible. Signals (smoke or flags), gestures (deaf mutes), whistling (*cf.* Harpo Marx), and writing (letter romances) are alternative modes of communication. So is pantomine. This would suggest that speech is not the "cause" of language, but that language prompts speech and other means of communication.

Eric H. Lenneberg shows that at the age of 21-37 months the age of "acquisition of language," the "right hemisphere can easily adopt sole responsibility for language and language appears to involve the entire brain..

though the left hemisphere is beginning to become dominant toward the end of the period."[5] By the age of fourteen language is markedly left-lateralized, irreversibly. I conclude that the internal language code is first set up; then the physico-motor apparatus and left-brain dominance usurp language for external and public behavior. The road is clear, then to consider whether self-speech may prompt public speech, admitting that public speech may govern self-speech to a degree. Or, more appropriately, we should assert that self-symboling prompts public symbolism.

ANATOMY

Speech occurs similarly in all humans: sound waves are made by muscles and tubes, and consist of phonemes (vowels and consonents, etc.), combining into morphemes (e.g. words), which acquire a morphology (sentences, etc.) and broader levels of syntactical patterning — the whole largely unconscious except on the superficial level of the "spelling bee."

No specific speech center occurs in the brain, a fact of large significance: there is no speech organ, no lobe, no sign of an organic mutation, no high density concentration, no neural bunch, no exclusive territory. Speech is controlled from a large cortical area extending from just in front of the visual area, across the auditory to the edge of the motor region. The area can be tested functionally in the left hemisphere for the right-handed person, and in the right for the left-handed.

The tongue and larynx have muscles and the brain accords them special motor areas. The area for the tongue is much larger than for the whole leg, one more instance of the dys-economy, or at least "indifference" of "nature," assigning to the "less important" a large housing while the more worthy tenant sleeps wherever he can. The whole central nervous system supplies the messages that are framed by the lips and tongue.

The chimpanzee enjoys no such grandeur, says Ralph Gerard, "I strongly suspect that you could not teach a chimpanzee to speak chimpanzee, let alone English,

because he doesn't have large enough areas for his
tongue and his larynx."[6]

We are not convinced: an ape can make several distinct sounds, say six; this would allow about 2_6 or 128
unrepetitive combined sounds, many more if repetitive,
viz., "hubba, hubba."

Attacking the assertion of one pongid researcher, that
"language is no longer the exclusive domain of man," one
group of scientists has concluded from its study of a
chimpanzee called "Nim," and an analysis of other pongid and infant studies that an "apes's language is severely
restricted. Apes can learn many isolated symbols (as can
dogs, horses, and other non human species), but they
show no unequivocal evidence of mastering the conver-
sational, semantic, or syntactic organization of language."[7]

But all this is not because of a lack of tongue-motor.
The brain stores, exercises as memories, and emits signals according to its history. What is used is banked and
what is not used has no bank account to draw upon. If
apes cannot talk, it is not because of a lack of these
evanescent motor centers of the cortex. Nor is it because
the brains of apes are too small. Fluency of speech is not
correlated with brain size in humans, with a span of difference of hundreds of cubic centimeters, as much as one
fourth. For that matter, the human brain is largely
disused, so an ape ought to have brain-room for talking,
even if only "small talk." The chimpanzee also has space
for data storage in his brain, beyond motor areas. Nor are
apes untrainable, witness the responses obtained by dedicated keepers over a period of time; they can be made to
imitate man closely. Yet, as claimed above, very little
speech ensues.

Is it then that the ape does not want to talk? Yes, that
hits at the central problem. There is not enough internal
conflict in the primate to "justifiy" the installation of a
symbol and signal system. Even if it were to be, or has
been partially installed, the animal is not schizoid
enough to levy continuous demands upon the system,
and it deteriorates from desuetude. George Miller says,
agreeably, that "talking and understanding language do
not depend on being intelligent or having a large brain.

They depend on 'being human.'"[8] So long as the source of human nature cannot be pinpointed, it is well to put "being human" in quotation marks. But I think that we shall no longer be required to do so. Perhaps to get apes to talk, infant apes must be first neuroticized by continuous injections of chemical sensory excitants and neurotransmitter depressants.

NEUROLOGY OF SPEECH

Monod (1971) maintains that the instructions for building human language may be contained in the genetic code. If so, the instructions are probably not complicated, as we shall explain. Writers are verging towards the concept of outer language being the language also of inner thought. Johnson writes:

> Although it must be recognized that language is not the only tool of thought, for we have unconscious thinking as well, it remains true that most of the mental processes of humans actually use verbal symbols as stimuli for nonverbal responses. Inner speech is produced, and it can be used as an instrument of rational processes such as voluntary movements. Herrick (1956) states: 'I repeat my conviction that some form of symbolism is requisite and that without the invention of language symbols the human type of mentation is impossible.'[9]

Schizophrenic patients show a profound intuitive understanding of symbolism while trampling the rules of grammar. Otto Fenichel holds that their symbolism is not a tactic of distortion but an archaic form of thinking, thinking by metaphor, we would say. The right hemisphere can assemble word forms by itself, when cut off from direct communication with the language apparatus of the left brain; this would only confirm the residue in both brain hemispheres of the bilateral primate ability to utter a variety of sounds. The chimpanzee can use words, if strongly trained to do so; one of them, Washoe, used veritable sign language, derived from American Sign Language, leading Pribram to say that "primates *can* construct and communicate by signs, context-free, consistent attributes of a situation which are discriminated and recognized."[10]

In accordance with the theory of human hologenesis, to be advanced later, and in striking coincidence with the philosophy of pragmatism, we can argue that language is thought, and thought is language. What happens interpersonally also happens intrapersonally. Since, as we have just argued, the brain treats "inner" and "outer" indiscrimately in relevant ways, the brain may actually employ language without discrimination as to the location of its referrents. The infant babbles; a year later he utters a "word", that is, a reference that outsiders can comprehend. Whether one is talking to an audience or talking to oneself may be a reference that is learned. It is within the ken of many people to hear a victim of trauma — an exhausted survivor, a tired soldier, a mourning widow — range back and forth from talking to the outsiders to talking to oneself and to "insiders" of the self.

> Black (1971) has reviewed recent work which demonstrates that hallucinated words and sounds can affect the EEG [electroencephalogram]. The normal production of alpha waves are changed by such experiments, and evoked potentials are altered in hallucinating situations. The conclusion was that the EEG responds in a manner which demonstrates that hallucinatory material is processed as a reality to the nervous system just as any other phenomenon might be perceived.[11]

And again:

> It is a fact that Gould (1948, 1949) used a stethoscope to listen to the hallucinated

> inner speech of a patient. The external-
> ized sounds can be heard when the
> instrument is placed in front of the
> patient's mouth, and normal speech can
> be heard at the larynx.[12]

It is suggested that inner thought forms itself as a neural network of neutral references among cerebral engrams (gestalts, holograms). Consequently the network itself becomes a code for interaction among the references. That is, the holograms are indexed, or given names; then grammar becomes the rules for drawing upon the names. The basic linguistic expressions, such as: "Dogs fear men"; "Gods exist"; "Go away"; "Spring will return"; are references to a key set of holograms engaging the attention, to expectations based upon their summated behaviors, to egocentric wishes that can be couched as demands or "laws of nature." The "decision" to employ sound for language is partly unconscious and habitual, since sound is an old underemployed facility, and then an invention. Sounds can readily be correlated with the thought code. Silent speech connects with the speech motor system and springs outward, with striking effects.

The outer world responds to the degree that it is human, or it seems to respond. Furthermore, experientially, the world responds to the thought rather well than badly. What begins as ejaculations, develops into propaganda, and propaganda in turn becomes principles — ethical and scientific. The language changes by feedback and alteration. Meanwhile, the patterned object of the grammar becomes himself a subject, if single, and a game between two subject-objects produces a "universe of discourse." Consensus on words and syntax develops. What happens "outside" happens "inside": the code one uses internally is never much different from the language used in dealing with the world. The private language of schizophrenics or anybody is merely a paranoic secret like the "Pig Latin" of children within hearing distance of their guardians.

If displacements are infinite, so are codewords for them; indeed, the wide variety of displacements determines the scope of the language. Economically, efficiently, quickly, energy-conserving: language proceeds. The words need be very few to refer to everything and all the interactions among them. A half-century after Shakespeare's niagara of words, Racine's 1000 words and even less were deemed adequate to say everything in French, and for a long time thereafter anyone inclined to be more verbose was obsessively resisted.

THE STRUCTURE OF SPEAKING

What produces systematic symbolling in the human? The elements of the process are self-dispersion, anxiety, self-collection, coding, metaphor, and algebra. There is a sequence in all of this, but it happens so quickly and continuously, and with so much overlapping, that it is misleading to make neat phrases. Of self-dispersion, anxiety, and self-collection we have already spoken. The self, split by instinct delays that scramble the ego, undergoes heavy anxiety, and strives for reinstinctualization or any other forms of what is hoped will be self-control. For this purpose it ranges through the world and time by its techniques of displacement, lodging everywhere but then having to control these lodgements, too.[13]

The displacements do not enter the brain pell-mell and without discrimination. The impulse that identifies them in the first place is motivated. A displacement must belong to a realm of control associations; it is metaphorical. The brain codes it by an ever-so-slight but significant tag so that it resolves into a data bank whence a code-symbol can retrieve it. If it is to be used to characterize an individual thing, it is pulled out in its entirety, sign upon sign, until it becomes a vivid picture. If it is to be used as part of a category, it is retrieved more or less as a naked index reference. As Benjamin Whorf once said, no word has a precise meaning. Mathematicians hate to admit it, but no mathematical symbol or arithmetic number has a precise meaning, either.

The poly-selves are pocketed or diffused all over the brain, the body, and the outer world, including the past; the poly-self is in millions of places, a shepherd, or better, lead sheep, of a gigantic flock. Wherever and whenever perceived, they return, finding their coded abodes and reinforcing their electrobiochemical walls. Given the strength of the major ego components, the selves or roles, the coded items are not randomly distributed in the brain, but aggregate according to an abstract hierarchical classification item. If this seems like a metaphor of the rational human operation of classifying subjects, the metaphor is reversed; I would conjecture that the external work of classification in every walk of life derives from an intuitively perceived basic classifying going on naturally in the brain; man is imitating his internal central nervous system operations, just as he copies, often subconsciously, his legs, musculature, eyes and other parts of the body in designing tools.

The permutations and combinations of the stored and coded material are practically infinite. The coded item, which is both an abstraction and a metaphor, is "willed" to collect a sentence. (By "will," here, let us mean the set of determinants representing past operations which now demand a new operation.) The brain performs its algebra, imitating itself, and then speaks the presumedly understandable words to the communicant.

The algebra is simple, such as a/b; c/d; a=b, or a=c; or a-b = c. After all, once the wish is present and the analogues are retrieved, what still needs to be said can be formulated according to a few basic functions. Formal characteristics of the statements are not required, nor are verbs and nouns, nor singular and plural, etc.; languages have varying codes for these; they produce interesting ideological configurations in their speakers but are probably not of essential importance in creating sub-classes of human nature.

Description, interrogation, demand: these three may suffice. Basically the mind works with such statements, putting into them the information bits supplied or wanted. "Fence-sitting tobacco-chewing man;" "name?"; "Down, John." The first is additive of qualities, but could be of quanitities; then comes the specification of an unknown blank in the "man" code data bank; finally an attempt to impose one's will.

The public words needed are the question of the

name, the name "John," and the command "down!"
Really, only the command is needed if the intent (and
power) are clear. Even a glance would suffice, if the John
had been half-trained not to sit on the fence. But the little
that needs be uttered hardly represents the internal processing; very rapid speech signifies a disturbing problem, not that a speaker can talk as rapidly as he can think;
this is an impossible feat, though listeners tend to corre-
late the two.

Noam Chomsky was probably on the trail of such facts
when he foresaw the road that linguistics was taking.

> Contemporary work has finally begun to
> face some simple facts of language that
> have been long neglected, for example,
> the fact that the speaker of a language
> knows a great deal that he has not learned
> and that his normal linguistic behavior
> cannot possibly be accounted for in terms
> of "stimulus control," "conditioning,"
> "generalization and analogy," "patterns,"
> and "habit structures," or "dispositions to
> respond," in any reasonably clear sense of
> these much abused terms.[14]

Also, "The speaker has learned his art by internal processing."

Ernst Cassirer discussed the case of Laura Bridgeman,
who was a deaf, dumb and blind child. She made distinctive sounds for people she knew, when she encountered
them. Later on, like Helen Keller, she was delighted to
discover that various objective (external) community
names for things and people existed. Both girls wanted
immediately to learn the name of everything.[15] This fact
supports the theory of *Homo Schizo I*, that language, like
culture as a whole, was hologenetic with the first
humans.

Many more coded messages are circulating interiorly
than find their way into vocal utterance. They are of the
same kind. The most brilliant and learned voices play
upon these simple themes, so that we may follow for a
considerable distance those students who have reduced

brainwork to an immense computer, only we say, as we shall again in the next chapter, that a combined analog and digital computer is at work. Further, the computer invention is an intuited imitation of human ratiocination. The computerized robot is man's high hope for recapturing his primate instinctive behavior.

VOX PUBLICA

Symbolism is a neurological network set up to cope with the polyego predicament. Talking with oneself is not to be separated etiologically from talking with others. Basically, the same motives and the same sensory manoeuvers are implicated, with the same basic effects.

Once again, we encounter the *hysteron proteron* phenomenon, a normal logical delusion: it is believed that language is a social achievement enabling people who are apart to exchange meaningful messages, and, further, that these messages are sometimes initiated by the insane to talk to themselves.

Instead, language develops as a solipsistic and holistic control of inner and "outer" messages. Without the compulsion to talk to ourselves, we would not talk to others. The outer messages are still messages to ourselves; the selves in this case are the identified, displaced objects outside of our bodies. And the aim of the outer-directed messages is to control the outer world.

Carl Jung stressed the psychological difference between extraverts and introverts. Certainly the consequences of inward as opposed to outward displacement-biases are many and important for analysis and therapy. No doubt the human race can be divided into the two groupings. But both groupings derive their existence from the same, more basic human polyego origins of speech and the dilemmas of choosing internal as against external modes of polyego integration. The greatest and most urgent need of the poly-self is to "put one's house in order," part of which task, because of the excessive and demanding fear, is delegated to outside persons and objects.

The feedback is extensive and compelling. The only

way, or at least the best way, to control the world outside
the body is to communicate with it, and the most effective mode of communication is by code or symbol, and to
control by symbolism requires accepting a common
medium of exchange, signs and words which prompt
external behavior that reduces the anxiety of the person.
The solipsistic origins of the language are clearer in
an oral culture. Writing assures the objectification and
authority of language; it takes people out of themselves
and helps to delude them into believing that they are not
talking to themselves. Thus, writing disciplines and
socializes the people, taking up a centralized responsibility for their fear therapy and not permitting them to go too
far towards anarchic solutions. The origins of the alpha-
bet, proclaimed among the greatest of inventions and
originating, says Santillana, from astronomy and games,
shows a great capacity to generalize from observation
(hearing sounds, especially). Thus 20 or 30 letters are
given the task of abstracting all speech. Pictograph and
syllabic writing employed symbols much more exten-
sively, revealing a lesser application of the human power
of generalization.

A schizophrenic patient often invents "outer" language, swinging his clever symbolic manipulations of his
dissociated egos to others, usually to ill effect, so far as
his controlling them is conceived, but in certain cases, as
when he "speaks in tongues," actually converting others
to his will. The typical internal struggle to accommodate
one's egos often requires relinquishing attempts at controlling the outer world by the language that the "egos"
understand: first things first.

F. de Saussure distinguished general language from
speech, which is uniquely individual, like a fingerprint
of structure and content. No two people speak alike. Each
person has his own code, but the codes are forced
together by the felt need to communicate on the part of
both individual and group.[16]

CULTURAL DISCIPLINE AND SPEECH DIVERGENCE

Emperor   Frederick   II   of   Sicily,   Holy   Roman

Emperor, yclept "Stupor Mundi," set up in the 1300's a nursery of neonates attended by mutes, to discover from their untutored babbling how the original natural human tongue might have developed. The infants died from various causes before they could arrive at speech. As with experiments to isolate existential fear, experiments to discover the origins of speech are difficult to contrive. Psamtik I of Egypt tried a similar experiment two thousand years earlier, and James IV of Scotland also did so two centuries later. And there now is a humanistic topic for a master's degree in educational psychology. Lingua Adamica, it came to be called, whatever it might be.

Cultural agents teach the infant a language. The discipline is severe; rewards and penalties are numerous: "Speak our language or not at all." Teachers of immigrant children recognize this dilemma; children sometimes stop talking altogether. Exceptions occur privately, in dreams. 'Mad poets' can speak differently. So can scientists. Drunks can babble. Religiously-inspired persons can "speak in tongues" unknown. We can learn other languages, best when very young and the process is approved by our attendants.

It is not uncommon of old people, who have practiced a second language, an accent, a dialect or a jargon to perfection during their lives, to relapse in their final months into their infant and childhood language. The reason may be not that they performed best in their original language, or that the memory traces of the original words *in themselves* were more deeply imprinted, but rather that they established their poly-ego system and its embedded network in the earliest years of life. The strength of their original tongue is in fact the strength of their ultimate ego defenses, holding together against the dissociations brought about by the erosion of approaching death.

Feral children do not speak a language, but can learn one very slowly. Some pygmy tribes are said to possess no pygmy language, but to speak the language of non-pygmy tribes with whom they associate, giving a special accent of their own to the speech that makes their tongue incomprehensible to ousiders.

Kester in his book on Upper Paleolithic language sees six basic roots in all languages and finds thousands of analogous idea-centered words surrounding each root.[17] The roots are *ba, kall, tal, os, acq,* and *tag.* I agree with Lowery, who, in an unpublished manuscript, asserts that Kester has not succeeded. Nor probably did Cohane in his book, *The Key,* where several sacred root words such as *haue, og, ash,* and *ber* were pursued into hundreds of presumably derivative geographical sites around the world. Yet I have been long in sympathy with Whorf, who in a fellowship application to the Social Science Research Council, in 1928, talks of "restoring a possible common language of the human race or in perfecting an ideal natural tongue.. perhaps a future common speech into which all our varied languages may be assimilable, or, putting it differently, to whose terminology or.. to whose terms they may all be reduced."[18]

There is a question of course as to whose code, whose exclamation would be authoritative for any given object, but the primordial scenario, which I portray in *Homo Schizo I,* has only siblings or mother and offspring as the communicators, and we must suspect authority in the second case to be in the mother and in the case of the siblings the same authoritative situation as arises in a gang of children coining new and secret words at "play." Language is essentially symbolism, a code that shortens inner and outer communication in respect to economy and speed of transmission.

More plausibly than not, it may be maintained that whenever and wherever *homo schizo* originated, he spoke one language and it is from this language that all subsequent ones have descended. We may also premise that, in the beginning, descriptive epithets (Great Zeus!) were ejaculated and a vocabulary of names that included the state of the object grew rapidly until every displacement was given a name. In part simultaneously, the equal sign of the "is" was generated, with its opposite, the "is not," and sentences began.

Little else need be said here: speech is basically an agreed-upon code referring to classes of objects and to their losing or gaining qualities. "Dog is wolf not wild;" "Sun is not, Moon is." But one cannot imagine a simple vocabulary and syntax enduring even for a few years. Nor can we imagine new features being deliberately

invented. Language came in a rush — originated sponta-
neously, says Levi-Strauss. It was a cultural and organic
quantavolution. Why should the first speakers stop at one
or one hundred words, as if they were apes in training.
There were, as I speculated in Chapter Two, impelled by
the breakdown of the instinctive mammalian ego to busy
themselves with coding inner communications and outer
communications to their ouflowing identifactions.

Genera and families of language in the world are few,
but derivative languages, comprehended by outsiders
only with much learning, number in the thousands. It has
been estimated that at the time when Columbus arrived
in America some 2000 distinct languages were in use.
Europe is dominated by Latin, Germanic and Slavic
tongues with many national and sub-national derivia-
tives. The North African littoral speaks Arabic, while in
Central Africa hundreds of diverse languages are spoken.
We do not know what produces many tongues and what
causes a single speech to prevail without much change
over a long period of time.

All effort is made to discipline people to a common
tongue; yet languages ramify profusely. As propellants of
divergences in speech among groups once linguistically
united, several factors can be imagined on the basis of
instances from history. Physical or social isolation is a
necessary basis for most, if not all, cases of linguistic divergence. Movements of population with the associated
ecological change promotes new terms and disuse of old
ones. Differential increments of new technology add new
postures towards linguistic content and style. Partial
incorporation of the language of groups newly encountered, whether as subjects of conquest or the conquerors,
is often a factor.

Religious divergence is especially important when
disasters of various kinds occur, focussing intense attention on new sacred beings of the world and all objects
and relations supposedly touched by their holy hands.
The practice of tactical secrecy, at first in sub-groups,
then in dominating groups accompanying the fragmenta-
tion by violence or politics of the principal group, must
also be considered.

Memory failures, collective amnesia, accompanying

abrupt splits of human groups regardless of the source, can select and discriminate vocabulary, style and usages. Conflict, competition, accompanied by hostility, snobbery, and "trade secrets" can accelerate linguistic divergence as well. Most divergence is unconsciously generated; a little is deliberate.

Without a chronology, which is rarely discoverable, one cannot tell time by divergence, because the aforesaid causes may be quantavolutional or uniformitarian. The Australian dog, the dingo, is thought to have arrived 7000 years ago, but all tribes have special names for it.[19] The multitude of American tongues might have occurred in 12,000 years, or in much less or more time. Nor do we yet know how many languages were extinguished during the period, or whether the full impetus to change affected a single Asian mother tongue or also other Asian along with some proto-American tongues that preceded the conjectured recent invasions *via* Bering Straits.

We would stress that languages can be constructed rapidly. In a few years, a youthful cohort aged thirteen to nineteen, granted libertarian linguistic practices, can fabricate an argot that is incomprehensible to the general society. The extent of the divergence and the rapidity of change are partially concealed because the argot is discouraged in youth-to-adult contacts and the written media go their own way linguistically. Charles Morris describes the various special languages of political, poetic, bureaucratic, religious, and other cultures in his book on *Signs, Language and Behavior*. Zvi Rix points out[20] that "the accurate placing of by-gone happenings on the time-coordinate is the precondition for the understanding of reality. Reduction or loss of the time-component (i.e. flattening the four dimensional space-time universe into our less plastic three dimensional world) leads by consequence to misconceptions and delusions of paranoic character." It can lead to other forms of schizotypicality. The Hopi, for example, who are said by Whorf to lack a word for time, are said by him and others to have a global immediate consciousness that would be regarded as abnormal if encountered by a Euro-American.

That is, we are under the influence of symbols but we do not know their origins and time of origination. Note how the invention of new words and language are attempts to get us out from under the influence of old behavior and ideology, while the opposition to new words and language is a conservative attempt, knowingly or unconsciously, to keep us under the influence of ancient symbols.

It matters not what is the elapsed time since the generation of a language, in judging its sophistication. Languages, like cultures, may be tribal, but they are never primitive. No scholar has yet advanced a viable method of differentiating old from young languages, or developed from undeveloped, this despite the availablity of such recent historical models as Italian-Latin and American-English. Much less has anyone been able to demonstrate the primitivity or even the irrationality (except in missing technological terms) of a language. "Many American Indian and African languages," declares Whorf, "abound in finely wrought, beautifully logical discriminations about causation, action, result, dynamic or energic quality, directness of experience, etc., all matters of the function of thinking, indeed the quintessence of the rational. In this respect they far outdistance the European languages."[21]

INNER LANGUAGE

We return now to the internal constitution of language. Language is useful in the animal-work of humans, as in hunting, growing, working, co-operating, and also in the displacement labors of worshipping and sacrificing. Still, language does not exist for these purposes. It exists as an internal message center. We note how words come out in a flood from a "quiet child;" the child has been talking to itself and belatedly concedes that it will have to talk to others. I think that in the behavior of Kamala, the India wolf-girl, who took years to emit words and then progressed rapidly,[22] one can detect an inner speech, just as in mental patients who refuse to speak but who can be heard to talk to themselves, even their speech-muscles and EEGs betraying the fact.

The utility of internal speech can be identified as a

message exchange in lieu of a missing automatism. A machine that is set to imitate a perfect animal, which receives and responds to stimuli undeviatingly, does not need a language. But the human mind is out of control and messages have to be sent throughout and back and forth in much greater volume than in the animal. The flock that is scattered everywhere has to be gathered. "Instead of dealing with things themselves, man is in a sense constantly conversing with himself," said Ernst Cassirer.[23]

Inner language is not identical with outer language. A mad person may abandon society to control his selves, speaking a "disordered" language, which must bear significantly upon his struggle for self-organization. He does not care whether his speech helps others to coordinate the world. The effort seems not to be worthwhile; he is demoralized because he is depersonalized. If you cannot speak the language, you cannot be a citizen; and *vice versa*, in a radical double meaning.

Working inside the social system, there is leeway to use a broader and richer language, still recognizable but suspect by those who control the system. The language of politics and power is normally barren; clichés abound; conventional images are recommended in rhetoric. As is true of language and culture so with language and politics: each can stupefy the other. But collective enterprises cannot move without rules, and rules, including language, stupefy. They do so insolently, too, and arrogantly, because connected with power and unconcious of their roots.

IDEOLOGY AND LANGUAGE

What appears as speech is a voiced code shared by the speakers. The silent or unexpressed language is both the full code and the key to the voiced code. When Whorf says that the voiced code represents an ideology or *weltanschauung* that is peculiar to its speakers, he may be criticized for comparing the overt results of linguistic expression of two or more peoples. This enables them to assert a more marked difference between humans than may be the actual case.

As Whorf and kindred scholars have established, a group's spoken language, properly studied, reveals many affinities, more or less cryptic, with the special outlook of this group on the world. Call this "the overt linguistic ideology." But now Whorf may be making too much of what is spoken. First, he assumes a mirroring of the overt language by the covert language of thought, especially since he can decipher subtle aspects of the logic of the speech. However, the covert language may contain precisely those elements of thinking seemingly absent in speech. Seen from the surface, a flounder is a brown fish with eyes; seen from the sand it is a white fish with a mouth. But it is a fish like other fish in most significant respects.

If this is so, then the many linguistic groups may not represent such profound ideological differences as Whorf maintains. What surfaces as speech, that is, may be phenotypical and the genotype may be even universal. This condition, if real, has much importance for our theory of human nature. Put bluntly, "Man thinks the same everywhere, but you'd never know it to hear him talk."

Whence, to appraise Whorf's original contribution, we would say, "Yes, the language that surfaces limits what can be readily communicated. Yes, the surface language, properly analyzed, shows many connections with the internal thinking processes. Yes, the surface language plus its discoverable connections with the subsurface language gives an operating distinction between two languages that can be called an ideological divergence. Yes, too, although Whorf does not digress upon it, gestures, timbre, amplification, inflections, posture in speaking, and facial expressions are part of linguistic communication, and can distinguish speakers, even of the same language; Adenauer did not speak the same German as Hitler.

But no, now, these sub-liminal linguistic ideologies are not the human ideology; they are not basic. Language, linguistic analysis, even Whorf's penetrating analysis, does not mirror human nature. It is not the key to open all doors. The whole study of human behavior, human action, is the master key. Language, as a portion of

behavior, deserves its place. If we were to bring together
two strangers and they were urged not to speak, write or
use conventional gesture, that is, forbidden to symbolize
conventionally, they would begin to communicate by
actions and imitations; emotional expressions, perhaps
touching, would play a role. They would be almost inca-
pacitated in the beginning but their activity would soon
graduate into a new symbolism, and before long a common discourse would unite them. Perhaps some such
mode of arriving at a universal language is better than the
Basic English that Whorf so trenchently criticizes for
being so very English.

Language, Whorf properly insisted, is not merely a
technique of expression, but "first of all is a classification
and arrangement of the stream of sensory experience
which results in a certain world-order, a certain segment
of the world that is easily expressible by the type of symbolic means which the language employs."[24]

For instance, "the Hopi language contains no reference to 'time,' either explicit or implicit." Yet the Hopi
"equally account for all phenomena and their interrelations, and lend themselves even better to the integration
of Hopi culture in all its phases."

The Hopi language is rich in verbs and verb forms
(but not tenses) whereas the Etruscan language prefers
nouns. "Most metaphysical words in Hopi are verbs, not
nouns.." Whorf finds the Hopi possess two "grand cosmic
forms," the objective and subjective, or the manifested
and manifesting.[25] I would venture that these resemble
the ancient Greek notions of Being and Becoming: whatever exists, is material, and what is historical must be distinguished from what does not exist (or is on its way), is
subjective and is in the future.

A most impressive feature of Whorf's analysis of languages is his demonstration (which I am extending logically) that languages can be graded according to how
much of the logic and philosophy of the users is buried in
the language as opposed to how much must be added in
speech.[26] Whorf regards "thinking as the function which
is to a large extent linguistic." Then, "silent thinking is
basically not suppressed talking or inaudibly mumbled
words or silent laryngeal agitations..." It is the "*rapport*

between words, which enables them to work together at all to any semantic result."[27] These are neural processes (Whorf makes an unsatisfactory distinction between motor and non-motor processes in order to get rid of the 'mumbling' and agitations) that are, "of their nature, in a state of linkage according to the structure of a particular language, and activations of these processes and linkages in any way, with, without, or aside from laryngeal behavior... are all linguistic patterning operations, and all entitled to be called thinking."

He writes, later on, "Every language is a vast pattern-system, different from others, in which are culturally ordained the forms and categories by which the personality not only communicates, but also analyzes nature, notices or neglects types of relationship and phenomena, channels his reasoning, and builds the house of his consciousness."[28]

Whorf takes pain to elucidate that "in linguistic and mental phenomena, significant behavior... are ruled by a specific system or organization, a 'geometry' of form principles characteristic of each language. This organization is imposed from outside the narrow circle of the personal consciousness, making of that consciousness a mere puppet whose linguistic maneuverings are held in unsensed and unbreakable bonds of pattern."[29] And he insists that the savant and the shepherd are bound alike in the toils of their mother tongue.

Actually when we reach the pith of Whorf's message, it is that different linguistic groups express the same idea in different ways. And these different ways expose the falsity of thinking of language in its acceptable European form. But this is what we have been waiting for. We have now a genius in linguistic analysis to tell us that the same basic process is occurring, but is independent of our logical, grammatical, syntactical forms.

Speech does not determine psychology, but the psyche finds many ways of expressing itself. There are many codes. They arrive at similar ends. To take an example from Whorf: in English, it may be said: "He invites people to a feast." In the Nootka Amerindian speech, a long word says: "Boiling - cooked - eating - ers - he goes for." (tl'mishya/is/ita - 'itl - ma).[30] But the

English-speaking poet can say: "Boil-feasters he invites,"
or "Feasters he fetches." I am sure that the Nootka word
sounds no more one than the English words when these
are rattled off.

Whorf in several essays adverts briefly to the

> schemes like Basic English, in which an
> eviscerated British English, with its
> concealed premises working harder than
> ever, is to be fobbed off on an unsuspect-
> ing world as the substance of pure Reason
> itself. We handle even our plain English
> with much greater effect if we direct it
> from the vantage point of a multilingual
> awareness...; Western culture has made,
> through language, a provisional analysis
> of reality and, without correctives, holds
> resolutely to that analysis as final. The
> only correctives lie in all those other
> tongues which by aeons of independent
> evolution have arrived at different, but
> equally logical, provisonal analyses.[31]

Whorf would seem here to reach backwards for a
larger truth than linguistic-thought-relativism, namely: a
language whose practitioners are acutely self-aware and
ingenious can be coaxed into ways of speaking that are
like those of any other language. Is this not what occurs,
actually, when an English dialect becomes after some
time an American dialect, reflecting a new ideology and
lifestyle? And what occurs when a science takes hold of
its mother-tongue and reflects and creates a new logic, an
ideology and philosophy with it?

The tasks of logician, poets, and anthropological ling-
uists should center, then, upon the interpretation of naturally emergent speech, upon what a culture does to it,
upon what it does to the culture, and how cultures interact through speech.

Language is here regarded as an immediate, primary
function and manifestation of human nature. It is not, as
often portrayed, a sort of luxury that the mind resorts to
after its job of running itself is completed and it wants to

communicate with its fellows. One should avoid the grand conceit that humans have a natural, built-in, realistic, and rational way of dealing with themselves and their environment, despite occasional vagaries.

What is rational is not to be demeaned. There is a pragmatism of the human that extends to his speech. It begins with the kind of problem-solving that besets and befits a dog or ape. The primordial needs of food, warmth, security, defense, and sex are addressed in recognizably mammalian ways. But, quickly, lacking the instinctive definitiveness that turns one to a tunnel-like solution or none at all, the human shifts first to a schizophrenic state and then into a process of trial and error, retrial, and possible success. He requires a computer that stores, retrieves and manipulates data, and so copes with these problems in linguistic form. This is the most rational level of which the human being is capable. Here he fixes his mind as closely as possible upon the strict requirements of life as he views them.

But this is the farthest development from his born condition, the "buzzing and confusion" of William James' famous description of the infant mind. He has to pass through all the symptoms of madness before arriving at this accommodation, the closest to instinctual as he can ever be. His heads are pressed together by a culture and by the exercise of the structures dealt with in this chapter, along with cultural specifications. Between the animal and the pragmatic is the natural level of *homo schizo,* resisting and unmaking and remaking the animal and the pragmatic in the vicissitudes of life as *homo schizo.*

And, if the world is ever to be united in mind, it will be partly owing to a new language, in our sense a rational language, fashioned to its goal. The history of rational languages begins, like most scientific history, with a mistake. Thus one John Wilkins laboriously constructed, saved from the flames of the Great London Fire, and finally published in 1668 a treatise *Towards a Real Character and a Philosophical Language,* wherein for example, the word "salmon" becomes the word "zana," a river fish with scales and reddish flesh. Jorge Luis Borges wrote recently about his brilliant advanced ideas.

The socialists and communists, following Karl Marx,

produced in the nineteenth and twentieth centuries a handful of words and slogans that dissidents of many countries might share, feeling that they spoke a common tongue. It is not technically beyond our means today to fashion a language that is much more efficient and appealing that Pidgin or Basic English, or Esperanto or Marxese to facilitate communications among the sharers of a new world belief and participants in an accompanying grand movement. This language would of course become a cultural language after overcoming its severe trials as a rational language.

chapter seven

THE GOOD, THE TRUE, AND THE BEAUTIFUL

The good is what one wants; the true is how to get it; the beautiful is a mask of the good and true. Such is the frame of the argument here to come. The repugnance that should be aroused by it is one which I can feel as sensibly as the reader, for do we not appreciate that the good is what we good ones want? And the truth is more than mere means, but ought to be good means? And the beautiful is the subtle expression and adornment of our good means and good ends? But let us hide our light under a bushel and speak of others.

How does human mentation work on these matters? Most mentation, we should have to admit, is a muddle, testifying as a whole to the frustration and futility of humankind, but this is so widely known that we need not take the time to describe it. Mentation, like human behavior generally, seeks to recapture instinctiveness and, by so doing, to hold its poly-ego in a comfortable balance as near to automatism as possible. The closest it has come to this *Nirvana* is a state in which the rules for quickly achieving goals are routine and effective, and the sublimation of the instinctive ends and means is at a minimum. This is ordinary scientific and rational behavior. Man chooses art, and whatever else is blessed as voluntarism and beauty, because he cannot attain instinct directly, or finds himself stranded in the muddle.

A most apparent excrescence of the human mind is egotism. The human emits a plentitude of ejaculations, demands, and wishes, which he believes are reasonable simply because they emanate from himselves. To all of his positive identifications he ascribes a good, to all negative ones (and many are ambivalent) an evil.

He characteristically emits denials of whatever would appear to oppose his good, quite aside from the rules of logic or reason or justice, although to these he may even subscribe. His capacity for denial of the opposition extends to non-perception and non-recognition. The very sensing of things by eyes, nose, taste, ears, and feeling is broadly prejudiced. Nor is this selective sensing a "logical condition for survival" or "a preference — *de gustibus non disputandum est"*; it is a severe effort to destroy what threatens.

The human possesses a rudimentary notion of cause which labels whatever he dislikes as the cause of the evils he perceives and whatever he likes as the cause of the good. Guilt and blame are displaced liberally upon his negatively construed objects.

Everyday thought exhibits an abundance of what psychologists term "erratic cognition." Some Hindus say that "The Sun and the Moon rise and set only because the brahmin recites the Jayatri." The Aztecs, who were butchering and eating an estimated 200,000 persons per year when the Spaniards arrived upon the Mexican scene in the sixteenth century, claimed that, without a gift of human organs, the sun would not rise. Still, four centuries later, the Nazis, adorned with the prehistoric swastika, conducted a holocaust of millions of humans in the belief that they were purifying themselves and Germany. Among those killed were some persons institutionalized for mental disturbances.

In a related type of case, a disaster occurs; it is "normal" to believe that it happened because the victims had been bad. "They deserved what they got." The

reasoning is to be discovered both in the Bible and in
present-day Christian communities, whether in Alaska
during the 1964 earthquake or in the Wilkes-Barre, Pa.,
flood of 1973; it permeates every culture's ideology. Nor
is this universal reasoning simply a product of the lazy
human mind, which does not seek scientifically for the
antecedents of a disaster. It is an effort to control the
world. It gives humans a great collective responsibility,
an intolerable one. The destruction of the world itself is
laid to human wickedness. In order to believe in human
control, it may be necessary to believe that humans can
bring the world to an end!

Considering that the first psychic and social forma-
tions, such as religion, were put together under most
unfavorable internal and external conditions, the basic
mentation of humans is quite understandable. The forma-
tion of the logical person was a pragmatic process and
still is; to the instinctive animalistic behavior that yet
remained was added the ability to determine the consequences of actions and thenceforth to adjust one's behavior in accord with predictable consequences. But this
pragmatic process has always been stifling under a blanket of schizotypicality.

Human mentation is normally preoccupied with the
great battle for control of fear. This is and has been of
much more interest and concern to the organism and
society than the pragmatic concerns of the several areas
of life — work, sex, science, health. All of these life areas
— the immense structure of civilization — emerge from a
"madman" trying to control his head. That pragmatic
behavior is neglected in the frenzy for control is normally
observable in human thought and behavior.

Governments operate in the same muddle as individuals, whether they be democratic, communist, military,
traditional-authoritarian, theocratic, or tribal. It is quite
clear among them that the good is what they want, the
truth is how to get it, and the beautiful is what adorns
their good and true. The documentation of this statement
is so profuse that I can only allude to it here.[1] A century
ago, Ratzenhofer expressed the consensus of the most
discerning political scientists when he suggested classifying politics as a branch of psychopathology.

Raison d'état carries properly its cryptic original
sense: whatever the state wants is reason enough. "Do
not ask questions; it will do you no good." The governments consist of the men who run states; these men are
basically similar to those whom they rule; they are constrained by attitudes, ideology and capabilities. They
have the same or slightly more of the schizoid traits of
split personalities, fear, obsessions, paranoia, and immer-
sion in symbolism that are observable in ordinary people.

THE OMNIPOTENCE OF OUGHT

Man exercises from his gouty toe to the heavens above
what Freud has called "the omnipotence of thought." He
builds in his mind an image of a new reality that is under
his control and, further, will believe and act as if the corresponding events are occurring as planned. The concept
appears obviously when a physically constrained mental
patient claims a power to move the world and to consult
with others, such as gods and kings, who are engaged in
the same business. Thus it is a kind of megalomania.

Still the indulgence of omnipotent thought is ordinary, even usual. The notion of "free will" in morals and
law is an example. A person is expected to claim voluntarism and, if he does not, the community claims it for him.
It is appropriate behavior. He must practice affecting
himself, others, and the world with his mind, and he is
abetted and encouraged often in imagining his own
spheres of power; so heaven is attainable, as is hell, good
as well as evil, world destruction and world renewal, the
triumph of the Ideal, of Truth, of Order.

What grammarians say "ought to be" is obsessively
regarded as "is," that is, achieved: "God is on our side."
"Work is fun." "Parents are good." The distinction
between a preference and a fact is overriden, not because
some humans cannot comprehend it, but because they
cannot tolerate the world that exists. In the beginning,
and in the case of every infant, the "is" is painfully segre-
gated from the "ought" so we should not be surprised at
the universal recidivism from "is" to "ought." When philosophers like J.R. Searle, in a desperate spasm of

sublimity, attempt to derive "ought" from "is," they end up deriving "is" from "ought." Still the naturalistic fallacy is an indefatigable Sisyphus.

The overriding drive to control the self and everything else is the "should be" of all "should be's." The gods are made "to be" as they "should be," friends of ours, of our tribe, or perhaps even of humanity. No matter that they are also believed to have repeatedly destroyed the nations and that they will do so again; they remain, in Homer's cliché, "the source of all blessings."

Wishful thinking, in matters both small and large, is universal and practically ineradicable. Megalomania is but an obvious pathology, slightly out of step with the fundamental human delusion of making a wished world out of a real world. Masses of people who are helpless and frustrated by lack of control achieve miracles by prayer — for the cure of illness, salvation of the soul, and the recovery of popes and presidents who have been shot.

That will and morale are powerful agents cannot be denied. Not so long ago, in the dust bowls of empiricism, these words brought shudders. The development of psychosomatic medicine, the infiltration of the West by Hindu Yoga, the respectabilizing of consciousness-raising and, paradoxically, of suggestive techniques, brought them into new prominence.

Hilgard discusses the experiments of Spanos and others on suggestion.[2] Hypnotized subjects believe all the more readily that their arm is becoming stiff if beforehand they have been supplied with fantasies, as that the arm is in a splint or made of wood or iron, and therefore cannot bend. Spanos calls these "goal-directed fantasies." We regard them also as a type of psychosomatic conversion. We see in them evidence that will-power can become an operational concept, even in pracical affairs, after a century of ridicule and obloquy. Will-power in politics, religion, sports, or business must be an exertion upon external objects of the same physiological system that accounts for psychosomatism up to the point of the system impacting on the body tissue, which completes the operation if internal, but carries the operation only into an external activity if involving a displacement removed from the organism.

There is little question but that *homo schizo* can mobilize his mind for remarkable feats of organs, mentation and behavior. We note too, following the connection between so-called visceral learning and yoga, and of the omnipotence of thought. All serve to validate the very old supposition of *homo schizo* that he could do anything if he only wanted to do so badly enough. The fact that our contemporary world is so extreme a chaos of wills and wants obscures the enormous potential that this age-old idea possesses when harnessed to modern psychology. "We demand a character for which our emotions and active propensities shall be a match. Small as we are, minute as is the point by which the cosmos impinges upon each one of us, each one desires to feel that his reaction at that point is congruous with the demands of the vast whole — then he balances the latter, so to speak, and is able to do what it expects of him."[3]

Once again we must allude to the enormous impact on the world of the drive for control genetically engendered in *homo schizo* by the failure of animal instinct and the fearful balkanisation of the human self.

SECRET WORDS AND PANRELATIONISM

Ordinary language is like the language behavior of primeval humans and of the mentally disturbed. There are many repressed inutterables and also blasphemous ejaculations. Words are kept secret; words are coined in profusion. Words are made to be deceiving and used to deceive the self, others, gods, animals. Words are given reality, made more "real" than the real. Names, too, are often secret; to name a person or thing is believed to possess it. Words are sacred: "In the beginning was the Word."

God-words are addressed to those who appear both in the skies and on earth as controllers of the world and these have nevertheless to be controlled to relieve one's fears. Words are played with like fire-crackers: known to be dangerous they are yet thrilling and give relief to anxieties. They are covered up or sublimated — all through poetry and philosophy.

From Plato to Rudolf Steiner philosophers and poets have been word-players and handlers of words as sacred and secret. Words are regarded as absolute: one is forbidden to touch them. There is a fear of clarifying them or defining them operationally: to define a word instrumentally is to murder it. There is much of this in philosophy, as well as in politics and aesthetics.

The animate world has never been and is not now limited to life. Animism is rife. Everything is alive. Thus the world may be controlled by incorporating it in oneself. Considering the "natural reason" supposedly granted to humans, it should be simple to draw a distinction between natural forces and animate forces. Yet it was not and is not done. In fact, the more disturbed that people are, the more they see themselves in animals, plants, rocks, and skies. This phenomenon is of course closely related to paranoia, as for example, in the belief that eyes are watching one from everywhere. The "all-seeing eye" is one of the earliest and most nearly universal symbols. It is, incidentally, inscribed upon the "Almighty Dollar" and the Seal of the United States of America.

The "eye" of myth and symbol relates to primeval and schizoid thought. Isaac Vail believed that the primordial eye was the boreal opening from which Saturn on his throne looked down upon his domain.[4] He thought that it was an illusion of solar light playing upon a hole in the thick cloud canopy covering the Earth. That is, it was based on reality and psychologically perceived as an eye, and it is in keeping with the universal association fallacy: "like" means "same."

Homeopathic magic, superstition, homeopathic medicine, and many more behaviors rest upon the belief that things that appear to be alike are "in each other." The "cosmic egg" is the vault of heaven and bird's egg. Both become broken. Each is the other. It is by means of such associations that mankind is not only deluded but also charged with an interest in the mundane; for the mundane is infused with the sacred. It is only then worth much attention, control, development.

Pan-relationism, the stretching for analogies in all of existence, is typical of mentation. The "most remote"

things are brought together by a fancied resemblance.
This would seem to contradict the schoolboy's resistance
to recognizing the "most obvious parallels," unless we
allow for his contradictory motives; and, of course, once
outside the schoolroom, his heart hangs upon a cloud.

Misplaced metaphors; the use of the part to indicate
the whole (and *vice versa*) the tendency not only to dis-
sociate analytically unanalogous things but to super-as-
sociate ("to flounder in a mire of uncontrolled associations," as Bleuler put it); to coin many neologisms — all
of these "illogical" techniques of mind along with those
mentioned before are rife in primordial thought, in psychopathic thought, and when dispassionately analyzed,
in individual and social thought today.

In German legend and folk tale, Erlkoenig (King of
the Alder trees) is vaguely an ogre, who skulks in the
fogs, a pedophile who then disposes of the young bodies;
he is also a late descendent of Odin (identified as Wot-
man, a complex of Saturn and successor gods). He is also
related to Rubezahl, the threatening companion of Santa
Klaus (Saturn). Whence one is permitted to connect oral
ingestion (cannibalism) with the sexual (especially the
sexually aberrant). One does not elaborate a major connection here, but only a typical overlapping and transacting of cultural and religious displacements, according to
what should be understood as the omnipresent holistic
character of culture and religion. We leave it to psychiatrists to search in their practice for the suggested connections and refer to other passages in our works, *Homo
Schizo I* and *The Divine Succession*. Folk tales, mytholo-
gists now generally agree, are a happy hunting ground to
the sublimations of the culturally perverse, as well as for
the most ancient images and experiences.

If a group were miraculously to be deprived of its illogical schizoid forms, it would collapse immediately, for it
has been founded upon them and penetrated by them
throughout its existence. That "language loses its power
to communicate on a rational level" under all of these circumstances, is true and expectable. It is also operationally and structurally not so significant as one is given to
believe; for there is only a highly limited rational level in
language. The human does not distinguish well between

"friend" and "foe," even on the level where these interact personally with him as people and animals, much less
on the level of spirits, ideologies, and gods. Again we
hear that he does distinguish, but the task is difficult,
"causation being often impenetrable by rational means."
More likely, the human elects friend and foe out of a
need to like and dislike and as part of his translation of
reality into opposites.

Quantitative thought is difficult for the human, at best,
and even a slight anxiety will cancel his efforts at shading
his distinctions. Useful though this latter shading may be
for other purposes, it is not so comforting and reassuring
to a temporary ego stability as a clear-cut invidious distinction. Whenever A is not identical with B, either A or
B is deemed bad. Under conditions of the highest sublimation, A * B becomes Yin and Yang, logos and mythos,
and other concepts that lend themselves to disputation,
and provide fuel for the everpresent ambivalence, which
is conveyed by the everpresent anxiety into doubt, distinction, and dislike.

Most of the mentation that occupies the human mind
is composed of operations such as the foregoing. They are
the easiest way to believe. They arouse the least internal
resistance, even though they hardly make the human
consistently successful. They rather lend to his life and
history that miserable erraticism upon which thrive mor-
alists and mind healers.

RATIONALIZATION

In this age that is dominated by a belief in
"rationalism," much that believed not to be rational is
gathered together in the concept of "rationalization."
Rationalization is supposed to be finding persuasive
arguments for doing what one thinks one wants to do. It
therefore depends upon the sophistication of the per-
suaded and upon the demands that the rationalizer makes
upon himself. Rationalization is assigned to linguistic
emissions whose purpose is to conceal real mentation by
describing it in acceptable linguistic, moral and logical
forms. Thus, as in the case of the anarchist, G. Zangara, a

man hates his father, displaces his hatred upon a remote authority, the president, and tries to kill the president, believing and asserting that the sole source of his action is in the policies of the president.

The idea of a separate process of rationalization characterizes all human communities, but especially modern communities, where all behaviors are supposed to become "rational," tied in as cause-and-effect with appropriate and approvable community conduct, or at least with an ideal ethic recognized as such, even if opposed, by the community.

In the theory of *homo schizo*, rationalization is nothing but a pandemic mode of discourse; it is the "rational," but defined and shaped by whatever level of rationality that the community manifests. The most exalted philosophy, as well as the lame excuse of a malingering schoolboy, are equally rationalizations. The human does little but rationalize its wants; it does not do something extra and special called "reason."

Where is the line to be drawn between rationalization and rationality? Out of the clouded mental sky do not some few stars of intelligence shine? If intelligence exists, we would say, it is a rare ability to continuously compress mental operations according to symbolized rules along a track of highly correlated "cause-effect-cause-efect... n" ties, and to make many track-switching associations, as we shall soon discover. But it is worth investigating.

THE DISSOLUTION OF LOGIC

The digital (or linear) and analog logics can perform all mentation thus far ascribable to "reason," it would appear. I know of no computer designer who would admit an inability to program any sharp rational process on one or the other or both kinds of machine. As I would portray these logics, in *homo schizo* theory, the digital or linear is a coding to take care of "elapsed time" on delayed instinctual reactions, while the analog is a coding to utilize the displacements engendered by the same glitch. In both cases a language appears, which when working "as it should" accomplishes "rational thought."

"Rational thought" is defined as appropriate public symbolic behavior aimed at a solution. The public may be anyone or everyone. A trite lesson in logic goes: "all men are mortal; Socrates is a man; therefore Socrates is mortal." (All X is Y; S is X; *ergo* S is Y.) Presumably, the lesson is based upon reality. We characterize many men, and then observe that Socrates shares their modal characteristics. Further, one observes that, among other happenings, they all die; whereupon Socrates must die, too. It helps to observe that Socrates did die, unfortunately.

Obviously, all depends upon whether Socrates is accurately placed as a member of the human species and whether any exceptions to death occur. It is clear that Socrates can be deviant from all human norms except this absolutely inclusive norm of death. The problem is first one of analogy, then of algebra.

The procedure is called an Aristotelian syllogism and has long been regarded as the classic deductive proof, but, even as William of Occam surmised in the late Middle Ages, it is an emanation from the structure of the mind, not a quality of reality, that is being processed. The lioness who has seen and hunted many antelope knows that all antelope are mortal, and that the antelope she sees now is mortal, and she can expect it to die by her claw and fang like the rest. The philosopher has to prove it symbolically, cutting through a mass of confused human neurology before putting the major and minor premises together in a conclusion.

Modern psychology and pragmatism have pushed much of Aristotelianism into a corner and occupied its premises otherwise as well. Its three basic laws have become tautologies: that a thing is itself, 'A' is 'A'; that a thing cannot be both itself and something other than itself, 'A' cannot be both 'A' and 'not-A'; and that a thing must be either itself or not itself, 'A' being either 'A' or 'not-A'. These statements are suppositions of narrow utility, overwhelmed by the multitudinous demonstrations of modern psychology and anthropology that 'A' may or may not be 'A'; 'A' can be both 'A' and what 'A' is not; and 'A' can be either 'A' or not 'A' or both. That is, no thing, no occurrence, no process, no 'A' exists but exists holistically, in the company of its opposites. Causes and

anti-causes cohabit. This is the actual operation of the
human mind, acting out of its structure. It is also *homo
schizo* theory, which is non-Aristotelian and non-Carte-
sian.

The mind can recite "2 and 2 are 4" and is trained to
insist upon its rationality; it can apply the form in a number of cases in which it understands how numbers stand
for things. It thereupon resists "untraining," which is the
strenuous achievement of philosophers and psychologists; these say, "You must ask what the number-base is;
and what is '2' in each case; what do *'and'* and *'are'* mean,
and *'4'?"* So the mind resentfully goes from primordial
muddle to philosophical muddling.

The question of whether this is the actual condition of
the real world rather than of mind alone might not appear
germane to the present discussion. However, inasmuch
as *homo schizo* seeks to control the universe because he
is displaced throughout its time and space, he will presumably seek to know it for control purposes. Therefore,
he will wish to elaborate and perfect whatever human
apparatus is best adapted to that end. All of his efforts at
controlling the divine and the mundane, objects and existence, will be pragmatically judged. All of the non-logical
and logical procedures generated in all of human history
are so tested.

The modern age has proliferated not only forms of
non-Aristotelian logic to this end, but it also witnessed
occult ideas, cults, therapies, and countless other modes
of confronting reality. Every nook and cranny of psychiatry, philosophy, mysticism, magic, behavior, life as art,
group configuration, and of Siberia, the Caucasus, Egypt,
South America, the Caribbean, China, Indonesia, Ruma-
nia, Iceland, Tahiti, Africa and India — the whole geographical and ideational world and outer space, too —
have been poked, prodded, pierced into and opened up
for a better way. All are driven by the hope of discovering
and seizing upon a procedure that will give the longed-
for control and set the human mind once and for all at
ease. After reason has failed to prove reasonable, it is
every man for himself, *sauve qui peut.*

Internally, tha "appearance" of the linear and analog
logical forms must be "messy." That is, nothing is as clear

in neurological language as it is in public language; this
is a truism, since public language has to pursue a clearly
communicative format. When a few scientists first began
to speculate about the brain as a computer, John von
Neuman remarked that probably "it is futile to look for a
precise logical concept, that is, for a precise verbal
description, of 'visual analogy.' It is possible that the
connection pattern of the visual brain itself is the simplest logical expression or definition of this principle."[5]
Pribram, with the hologram image in the vanguard of his
work, can today supply much of what was missing then.[6]

In any event, preceding public speech, "the mess is
cleaned up," in anticipation that the company to be enter-
tained will be critical. In babbling children; senile
adults; persons with "thought disorders" or brain lesions;
"feral boys;" "mad" poets; flows of free associations pro-
voked by psychanalytic therapy or electric shock; dreaming; autistic reveries; or deliberate imitations of stream of
consciousness as in James Joyce's Ulysses — the internal
language is not sorted out and cleaned up prior to public
delivery. Such is accidentally true as well of what Freud
called "The Psychopathology of Everyday Life," the multitude of slips of tongue, memory failures, etc. that
accompany us through life — and, of course, we understand that the "accident" is not a "real accident," not for-
tuitous.

In ordinary cases, training maintains its grip on the
external communication. The mind selects the arithmetic
and analog rules which, it has been thought, are acceptable manipulations of terms. The mind "makes sense,"
publicly. The degree to which its public demonstrations
of logical mastery grip the mind, and influence it, can
vary greatly. The display logic may convey little of the
"true" thought processes; it may conceal them and in any
event express only some part of them. But, we stress, this
display is what excites much of the response in the transactions between external minds. So two people deal in a
currency that scarcely measures the internal values of the
exchange.

The language expressed by schizophrenic patients with
"thought-disorders" is reported to differ markedly from
the language of a comparable non-thought-disordered

group of "schizophrenics."[7] But it appears that the language of the second group, whose thought did not exhibit disorder is not somewhat disordered, nor is it normal; it is a guarded, more concise tongue, showing that the speakers are exercising stronger controls over language than either the normal or the thought-disordered patients are.

In general, what makes for intense memories in people also makes for obsession with "correct" logical expression and for following compulsively the dictates, or solutions, provided by the logic. People in logical or rational communication must convey what they intend to convey in all critical circumstances, whether football players or bankers or scientists, or else the language breaks down.

THE USES OF PUBLIC REASON

The languages of general and specialized social groups realize this principle, and they exact discipline in communication and impose heavy penalties for not speaking the language fluently and functionally. It does not matter much what "gibberish" the same people speak to their spouses in bed, or to themselves internally, or in their "free time," so long as they speak properly when "on duty."

The advantages and limitations of rational language and thought are now becoming more clear. When a Corrections Commisioner says to a Prison Warden: "your remission rates are 59%. You must do something about it," the Warden understands him on the level of the discourse. The Warden does not recite to himself the history of corrections in the world and in modern society, the history of the concept of "rate," the significance of rates, all that is known about his prison, changing economic conditions, the full background of the Commissioner, and all the options facing him along with their rationalizations. He takes the statement as close to its face value as he can and tries to deal with it as narrowly as he can. "Yes. I've already set up a pre-release rehabilitation program."

We can make much or little of the exchange. We can extol the marvels of speech, that lets a few words stand on top of a mountain of explanations. Or we can regret how pathetically little the words convey of the world in which the two men are operating. The language is acceptably "rational": a condition is quantitativly denotated. The condition is offered as a non-refusable challenge. The challenge is accepted, even anticipated, and a "step in the right direction" is assured. Released prisoners returning to jail may be fewer, future remission rates even decline (although the situation and the problem are grossly simplified here).

The example is fairly typical of the use of reason in human affairs. As the problem becomes more special and the need for a specific result becomes more acute, humans are capable of herculean efforts at instrumental rationalism. To despatch and recall a space shuttle, many thousands of highly trained people must work for years under the most intense discipline and supervision, and billions of dollars must be spent. Success of the venture can be said to represent every form of rational behavior known to man, from the navigational computers to the psychiatrist watching over the astonauts' social behavior to the public relations experts erecting a network to keep the public as intimate and yet non-interfering as communications technology and socio-psychology will allow.

Success of a shuttle flight does not include, however, full assurances of rational behavior. For example, no one doubts that space shuttles of the next generation will be more highly rationalized in their technical and human operations. Furthermore, the original decisions to attempt a space shuttle are not of the same order of rationality, but rather typical of political decisions. Would the resources have been better allocated to the construction of new American cities? Or to other presumably beneficial ends? In such a case, too, all known types of instrumentally rational behavior might have been exercised, as indeed they are when a military nuclear missile system is designed, organized and installed.

Knowing how such decisions are made does not solve the problem. Public opinion, interest groups, legislators, officials, scientists, and the media enter the decision-making process. With the increasingly rationalized tools of social science analysis, one can follow the course and

weight of influences leading to the final choice, just as a
radiologist, by employing chemicals, can trace the ramifications of a foreign element in the human circulatory
system. Even so, one cannot locate an ultimate rational
source.

One can only ascend to ever higher levels of instrumental rationalism, investigating choice-behavior, with a
mathematical precision that can win a Nobel prize, but
without ever reaching a heaven where choice is made
absolute by marrying "the Good." The Good forever
basely remains what one wants, hence what one is capable of wanting and trained to want, be it comfort, love,
landing on the Moon, ridding the earth of enemies, worshipping one's gods, or something else.

THE SECURITY OF CONSENSUS

Thus rationality is ultimately the practical ability to
achieve one's good, including all lesser goods or bundles
of goods that add up to the configuration of one's good.
Moreover, this good of one may be the greatest "evil" as
well as the greatest "good." It is only made "good" or
"evil" by persons, such as the readers and author. Finding the "good" is not a discovery of the treasure in a
sunken ship. It is the assembling of an internal psychic
code prompted and guided by external coded transactions resulting in futuristic code-images. If the emergent image possessed by "Jean Smith" and "John Doe"
coincides with your image and my image, we share the
good. By many means, some more logical than others, we
can determine the fit, thus the consensus. Thereupon, we
may proceed with this collective good, more or less in
logical language, in some cases foisting our codes upon
other people and things, obtaining a broader consensus.

The consensus, despite the brevity and vagaries of
external language, is reassuring. It unites our externally
displaced identities with our internal identities, making
us "one with the world." Our sense of control is heightened, our anxieties lessened. Credit must be granted to
logical processes for the welcome security, insofar as the
transactions are actually or apparently couched in logical

language. When children chant the table of multiplications together: 1 x 6 = 6; 2 x 6 = 12; etc., they are exchanging passwords for security, as well as confirming the validity of the terms and building habits of rationality. They also may chant prayers, identically, except that habits of non-rational belief are established.

Plato's *Timaeus* as interpreted by Taylor argues also that those who cannot do a sum take fear when the planets show oppositions, occultations and reappearances.[8] This is not the only indication from ancient legend and science, nor from modern psychology and behavior, that numbers are a *security* device as is measurement, hence astrology, astronomy and astrophysics. The universally-observed magic of numbers and the superstitions of numbers support this hypothesis.

Numbering may have originated in the fight against fear; numbers and measures may ultimately become logical-rational procedures; but thay may originally have been methods of fighting fear. Counting, ordering, measuring, have in them a fear therapy. So children are told to count sheep in order to fall asleep. "Hail, Mary's" are recited by soldiers until panic passes. Parachuters count before leaping. The count-down before space-vehicle launching is a public ritual of prayer, wish, and suppression of last frightened thoughts.

CAUSATION

For thousands of years, the leading forms of philosophy of truth have been directed generally at the destruction of commonsense truth. The analysis of discursive symbolism among the ancient Greeks affected human communications with these questions: What do you know? (perception and cognition) How do you know it? (logic and proof) Then, do you know yourself? (Socrates) The three questions cast much of what passed (and still passes) for knowledge into the realm of the non-rational. Strong currents even of scepticism and cynicism moved through the intelligentsia.

The classical Greeks were neither first nor last to go through the act of first constructing natural laws and then of finding out how to evade them. It would appear that this constructive-destructive process is characteristic of high periods of mental development, whether in the Arabic enlightenment, the high Middle Ages, the Renaissance, the Eighteenth Century Enlightenment, or the past century. The more man subjectivizes, the more he can control the outer world, but also the more he can see of the limits of his truths.

So it happened that in more recent times, we have seen the destruction of Euclidean geometric space as an absolutely existent phenomenon; "time" has been reduced to a relative, generically impelled habit and coincidence; and the "caused" has become a "function." Needless to say, the outlook of science has been forcibly affected by this relativism, but ordinary life has proceeded on its commonsense paths, carrying on faithfully the belief in absolute truths of knowledge while of course carrying along its full complement of illusions and delusions. Yet ordinary life has been always affected by the relativism of time and space, and the incidentalism of causation.

The concept of causality has caused philosophers infinite headaches, leading up to its final denial; but the path remains to support the commonsense belief that stress causes pain. Analysis of alleged "causation," freed of commonplace prejudices, quickly arrives at the conclusion that in any given case of "causation," everything in the vignette can be termed a casual factor, and that what is called "the cause" is whatever the judge deems it to be.

Thus, in the statement, "I rang the doorbell," "I" may be presumed to be the cause only because I, at least, am interested in my participation in the event. But, ultimately, the simple act breaks into infinite smithereens of the universal moment and of the endless past, eliciting statements such as, "if copper were not once geologically formed,... there would be no bell," so ancient deposits of copper are the cause; or, "my finger caused the ringing...etc.," or millions of other causes more or less as meaningful, *sub specie aeternitates*, as "I."

To make matters worse, lurking beneath the superficial determinism is a notion of free will that would furnish a potential "non-bell ringer." If I were completely free to not ring the bell, one would have to say that at least one and by extension millions of past decisions were unnecessary. The bell was rung, but by an unnecessary cause. Perhaps the cause was all the more unnecessary, since my excitedly expectant friend, say, opened the door just as I was about to ring the bell, and claimed that she heard it.

Quantum mechanics also would destroy ordinary causal theory, lending as it does an indeterministic element to the "decision" of a causally potent condition as to whether or not to actuate, that is, happen.

A given electron may or may not "choose" to leave its radioactive atom, for example. Or, in order to discover the momentum of a given particle (which is at the same time a wave), one foregoes by the conditions under which this can be observed and measured, the chance of discovering its location — and *vice versa*. With quantum theory and the Heisenberg principle of indeterminism (uncertainty), the following must be foregone: certainty; predictability; causation; space and time; Aristotelian logic (see above); nor can the quantum-uncertainty principle be proven true or false empirically. What remains, however, are statistical probabilities governing aggregate behavior. As we cannot ask an explanation of the basic fact that "inertia is", neither can we ask why there is a state of indeterminism.[9]

As if this were not enough, what we see in causality in the human mind is a spasm of incompleteness between two events that it is felt ought instinctively to happen in sequence. Here again is the instinct glitch. Anything once delayed builds a secondary displacement circuit or hologram. The circuit continues to be excited by analogous events and the analogous sets become grouped into perceived casual classes, as, for example, "stress causes pain."

When I press the bell button by a door, millions of past events, known and unknown, are bridged, but to the self-aware human, the act (or the hesitation before the act) is interpreted in the light of many analogous actions. The principle of causation seems obvious even to a child: "Go ring Auntie Mabel's bell to see if she's home."

TIME AND SPACE

The world, it may be agreed, is essentially vacant of time, space, or causality. So is the human mind. No time-clock as such registers impressions and expressions of the central nervous system. However, what comes to be sensed as time is the neurological superposition of halos imprinted upon neurons as they occur. Then, typical left-hemisphere operations ensue, ordering impressions by digital logic, cleaning up inner time for incorporation into external and especially cultural time schedules.

The past tense of time is perceived as one's recall reaches for lower figurations in the "stack" of impressions. The "lower," the older. When a women tells a man, "you remind me of my father," perhaps tens of thousands of circuits are retrogressively lighting up. In her mind, a coded representation of his behavior is vigorously seeking analogs (holograms). If, is as likely, she is engaging in wishful thinking, non-analogs and distasteful analogs are being censored.

As with practically every other human trait, a rudimentary time sense is invaluable to the communication of animal instincts, and the storage of time in memory as well as the projection of time are readily observable. A dog will crouch patiently besides a hole, from which once a squirrel emerged, in the hope that he will once again appear. We resort, as usual, to the human glitch and the splatter of displacements to account for the rich human display of temporal effects.

No matter what philosophers may say in derogation of time, every cell and every species, even every grain of sand and atom, enjoys its bio-sequences and bio-rhythms. Not only are all things in change; they are also changing in patterns, and uniquely, hence a kind of triple paradox of change, pattern, and uniqueness occurs.

"Our fearful mind anticipates the future but we can only understand what was in the past," declared Kierkegaard. Something has been said earlier of the sense of dread regarding death, the divine, and the future. To the schizophrenic, writes Meerloo, "the past is something demonic. The feeling of unbroken homogeneity with the

present has been lost... 'The world clock stands still,' says
one patient."[10] Mendel perceives the dissolution of his-
toricity and with it the future as a major characteristic of
disease.

Exaltation, which can be viewed as an agitated nervous crisis of the present moment, of which the use of the
historical present in literary style partakes, is frequent in
mental states pronounced insane as well as divine. It collapses both history and the future. It also reverses time.
The ancient prophets — the Hebrew Isaiah, Saint John
the Evangelist, the unknown Egyptian author of the
Ipuwer papyrus concerning the destruction of Egypt, for
example, used the future tense to say what had happened
in times past. Leonardo da Vinci, whose genius included
a set of *Profetie,* also refers in these prophecies to historical materials using the future tense.[11] Time becomes
like the chain that propels a bicycle, going backwards as
it moves foward. The faster a person or culture moves the
more its future and its history are changed. But a culture
denies that it can change, it denies the charge of *hubris,*
and celebrates continually its very beginnings as if they
were today and in the future. Time, man's great tool, is
repeatedly and deliberately destroyed. Time is projected
memory. To control himself, man must control his projections both past and future. Time, to him, is an event, a
fact, that must be controlled along with every other happening.

Left hemisphere brain damage interferes with the
perception of sequence but right hemisphere damage
does not.[12] If our theory that two types of logic form in
the brain, one analog, the other additive or digital, and
that the first is right-brain or bilateral while the second is
left-brain, the inability to perceive sequences may be
attributable to a disturbance of time-counting by digital
sequence coding. The analog contribution to sequencing
would be by superposition of images. It may operate like
holography, as was suggested earlier, allowing replicated
images to be stored in large numbers, so that the excision
of even a great many holograms in either or both hemispheres would not disturb the detection of sequences.

Future tense arises out of obsessional expectations of
the return of an event. For ordinary and minor events, the

future is helped to emerge by the transference of analogous major obsessions. The anniversary complex has deep roots in the human mind: an intense private celebration, when congruent with a public consensus, forms the peak type of human memory event. When an anniversary is forgotten, whether private or public, it is because of dread of the reoccurrence. Ordinarily, a deep enough trauma is quite suppressed and is celebrated only unconsciously, with depression or psychosomatism or displacement behavior. Thus any of these neuroses may befall a woman upon the anniversary of the painful death of a dear mother, especially if her age approaches the age of her mother at death. Public trauma can be bifurcated to give a mourning occasion followed by a saturnalian or joyful one, as before Christmas, or at Eastertime, among Christians and Jews, for different reasons , the Judaic mourning and joy in these cases relating to the great Deluge of Noah and to the Passover of Exodus, respectively. Thus we both remember and forget.

Space may be dependent upon time. That is, without time, space might be inconceivable. An animal is master of the space around it, more than the human, who probably suffers more awkward bumps and falls in the house he has built than do the animals that may share it with him. But only the human is driven to conceive of, measure, and manage all space, so that one must guess that he is the jack of all space for being master of none.

Human concepts of space are perhaps built upon an infrastructure of time. Once the sense of time is developed, space can be calculated as elapsed time between the self and the displacements of the self, where they were in the memory, where they occur now. Thus we think of primitive space as distance in time from an object or event to the experiencing self. Direction is also a point of reference from one's body — front, behind, right, left, up, down. Accurate mapping of space within the confines of experience becomes possible. What is beyond direct experience — over the mountains, the stars above — may be naively construed as far away, but much less far than they really are. The celestial bodies are measures of space — "I live a day's walk from you." or "six hours by airplane." But, thus, too, is time.

James Fraser, a century ago, explained the practice of magic by two principles. According to a law of similarity, like produces like; a magician can produce an effect by imitating it in advance. By sprinkling water, one can bring rain, providing other matters are attended to also. Second, the law of contagion maintains that things once in contact continue to interact ever thereafter. A spot struck by lightening is forever sacred to Jupiter. Such was the belief and practice of the ancient Etruscans.

These principles are found in current as well as ancient and trbal thought. Science often proceeds by imitating nature and unravelling strings of consequences. In them one can locate the operations of analogy that seem to be naturally produced in the brain. Analogy took the primary and more powerful role in the development of Greek science from magic and myth.[13]

We do not change brains or develop new organs in going from "falsehood" to "truth." We get rid of the "hocus-pocus" that accompanies magic. We make the magic public (open display and repetition of experiments). Then we increase the validity of the analogies and sequences until they become reliable.

The history of science shows us many a relation in tandem between magic, religion and scientific practice. Astrology as astronomy and magic is perhaps the most famous. The ancient Chinese could foretell eclipses, a major achievement of scientific observation and logic. But at the same time thay applied rituals and emergency policies to quell official and public fear of eclipses and to repel astral invasions. Mesmerism and hypnotism are another example, from the nineteenth century, of parallel evolution of cult practices and scientific method.

The discipline involved in the change from magic to science is intense, obsessive, and costly. An experiment by Liam Hudson performed upon students of history and engineering involved interrupting their sleep upon observing signs of dreaming and asking them to report their dreams. The engineers reported more frequently that they were not dreaming at all or could not recall the dreams. "The engineers' inhibition in dealing with 'primary process' thought — with ideas and images that have not been ordered in a conventionally rational way — is not a superficial aspect of their thinking; it is an integral part of the way in which their minds work."[14]

What we are observing here and in primitive magic are lesser and greater degrees of the conversion of obsession into bureaucratic and scientific habit and showing that, like a form of psychosomatism, the specialized disciplined worker over-develops a *point de'appui*, working from the conscious into the unconscious along a narrow band. This is not science as new theory or hypothesis, not science as poetry, which is an altogether different mental operation, distiguishing two types of scientists as night from day.

So must the routine administrator or bureaucrat be distinguished from the organizational innovators of the type of Epaminondas, St. Therese, I. Loyola, Thomas Jefferson, Henri de Saint-Simon, Mussolini, Trotsky, Henry Ford and Gandhi; a great many unnamable persons have produced the largest number of inventions — there were, after all, engineering students who did recall their dreams. The rational is the routine, true; but ought one not permit the term for the creative? But, then, the creative is non-rational. So it is both rational and non-rational, a contradiction if both are the same.

Therefore do we propose discarding the term "rational" or letting "rational" mean the ability to obtain what one wants, namely, "truth." We must disagree with those who, like Arthur Koestler, assert of the human dilemma, "No matter how much the symptoms vary, the pattern of disorder is the same: a mentality split between faith and reason, between emotion and intellect."[15] Faith and reason subsist cheek by jowl in the mentating process; we must abandon this medieval dichotomy if we would understand human nature.

So, too with emotion and intellect: emotion is intellective and intellect is emotional. At the turn of this century, George Mead was lecturing at the University of Chicago that: "It would be a mistake to assume that a man is a biologic individual plus a reason, if we mean by this definition that he leads two separate lives, one of impulse or instinct, and another of reason.. On the contrary, the whole drift of modern psychology has been toward an undertaking to bring will and reason within the impulsive life."[16] There is little neurological or pragmatic basis for the words. Nor do they help in programming policies for humanity.

Close in outlook to Mead, John Dewey, too, was long engaged in combat against traditional logic and psychology. In 1929, in his book *The Quest for Certainty,* he devoted a chapter to "Escape from Peril," where he continued his attack upon the philosophers' search for the immutable, the truth, by way of "pure knowledge." "The quest for certainty," he said, "is a quest for peace which is assured, an object which is unqualified by risk and the shadow of fear which action casts."[17] We would add that *homo schizo* normally wants to escape his perils and invented first historical religions, then thelogy, then philosophy, moving outwards into abstractions to develop the sense of certainty that would relieve his anxieties. But each further stage of abstaction displaces him farther, too, from the origins of existential fear in his inability to act like an animal.

SCIENCE AS INSTINCT

If theologians and philosophers vainly sought certainty in order to displace fear, are then scientists merely at another stage of displacement or sublimation? Would the counting of binary star systems be such, too? Might the rejection of the holistic term "human nature" be a collective schizotypical symptom of depersonalization among psychologists? Would perfecting solar energy systems fall in a similar category? Yes, we would say, but all with a notable difference.

Truth or the rational is how to get what one wants. Then "howling for bread" is true if it brings bread. So is prayer. Yes. What works, what is effective, is considered rational and true.

Would not bread be more certainly forthcoming if one farmed wheat and baked bread? Perhaps... in some cases... yes, on the whole... etc. The sparrows don't look to the morrow, said Christ; trust in the Lord. The infant

howls and is fed. The mob riots and is fed. The primitive
band gathers nuts and fruits and herbs. But we applaud
the ancient inventors of the science of agriculture. Now
they could feed more mouths while resting in place.

Science — and reason — are suppressors of unruly
processes.[18] They discipline the fearful selves to follow
rules which, they assert, will reliably bring desired consequences. "Get rid of the excess and costly baggage of
superstitious behavior: don't chant and dance around the
growing crops; hone your spades, plant more seed, dig
deeper; (then, reluctantly) it may help if you play music
for the crops to grow by."

The rules of science and reason are simple. All things
are sensible. They must be given exclusive denotations.
These must be acted upon in exclusively denotable ways.
They can then be grouped within a closed system of logical counting which is not so empirical. The process and
the consequences are to be watched and confirmed by
others. At no stage of the process should "wishing" be
admitted and given any weight. Scientific procedures
give *homo schizo* controls to add to his kitbag of controls.
To some extent they are more reliable controls, though
often for things that he wants to let be un-controlled or
cares little about, or are not what he wants most to control.

Behaviorally, what *homo schizo* has done, which has
come to be called "rationality" and "reason," is to select
out of his experience certain operations whose traits are
that, first, they give success (by test) in naming, and in
the transfer of naming (also by test), and, second, the
names can be counted and the count tested. Success in
testing is validated inasmuch as the names and their
manipulation produce psychic and material effects
deemed favorable. Why does man select these operations, and make so much of them that a wonderful science
ensues? He finds their effects *reliable;* he can make easy
and gratifying obsessions of them.

Is this all? This is a great deal. It makes the difference
between uncontrolled fear and a bearable equilibrium,
between helplessness and ruling the earth and all of its
denizens. It is the difference between a blank gaze and a
child counting apples, or even more, a computer guiding

a spaceship out and back to earth.

By temporarily giving up his chaotic mentation, by submitting to the controls determined by others, by obsessively dedicating his mind to the proven possible and proven practical, he can gain a share of control. The rules, the identifications, the promises, the secrets of language and experiments, the mystique and authority of science — all help him feel comforted and less fearful. The myriad displacements augment the normal complement of animal foci of attention and sources of stimuli.

The responses are the fantastically engendered capabilities of the human. Satisfactions emerge from a perceived coping with the stmulus by the selected responses. Science takes homo-specific urges, applies species-specific responses and obtains species-indulgent effects. To a foreign intelligence, none of these would make sense, much less truth. What the process resembles, in a sinister shocking way, is where it all began, the home that it never left, amidst the unselfconscious breeds of life.

The closest I find to this idea of the search to recapture instinct as inherent in pragmatic or operational science is in Mead's essay on the biologic individual.

After describing the physical world that faces the human as a biological and instinctive organism, Mead says "Just in so far as we present ourselves as biological mechanisms are we better able to control a correspondingly greater field of conditions which determine conduct. On the other hand, this statement in mechanical terms abstracts from all purposes and all ends of conduct."[19] Then he compares modern scientific method as a way of moving into the "now" to test reliability and truth.

On the whole, *homo schizo* would prefer more direct and easy methods of reaching the good, the true, and the beautiful, than science has thus far afforded him. If he were always comfortable, he certainly would not be rational; but then, if he were always comfortable (that is, had his quota of the values of sex, respect, health, knowledge, affection, and power) he would not be *homo schizo*, for there is no quota, only endless discomfort. Paraphrasing Heraclitus, we could say, "One can never bathe in the

same river of truth twice." But *homo schizo* would hate
this truth, even though he has had to live by it.

What *homo schizo* would most desire, because it
would bring him immediate surcease from his existential
agony, would be to become once more a generalized
mammal, whose mind fit its body, able to act decisively,
unconsciously, instinctively upon the presentation of a
stimulus. The good, and the truth that leads to it, depend
upon reestablishing the unitary ego, defining stimuli,
and affixing their specific responses, all to occur together,
holistically. Linear and analog science help. They build a
bridge over the stimulus-response chasm.

If only science might find a holistic way of bridging
the chasm, of healing the instinct glitch, man would feel
even better. The clue to this is in the incessant human
attempt to embrace the good, the true, and the beautiful
in one holistic motion where what is called ethics, science and art have no place and little interest, where he
feels at one with himself and the world, an intuitive
well-being. Although stoicism and Buddhism and Tao-
ism and many other formulas of conduct prefigure this
kind of confrontation that brings comfort and surcease
from fear, they cannot manage reliably to control the
"reality principle," that is, the persecution, hunger, massacre, frustration and demands visited upon them by the
unregenerate *homo schizo* outside the cult.

SUBLIMATION AS PREFERABLE DISPLACEMENTS

Sublimation is a concept that should desist and refrain
from spoiling clean scientific analysis. Originally it arose
out of an exaggerated interest in sex and purported to
designate how sexuality might be unconsciously suppressed, and disguise itself as a virtuous activity, so that,
for instance, a man who was inordinately and illegiti-
mately fond of his mother plunged obsessively into sofa
design, and thereupon was deemed to sublimate. Sublimation was looked upon as a socially welcome outlet for
unmanageable, if not perverse, sexual impulses, hence
applauded.

But a scientific definition of sublimation, divorced

from preferred behavior, must go rather like this: sublimation is a displacement activity whose original motivation is unrecognized publicaly. Then sublimation is for
all practical purposes identical with displacement, as in
Tinbergen's example of the stickleback fish quoted earlier. Why, then, use the term, unless it be to propagan-
dize a form of behavior, a way of life?

German youth leaders say, "When you are hiking and
hungry, sing to forget your hunger." Perhaps that is why
the child in the old English nursery rhyme "sings for his
supper." Here is a sublimation, quite explicit because the
locus of the displacement barely shifts around the oral
cavity. Sex, food, respect, well-being, safety, knowing,
capability: such are most activities, running on tracks dug
early in life, and taking up most of later life. All of these
values must be satisfied within the larger control frame-
work. No solution suffices, it appears, or succeeds exept
temporarily, with all of these goods, unless it carries with
it a quota of control. The human is readier than any other
animal to give them up, or compromise or complicate
them in order to get on with the business of the triple
control of his selves, others, and the world.

Ethically, of course, it is important how *homo schizo*
spends his time. As was said, the good is what we want.
And if we wish to call good ways of handling problems of
fear and control by the word "sublimation," noone may
interfere. We may apply our flighty word to an emaciated
artist who paints "still-lives," a gynecologist who is sexually unarousable, a politician with an adoring public
and no friends, a rich woman who hobnobs with bohemi-
ans, and a miser who leaves his wealth to his university
alma mater. What can we call a man who cannot paint but
loves to eat; a Don Juan who detests the physical apparatus of females; a strict parent who leaves a personally
irresponsible life; a "public enemy" whose friends love
him; a poor social-climber; a generous man who ignores
his community's needs? These are fixated on "primary
gratifications;" and then what?

The human is so displaceable, that one might even
put up stiff arguments against his having definite primary
needs, as have, for example, some advocates of homosexual liberation. As is often complained by western

generals, the Chinese soldier can fight on a bowl of rice. But then there was the Persian folk hero, Nastradin, who had just managed to teach his donkey to work without eating when, unfortunately, the animal died — showing that even animals can be trained to displace.

Superficially, *homo schizo* is infinitely devious, because basically he is terribly interested in sensations of control and will go anywhere into himself or into the furthest reaches of space and time to find surcease. Or he may not need to go very far but will sing, or dress like a peacock, rather than eat.

I trust that we are all in favor of fine arts, literature, history, and science and will do our best to commit homo schizo to their practice. Nevertheless, or should I say therefore, the analysis of cultural product must proceed apace. When we enjoy to witness the Amphytrion of Plautus or of Moliere, we must observe, too, the fascination which the plot holds because of its play upon the confusion of selves — Zeus and the Theban general two look-alikes, Hermes and the general's valet the same, and who is talking to whom? When we watch Shakespeare's *As You Like It*, there to observe the dissolution of court life into a forest of exile, where Celia receives the name Aliena and Rosalind becomes a transvestite and the philosophers speak schizophrenese, we realize in ourselves, the audience, the same transformations, the controlled momentary loss of control of ourselves and the world, joyful and comic when and only when we can reestablish ourselves afterwards. And so with the catastrophic underpinnings of *Hamlet*, *Midsummer Night's Dream* and *Anthony and Cleopatra*, as Irving Wolfe has shown.[20]

The same person, *homo schizo*, is operative in the creation and uses of science and history, the former already treated, the latter more adequately analyzed in *Homo Schizo I*. Only two examples are put foward here, to suggest the need for applying more trenchant theory to the "highest" products of *homo schizo*.

Proclus, the Neo-Platonist philosopher (410?-485), wrote of the planets and gods. In several passages, he described unmistakeably not only the rings of planet Saturn but also the bands of planet Jupiter, phenomena not

rediscovered until the nineteenth century. He explained
them by the self-discipline of the god, Jupiter, who, in
binding his deposed father, Saturn, to a new regime of
law and order, also righteously bound himself to his own
laws. A set of natural events in the sky was observed, and
was animated into a theophany; the gods were made to
behave as man wished they might, as guarantors of order
in the skies, and brought to earth as exemplars of order in
human affairs. The language of philosophy thoroughly
subdued the frightful story of the bloody struggle of gods;
a euphoria emerged from an age-old collective amnesia.
Thus have philosophers sought to create certainty, as
John Dewey claimed.

Ernst Cassirer, like Proclus a distinguished philosopher, a German refugee to America, wrote a book on
human nature, entitled *An Essay on Man*,[21] during
World War II. I studied it well among the first books coming to hand when I returned from long army service. The
book maintains throughout a high rational level of dic-
ourse. It is learned, soothing, endearing, acceptable — a
shimmering smooth amnesiac screen behind which other
types of *homo schizo* were destroying the total culture of
Europe which he was discussing. As in Ovid's *Metem-
orphoses* the most frightful activities are blended into a
lovely serene background setting.

So well was the philosopher's job done, that noone,
not even myself then, could suspect that here was as fine
an instance of the mind of *homo schizo* at work as was the
disastrous scene of slaughter and rapine from which I had
just separated. I say of these two examples of Proclus and
Cassirer, as might be said of the higher products of the
human mind in general, that they are all suitable candi-
dates for analysis by the conceptual implements of the
theory of *homo schizo*. Ordinary appraisals of art, literature, science, and philosophy are pathetic. This has much
to do with *Wissenschaftsoziologie*, the sociology of
knowledge. But the sociology of knowledge still requires
the appropriate launching pad for its flight of analysis:
this the model of *homo schizo* may provide.

In his work on *Schizophrenia in Literature and Art*,
John Vernon explains by way of Aristotle, Locke, and
especially Galileo how it came about that the world was

made to split into divisions of objectivity and subjectivity, so-called. Galileo, he reminds us, performed the schizoid feat of thinking "I do not believe that there exists anything in external bodies for exciting tastes, smells, and sounds, but size, shape, quantity, and motion, swift or slow." Thus came about the distinct "soft world" and "hard world."[22]

Says Vernon, "The threat the world presents for the schizophrenic is often a threat of control. In the West, the split of the world into two absolute principles, subject and object, has enabled civilization to control and manipulate nature.." This all "makes reality something unreal and makes the structures of classical thought that constituted that structure insane — that is, schizophrenic."[23]

Subjectivity appears to be fantasy and is relegated to the fantastic humanities. Now the same culture that creates the absolute reality-fantasy division also creates an absolute sanity-madness division."

But we have always had bifurcations and contraries that obsess philosophies, science, and religion, outlooks that we have said earlier may emerge from the essential ambivalence of *homo schizo*. The division of man into a body and soul is one such, which rationalizes the polyego to make it more logical, following the impression that there must be a sharp difference between ape and man and discovering this in the human soul.

So, too, the difference between mind and conscience, which even Freud could not evade and finds favor among many psychologists; there the attempt is made to have the split-selves appear to be an imposition of a "false reality" upon a "true reality," the former being subjective and the socially imposed whereas the latter is totally mammalian.

THE ORIGINS OF GOOD AND EVIL

The monarch of bifurcation is "good" and "evil." On the shoulder of every little girl and boy perches a good angel who speaks into one ear (the right ear?) while upon the other shoulder perches an evil devil who speaks into the other ear, as the catechist would explain. Human existence and fulfillment, it is generally believed, depends upon the recognition of good and evil and of their consequences. This juxtaposition of forces is certainly a crowning obsession of mankind.

No one knows where France's great dramatist, Moliere, lies buried, because he was a *comedièn*, an actor, a player of roles, a deviser and divider of human souls whose dividends did not equal the "angel" and "devil" into which the Catholic Church insisted and insists still, for reasons valid on its premises, that *homo schizo* must be divided. Unless an actor repented on his death bed, he (or she, as for example, Adrienne Lecouvreur, of whom Voltaire had something to say) is denied burial in hallowed ground.

The ordinary person thinks he understands this but often may not, believing, "Yes, actors are naughty and must repent their licentious and blasphemous lives." But, no, even a hypothetical blameless actor, who is punished on the stage for every sin he commits on the stage, must also be barred from consecrated soil. The culture, as authoritatively represented by the Church, decrees that the schizotypicality of man should consist of two contraries. Other poly-egos are regarded as culturally dysfunctional and are tabooed.

A common anthropological misapprehension, couched in sympathetic terms, would observe: "Unfortunately, humans are often superstitious and misguided, and go about seeking the good and bad, making a great many mistakes, exaggerating, failing to consider their own motives, casting stones at others and not looking into their own sins." Underlying such commentaries is the feeling that a rational procedure must exist somewhere for discovering and applying the good.

To the contrary. it is perhaps obvious by this point in our proceedings, that some mechanism of *homo schizo* is operating to perpetuate and maintain in royal style the distinction of good and evil. Good and evil are the product of ingenious and successful attempts of *homo schizo* to reduce his poly-ego problem to manageable proportions, in order to control himself and extricate himself from his predicament.

If a dominant self can be named head of the confederation — and let this be called "good" — and the other members of the confederation can be joined together as the opposition and called "evil," then we shall have a ruler and this ruler shall be preferred to the other — the evil devil — on all matters and decisions: and ego conflicts can be blamed upon the evil of the other. Further the evil other can be transferred almost at will, both consciously and unconsciously, among the inner selves, interpersonal relations, the natural world, and the divine world.

Ideas of "good" and "evil," we conclude, wherever they manifest themselves, function as schizotypical ways to control the world on behalf of *homo schizo*. It may be informative and intriguing to depict the nuances of value, the quantitative and transient nature of preferences, the complicated and multiform balances in concluding the truth of propositions or the desireability of behavior — so confesses *homo schizo*. But then he adds resolutely: "When the moment of truth appears, and a choice must be made, and my soul is tortured by doubts, then I must have the good, and only the good, and nothing but the good, so help me Good-God!"

EPILOGUE

The elephant's trunk is not a nasal tumor. The andro-vorism of the praying mantis is not a perversion. The seal's flippers are not a deformity. Nor is the human polyego a tumor, a perversion or a deformity. It is the humble beginning of his claim to rule the world.

In his immediate arrogance, like a newly ennobled baron, man invents his ancestry. The gods created him specially. The event was attended by the shaking of heaven and earth. All the beasts and flowers attended his dispositions. His every blemish became a sign of nobil-ity: fallen hair, clumsy toes, an appetite for everything that sprouted or moved, a jerky gait, a neverending anxi-ety, superstition, and suspiciousness. Compelled to count, he summed up everything. Compelled to displace, he permuted all objects into personal associations. When all is done, he looks at his work, and like Elohim, is satis-fied.

But he does not rest. He destroys. He tortures himself by inner contradictions. He attacks his fellows — not with the simple anatomical instruments of the beast but with an ever-elaborating paraphernalia and by all media — by the word, the organized onslaught, the manipula-tion of the whole range of the humanly valued — persons, objects, ideals, subsistence, affection, dignity, freedom, and life itself. No injury is too subtle, no injury too enor-mous. If it can be conceived, it must be developed for use. So goes history; so goes the world. All of man is good and bad, mingled inextricably, beyond separation, beyond therapy, probably even beyond meaning in his brain. What is to be done with this creature?

The chances that an intelligent, sharing, and peaceful creature can be formed of what exists are low, so low that it appears useless to bank upon them. Gross deficits exist in knowledge, in design, and in power.

We can imagine three different scenarios. One is organization. Another is selective breeding. A third is cloning. Organization has been the largest hope of theologians and philosophers from our beginnings. By its promise, evermore increasing with the advancement of the human sciences, a leadership would be recruited to promote all observable tendencies in the cultures of the world that elicit intelligence, generosity, and pacifism. These qualities would be so fortified by all that we know or may come to know about discrimination for "good" and against "evil" that opposing individual, popular, and organizational tendencies would be frustrated, and socially extirpated. Eternal vigilance would be required, and every investment provably promoting the three virtues would be jealously protected.

A second scheme is selective breeding. What is now unknown would have to be discovered: tests for genetic tendencies or docility with regards to intelligence, sharing and pacifism. This is not an impossible task. Ever more refined research may eventuate in methods of analyzing genetic correlates of these traits, as has already been done with intelligence. It might even be accomplished with crude means. Such would be the licensing of births, conditioned not only upon prospects of health, but also upon the prospects for intelligence, generosity, and pacificity, as judged by ancestry to the extent possible. Where at least some precision were obtainable, for a few if not for all potential parents, a sperm bank might be created whose use would become a condition for birthing, in the absence of positive criteria otherwise.

The third scheme would foster research into cloning, roughly considered as the substitution of certain undesirable genetic material in the egg of potential parents by desirable material. This would have an acceptability in that potential parents, who are often cognizant of their own deficiencies and those of their families, would accept just enough alterations to permit genetic gains while preserving most traits that are their own. All three visions have a probably fatal flaw: *homo sapiens schizotypus* fears them, naturally, as he fears all things. Fearing them, he will wish to control them. The more obsessive, selfish, and violent his efforts at control, the more likely he will succeed in obstructing, or suppressing, or perverting the three types of human reform.

At the very best, a determined group, thoroughly dedicated to the visualized plans, and agreeing to subject themselves ultimately to them, would come to command the power to put the plans into effect, and, once in power, would do so. There are isolated instances of this kind of behavior in the world, but no indications of their having broadened into a world revolutionary movement without losing their *raison d'être*. Cincinnatus resigned his post as Dictator of the Roman Republic and returned to his farm and plow. Not only are there few persons like him, but retiring from the scene is forbidden under the rules of the utopian game under discussion. We must conclude that even were science to guarantee high probabilities of success for these proposed solutions of *homo schizo,* we would not be able to obtain the power for the solutions without losing the dedication to them.

Under such circumstances, only one course can be recommended — that whoever believes, should do what he can, no matter that it may be an iota of the envisioned state of affairs. Devise a politics — call it "kalotics" — and apply it. Invent a therapy and proceed to apply it. What else can one do without doing evil?

We know this: that *homo schizo* has the capability for anhedonic, obsessive identification with an ideal, and he may as well work to transform himself as to destroy himself. Then, one day, just as a humble change made *homo schizo,* another humble change may be discovered to remake him. What a great day, when *homo sapiens schizotypus* becomes *homo sapiens sapiens.*

FOOTNOTES

Chapter 1: The Normally Insane

1. Letter to Francesco Vettore, 10 Dec. 1513, trans. and reference from paper of S. de Grazia, citing F. Gaeta, ed., *Nicolò Machiavelli: Lettere*, Milano: Feltrinelli, 1961, 304.
2. See Paul Meehl, "Schizotaxia, Schizotypy, Schizophrenia," in Arnold H. and E. H. Buss, eds., *Theories of Schizophrenia*, Atherton, New York, 1962, 21-45, 27. Here I use schizotypy, schizoid and schizo as interchangeable forms.
3. Fred Johnson, *The Anatomy of Hallucinations*, 1978, p. 29.
4. In Robin Fox, ed., *Biosocial Anthropology*, London: Malaby Press, p. 62.
5. Dorothea C. Leighton, *et al.*, *The Character of Danger: Psychiatric Symptoms in Selected Communities*, III. N.Y.: Putnam, 1977, 56.
6. Leo Srole, *Mental Health in the Metropolis*, N.Y.: McGraw Hill, 1962.
7. John F. Tallman, *et al.*, "Receptors for the Age of Anxiety," 207 *Science* (Jan. 18, 1980), 274.
8. Johnson, *op. cit.*, 1978, citing Cole's Survey of 1970.
9. Quoted in Johnson, *op. cit.*
10. H.D. Lasswell, "Democratic Character," Glencoe: Free Press 1951; *Power and Personality* N.Y.: Norton, 1948.
11. George G. Gallup, Jr., "Towards an Operational Definition of Self-Awareness," in R.H. Tuttle, *Sociology and Psychology of Primates*, The Hague: Monton, 1975, 310-41.
12. Eugen Bleuler, *Dementia Praecox or the Group of Schizophrenias*, 1911, J. Zinkin, tr., N.Y.: Intl. U. Press, 1950, 266ff, 304ff. *Cf.* Am. Psychiat. Assn., *Diagnostic Criteria for Schizophrenia*, 1978.
13. Dunham, cited in Johnson, *op. cit.*
14. "Psychiatric Labelling in Cross-Cultural Perspectives," 191 *Science* (1976), 1019-27.
15. D.C. Leighton *et al.*, *op. cit.*
16. Farley, *et al.*, "Brain Norepinephrine and Dopamine in Schizophrenia," 204 *Science* (1979) 94.
17. K. Meninger, *The Vital Balance*, with Martin Mayman and Paul Pruyser, N.Y.: Viking, 1963.
18. "Estimating the Genetic contribution to Schizophrenia," 133:2 *Amer. J. Psychia.* (1976), 185-91.
19. "A Sociobiologic Model of Schizophrenia," unpubl. paper, March, 1976, 11.
20. The quotations are from the *National Observer*, March 6, 1976, 1, 14.
21. Bleuler, *op. cit.*

22. Meehl, see fn. 2 above.
23. F. Lemere, letter, 132:1 *Amer. J. Psychia.* (Jan. 1975), 86.
24. *The Psychology of Fear and Stress,* N.Y.: McGraw-Hill, 221-2, citing studies of Eysenck and Cattell.
25. *The Neurotic Constitution,* N.Y.: Dodd Mead, 1930, trans from 4th German ed. 1912, 219.
26. "Schizophrenia," in *The Psychology of Dementia Praecox,* Princeton U. Press, 1960, 180-1.
27. *The Political Community* (Chicago: U. of Chicago Press, 1948) and the *Errors of Psychotherapy* (New York: Doubleday, 1950).
28. *Surviving and Other Essays,* N.Y.: Knopf, 1979, 29.
29. New-York: Pantheon-Vintage, 1965.
30. New York: Basic Books.
31. *Op. cit.,* 258.
32. R.C. Bland and J.H. Parker, "Prognosis in Schizophrenia: A Ten Year Follow-up of First Admission," 33 *Arch. Gen. Psychia.* (Aug. 1976), 949-54.
33. Werner M. Mendel, *Schizophrenia: The Experience and Its Treatment,* San Francisco: Jossey-Bass, 1976.
34. William Sargant, Eliot Slater, and Desmond Kelly, *An Introduction to Physical Methods of Treatment in Psychiatry,* N.Y.: Science House, 1972.
35. W.R. Thompson, "Genetics," 8 *Ency. Britannica,* 1973, 1149.
36. *Ibid.*
37. M. Gray, 90.

Chapter 2: The Search for Lost Instinct

1. *The Trauma of Birth,* London: Kegan Paul, 1929, xiii., 104-5.
2. *Realms of the Human Unconscious,* London: Souvenir Press, 1979.
3. *The Ego and the Mechanisms of Defense,* N.Y.: International Univ. Press, 1966.
4. *The Future of Man,* N.Y.: Harper and Row, 1964; *The Phenomenon of Man,* N.Y.: Harper and Row, 1961.
5. *Essay Concerning Human Understanding,* I, Bk 2, 448ff, N.Y.: Dover ed., 1959.
6. *Mind, Self and Society,* Chicago: U. of Chicago Press, 1934, 136-7.
7. 350, 349, *et passim.*
8. Ernest Hilgard, *Divided Consciousness,* New York: Wiley, 1977, 1.
9. *Op. cit.,* 142.
10. Highland, *Op cit.,* 249.
11. Jeffrey Gray, *op. cit.,* ch. 2; Stanley B. Rachman, *Fear and Courage,* San Francisco: Freeman, 1978.

12. Rachman, *op. cit.*, 145.
13. *Op. cit.*, 34.
14. *Op. cit.*, 29.
15. *The Idea of the Holy*, London: Oxford U. Press, 1928.
16. *New Introductory Lectures in Psychoanalysis*, N.Y.: Norton, 1933, 118-9.
17. *The Study of Instinct*, London, 1950, ch. I.
18. *Beyond the Pleasure Principle*, N.Y.: Liveright, 1950.
19. *Ibid.*, 2.
20. *Ibid.*, 30, 32.
21. 1968, 13-4.
22. M.R.A. Chance and C.J. Jolly, *Social Groups of Monkeys, Apes and Men*, London: Jonathan Cape, 1970, 165-8.
23. Quoted in Trevarthen, *op. cit.*, 1951.
24. Hicks and Kinsbourne, in Marcel Kinsbourne, ed., *Asymmetrical Function of the Brain*, N.Y.: Cambridge U. Press, 1978, 523. *Cf.* Trevarthen in the same work, 379.
25. Trevarthen, *Ibid.*

Chapter 3: Brainwork

1. "Pituitary-Brain Vascular Relations," 204 *Science* (6 April 1979), 23.
2. Tinbergen, *op. cit.*, 27.
3. *The Ghost in the Machine*, N.Y.-Macmillan, 1968.
4. MacLean's theory is discussed by Koestler, *ibid.*
5. Niels A. Lassen, D.H. Ingvar and E. Skinhoj, "Brain Function and Flow," *Scientific American* (1975), 71.
6. *Ibid.*, 65-6.
7. Related by Kluver in Jeffress, ed., *Cerebral Mechanisms in Behavior*, N.Y.: Wiley, 1951, 78.
8. In J.N. Spuhler, *Evolution of Man's Capacity for Culture*, Detroit: Wayne U., 1959, 16.
9. *Ibid.*, 18.
10. Fred Soyka and Alan Edmonds, *The Ion Effect*, N.Y.: Dutton, 1977, 23, 146-7.
11. *The Geomagnetic Field and Life*, N.Y.: Plenum, 1978.
12. Fletcher, *op. cit.*, 164.
13. "A Decisive Step in Evolution: Saltatory Conduction."
14. "Bilateral Organization of Consciousness in Man," 299 *N.Y. Acad. Sci.* (Sept. 30, 1977), 454 *et passim.*
15. Swanson and Kinsbourne, in Kinsbourne, ed., *Asymmetrical Function of the Brain*, N.Y. Cambridge U. Press, 1978, 284.
16. Kinsbourne, *ibid.*, 289.
17. Gail Marsh, in Kinsbourne, *ibid.*, 308, 295 *et passim.*
18. H.T. Chang, "Cortical Response to Activity of Callosal Neurons," 16 *J. Neurophysio.*, (1953), 117-31.

19. The works cited here can be supplemented by up-to-date references in the *Psychological Index* and a reading of Joseph Boger's "The Other Side of the Brain," in Ornstein, *The Nature of Human Consciousness*, San Francisco: Freeman, 1973, 101-25.

20. Quoted in Ornstein, *op. cit.*, *The Psychology of Consciousness*, San Francisco: Freeman, 1972, 58.

21. M. Le May and N. Geschwind, "Asymmetries of the Human Cerebral Hemispheres," in A. Caramazza & E.B. Zurif, eds., *Language Acquisition and Language Breakdown*, Baltimore: Johns Hopkins Press, 324.

22. J. Semmes, in Ornstein, 1972, 63-4. Typically, new ideas generate many metaphors (the right brain at work?), some of which, relevant here, are carried forward in Marilyn Ferguson, *The Aquarian Conspiracy: Personal and Social Transformations in the 1980's*, Los Angeles: Tarcher, 1980.

23. Tadanobu Tsunoda, *The Japanese Brain: Brain Function and East-West* (in Japanese), 1978.

24. Karl H. Pribram, *Languages of the Brain*, Englewood Cliffs, N.J.: Prentice Hall, 1971, 149-151, 369-70.

25. Gazzaniga *et al.*, "Language, Praxis, and the Right Hemisphere," 27 *Neurology* (1977), 1144.

26. "Brain Circuits for consciousness," 13 *Brain Beh. and Evol.* (1976), 376.

27. Paul Giraud, in 40 *Evol. Psychiatrique* I (1975), 41.

28. 1970, 232.

29. Trevarthen, *op. cit.*, 378.

30. *Op. cit.*, (1979), 6.

31. *Op. cit.*, (1974).

32. Klaus D. Hoppe, 29 *Psyche* 10 (1975), 919.

33. *University of Chicago Magazine* (1964).

34. Trevarthen, in Kinsbourne, *op. cit.*, 379,376.

35. In Kinsbourne, *ibid.*, 523; also Trevarthen, 379.

36. See the photo, p.280, pc, in J.P. Hallet, *Congo Kitabu*, N.Y.: Random House, 1966.

37. "The Great Cerebral Commissure," *Sci. Amer.* (Jan. 1964), 52.

38. S. de Grazia, "Left-Right in Politics: The Case for Symbolic Lateral Asymmetry," 29 *Pol. Studies* 2 (June 1981), 254.

39. L. Tiger, quoting Hutt in Fox, *op. cit.*, 115.

40. T.A. Parry, quoting Deikman, 6-7, in "The New Science of Immanuel Velikovsky," I *Kronos* 1 (1975).

41. A. Shimkunas, "Hemisphere Asymmetry and Schizophrenic Thought Disorder," in S. Schwartz, ed., *Language and Cognition in Schizophrenia*, N.Y.: Erlbaum, 1978.

42. R.G. Hoskins, *The Biology of Schizophrenia*, N.Y.: Norton, 1946, 75.

43. And *cf.* Margaret W. Gerard, "Genesis of Psychosomatic Symptoms in Infancy," in Felix Deutsch, *The Psychosomatic Concept in Psychoanalysis*, N.Y.: Intl. Universities Press, 1952, 82-95.

Chapter 4: Displacement and Obsession

1. Tinbergen, *A Study of Instinct*, 113-9.
2. *Critique of Practical Reason*, conclusion.

Chapter 5: Coping With Fear

1. *Op. cit.*, 234-5.
2. Jay Tepperman, *Metabolic and Endocrine Physiology*, Chicago: Year Book Medical Publishers, 1962, 136.
3. *The Physiology and Pathology of the Exposure to Stress*, Montreal: Acta, 1950.
4. *Op. cit.*, 195.
5. *Op. cit.*, 136-7.
6. Cf. Melvin Gray. *op. cit.*, 97ff for a list.
7. *Ibid.*, 93.
8. *Baudelaire*, (Penguin ed., 1961), 160.
9. *I and Thou*, 1937.
10. M. Gray, *op. cit.*, 131.
11. *Op. cit.*, 415-6, 27.
12. Theodor Reik, *Myth and Guilt*.
13. J.A.B. van Buitenen, "Manu, Ut-Napischtim, and Noah," *U of Chicago mag.* (Winter, 1975), 10-3.
14. *Totem and Taboo*, 1913, N.Y.: Norton, 1950, 45.
15. Bleuler, *op. cit.*, 180.
16. Mc Ghee and Chapman, 63, Patients 12, also patients 3, 5, 20, 14, 1.
17. Harold D. Lasswell, "Psychology of Hitlerism," in *Political Behavior* (studies), London.
18. Warner Sizemore and John V. Myers "Schizophrenia and The Fear of World Destruction," I *Kronos*, (Spring, 1975), 75; cf. W.A. Spring, "Observations on World Destruction Fantasies," 8 *Psychanal. Q.* (1939), 48-56.
19. K. R. Eissler, *Leonardo da Vinci: Psychoanalytic Notes on an Enigma*, London: Hogarth Press, 1962.

Chapter 6: Symbols and Speech

1. "Culture and Continuity," 9 *Tech. and Culture* (April, 1968), 210.
2. See this author's review of Ernest Dichter, *Handbook of Consumer Motivations: The Psychology of the World of Objects*, in 8 *Amer. Behav. Sci.* 2 (Oct. 1964).

3. Malcolm Lowery, letter to the author, 4 Dec. 1976.
4. J.B. Gleason, "Gestural Linguistics," 205 *Science* (21 Sept. 1979), 1253.
5. "The Natural History of Language," in F. Smith and G.H. Miller, eds., *The Genesis of Language*, Cambridge, Mass.: MIT Press, 1966, 248, 219-52.
6. "Brains and Behavior," in Spuhler, *op. cit.*, 17.
7. H.S. Terrace *et al.*, "Can an Ape Create a Sentence?" 206 *Science* 4421 (23 Nov. 1979), 901.
8. *Psychology of Communications*, New York, 1967, 104-5.
9. Johnson, *op. cit.*, 170. He cites Monod.
10. *Op. cit.*, 309.
11. Johnson, *op. cit.*
12. *Ibid.*
13. Cf. T. Thuss-Thienemann, *The Subconscious Language*, N.Y.: Wash. Sq. Press, 1967 on the thoroughly metaphorical and associational development of language.
14. *Cartesian Linguistics, A Chapter in the Historical Rationalist Thought*, N.Y.: Harper and Row, 1966, 73.
15. *An Essay on Man*, New Haven: Yale U. Press, 1944.
16. *Ibid.*, 122.
17. *Sprach der Eiszeit*, Berlin: Herbig, 1962; mss. trans. by Malcolm Lowery, 1976.
18. Carrol, intro. to Whorf, *Language, Thought and Reality*, Cambridge, Mass.; MIT Press, 1956, 12.
19. Norman B. Tindale, *Aboriginal Tribes of Australia*, Berkeley U. of California Press, 1974, 118-20.
20. Letter to Peter James, Aug. 28. 1977.
21. *Op. cit.*, 80.
22. J.A.L. Singh and R.M. Zingg, *Wolf Children and Feral Man* (N.Y.: Harper, 1942).
23. *Op. cit.*, 25.
24. *Op. cit.*, 55.
25. *Ibid.*, 58-61.
26. *Ibid.*, 85.
27. *Ibid.*, 67.
28. *Ibid.*, 252.
29. *Ibid.*, 257.
30. *Ibid.*, 242-3.
31. *Ibid.*, 244.
32. London: Royal Society Printers, 1668.

Chapter 7:
The Good, the True, and the Beautiful

1. H.D. Lasswell and A. Kaplan, *Power and Society* (1950) and D. Truman, *Governmental Process* (1951), both dependent to

some extent upon prior works, such as Machiavelli's *Prince*
(1532), Michels' *Political Parties* (1915), Pareto's *Mind and
Society* (1916), Mosca's *Ruling Class* (1890), Bentley's *Process
of Government* (1908), supplemented by many case studies
such as N. Leites' *Operational Code of the Politburo* (1951),
where he reconstructs the logical and thought systems of the
leaders of the Soviet Union until 1950, and one can nitpick the
"rational" from the multi-colored weave of ideology. Perhaps to
be mentioned also are such works of this author's as *Politics for
Better of Worse* (1973); the more formal *Elements of Political
Science* (1952); and, as a case study, *God's Fire: Moses and the
Management of Exodus* (1983).

2. Ernest R. Hilgard, *op. cit.*, 230.
3. W. James, *Essays in Popular Philosophy*, 84.
4. Isaac N. Vail, *Selected Works*, Santa Barbara, Calif.: Annular
    Books, 1972.
5. "The General and Logical Theory of Automata," in L.A.
    Jeffress, ed., *Cerebral Mechanisms in Behavior*, N.Y.: Wiley,
    1951, 24.
6. *Languages of the Brain, op. cit.*
7. Rochester and Martin, *Thought Disorder and Schizophrenia*,
    also Steven Schwartz, *Language and Cognition in
    Schizophrenia*, N.Y.: Wiley, 1978.
8. Thomas Taylor, *Timaeus* of Plato, e.q. p. 244. on counting, fear,
    and planets.
9. F. Waisman, "The Decline and Fall of Causality," in A.C.
    Crombie *et al.*, *Turning Points in Physics*, N.Y.: Harper, 1961
    84-154.
10. "Father Time," 22 *Psychiatric Q* (1948), 599.
11. Eissler, *op. cit.*, 247.
12. Carmon and Nachshon, 7 *Cortex* (1971), 410-8 cited in Ornstein
    op. cit., 1972, 89.
13. Bruno Snell, *The Discovery of the Mind: The Greek Origins of
    European Thought*, N.Y. Harper, 1953, chap 9.
14. "The Limits of Human Intelligence," in Jonathan Benthall, *The
    Limits of Human Nature*, N.Y.: Dutton, 1974.
15. *The Ghost in the Machine*, 259.
16. G.H. Mead, *Mind, Self, and Society*, Chicago: U. of Chicago
    Press, 1934, 347-8.
17. N.Y.: Putnam's, 1960, 8.
18. *Cf.* J.R. Kantor, *The Logic of Modern Science*, Bloomington,
    Ind.: Principia Press, 1953, Part II
19. *Op. cit.*, 352
20. "Heaven and Earth: Catastrophism in *Hamlet*," III *Kronos* 4
    (1978), 3-18; IV 1 (1978), 67-89; "The Seasons Alter:
    Catastrophism in *A Midsummer Night's Dream*," VI *Kronos* 1
    (1980), 25-47. *Cf.* R.J. Jaarsma, with E.L. Odenwald, "Nor
    Heaven Nor Earth Have Been at Peace: The Contemporary
    Foundations of Shakespeare's Cataclysmic Imagery," VI
    Kronos 1 (1980), 12-24.

21.   New Haven: Yale U. Press, 1944.
22.   Urbana, Illinois: U. of Illinois Press, 1973.
23.   *Op. cit.*, 28, That science may not pursue this dichotomy much
       longer is evidenced, e.g. in Judith Wechsler, ed., *On Aesthetics
       in Science*, Cambridge, Mass.: MIT Press, 1978.

INDEX

About the author

Alfred de Grazia taught social theory, political pyschology and behavior, and social invention for some years at Minnesota, Brown U., Stanford U., and New York University, after receiving his doctorate from the University of Chicago in 1948. His works on politics and theory helped to establish scientific method in the field of political science. He worked at military psychological operations in three wars. A lifelong occupation with social invention was reflected in the founding of the American Behavioral Scientist, the design of information systems, and in public policy studies that began with the First Hoover Commission on the reorganization of the federal government and continued through a syllabus for the National Endowment for the Arts entitled *1001 Questions* on national culture policy (1980). In 1963 he began a new series of studies on ancient catastrophes and their effects upon natural and human history, which eventuated in the Quantavolution Series, now being published.

The Quantavolution Series

Chaos and Creation: An Introduction to Quantavolution in Human and Natural History.

The Lately Tortured Earth: Exoterrestrial Forces and Quantavolution in the Earth Sciences.

Homo Schizo I: The Origins of Mankind and Culture.

Homo Schizo II: Human Nature and Behavior.

God's Fire: Moses and the Management of Exodus.

Solaria Binaria: The Origins and History of the Solar System. (with Prof. Earl R. Milton.)

The Divine Succession: Gods Dead and Alive.

The Burning of Troy: Essays and Notes in Quantavolution.

The Disastrous Love Affair of Moon and Mars: Celestial Sex, Earthly Destruction, and Dramatic Sublimation in Homer's Odyssey.

Cosmic Heretics: A Personal History of Attempts to Establish and Resist Theories of Quantavolution and Catastrophe in the Natural and Human Sciences, 1962 to 1983, (in four parts.)